To John,

With happy memories
& best wishes.

Brian Crosskill.

October 2009.

RECOLLECTIONS
of
GUNNER GOODLIFFE

Life of a National Serviceman in 1952 and 1953,
from his own diaries

BRIAN GOODLIFFE

25 Pounder Field Gun, Limber and Morris Quad

Vicky Saumarez

Published
2009

First Published March 2009

A catalogue record for this book is available from
The British Library

ISBN 978-0-9561814-0-4

Produced by Publicity Overload Ltd
45 Station Road
North Harrow
Middx
HA2 7SU

Tel 020 8427 2320
Fax 020 8427 0264

www.publicityoverload.co.uk

Printed in Great Britain

Further copies of this book are obtainable by writing to:
Brian Goodliffe C/O Belmont, Unit 1, Arisdale Avenue, South Ockendon,
Essex, RM15 5TT

For my wife Cynthia and our family:

Laura, Nicholas, Robert, Vicky,
Holly, Milly, Ludo, Jamie, Delilah, Cameron,
Casper, Finlay, Quinn and Wilfred.

***

And in memory of
David Nicoll,
National Serviceman in the Black Watch Regiment.
Killed in action in Korea, 8 August 1952,
when he was just 20 years old.

Contents

**25 Pounder Field Gun, on Firing Platform and
Ammunition Limber**

Vicky Saumarez

Preface

Over fifty years ago I made the fortunate decision to write a full diary during the whole of my two years of National Service, from 6 December 1951 until December 1953. The contents of these diaries were certainly no literary work, but luckily, I *did* write in sufficient detail for me to readily recall the events recorded during those two extraordinary years. The notes I made at the time have enabled me to recapture many of the happenings, the anecdotes and the relationships I had – most of which would otherwise have been lost in the sands of time.

Writing more than fifty years afterwards, means that we now view events and the world situation from a different standpoint. Many countries in 1951 – including Britain – were severely short of many supplies, and vast areas of Europe and Asia lay devastated as a result of the appalling wars perpetrated by Nazi Germany and the fanatical Japanese – both of which had ended no more than six years before. Also by this time, Eastern Europe was now firmly under the thumb of Soviet Russia's Communism.

Furthermore, the wicked and murderous dictators of the Soviet Union and China – Josef Stalin and Mao Tse-tung – with their immense armies arrayed against us, continued to do their best to promote turmoil, bloodshed and disruptiveness throughout the 'Free World' – unwittingly aided and abetted by the likes of Michael Foot, Aneurin Bevan and Wedgewood Benn, who apparently condoned and advocated much of the Communistic philosophy and actions.

It is easy to forget that during the decade after the war, the British Army – including many National Servicemen – was actively engaged in a bloody war in Korea (from 1950 until 1953), as well as guerrilla warfare in such places as Palestine (from 1945 until 1948), Malaya (from 1948), Kenya (from 1952) and Cyprus (from 1954).

Nowadays, that horrible monster Communism, which so dominated our world scene during the 1950s, has been cut down to size and thoroughly discredited, whilst in its place has emerged the equally threatening menace of widespread terrorism motivated by ungodly religious extremists.

Although I have thoroughly enjoyed revising and rewriting this account from my diaries, my original reason and stimulus for undertaking this task was *entirely* for the sake of our three children, **Laura, Nicholas** and **Robert**, and our grandchildren: **Holly, Milly, Ludo, Jamie, Delilah, Cameron, Casper, Finlay, Quinn** and **Wilfred**.

However, when some of my friends – who had also 'been through the mill' – read some early drafts of these *Recollections*, they strongly encouraged me to complete the work and to print extra copies of the finished book so that more people might also have the opportunity of reading this recent history, so seldom recorded in this way.

Finally, I say again, that nothing related in these chapters has been made up or embellished for effect.

Brian Goodliffe. – Beckenham, Kent, 2008.

More About the Author
and the Book

Brian Goodliffe was educated at Charterhouse, and started his National Service at the end of 1951. Like many others, he was just 18½ years old. Luckily, he decided to write a full diary during his next two years with the Royal Artillery.

After his initial training in Oswestry, Shropshire, and his further training at Mons Officer Cadet School in Aldershot, the remainder of his National Service took him to the Middle East, where he joined 29 Field Regiment Royal Artillery in the Suez Canal Zone. During the remaining fifteen months of his service there, he was lucky enough to travel extensively in the region.

He frankly records his recollections, friendships and experiences during the whole of 1952 and 1953; and he also tells us about the journeys he made in Sinai, Jordan, Syria, Lebanon and Cyprus – where he visited St Catherine's Monastery, Petra, Amman, Jerash, Jerusalem, the Dead Sea Valley, Damascus and Government House in Nicosia. During those memorable two years, he also took many photographs with his Leica IIIc camera which have been used extensively to supplement his verbal observations.

After demobilisation at the end of December 1953, Brian joined the family business, Office Cleaning Services and the New Century Window Cleaning Company (later renamed OCS Group). The original company had been founded in 1900 by his grandfather Frederick Goodliffe – a window cleaner in London. By the mid-1950s, OCS had already grown to become the largest building cleaning organisation in London, employing over 10,000 people, and soon to branch out into laundries, security, catering, pest control, and the cleaning of airports and hospitals, as well as many other ancillary services.

From the late 1950s onwards, Brian Goodliffe was instrumental in expanding the OCS laundry side of the business throughout the UK, as well as in the Netherlands and Spain. During those decades he also played his part in the Textile Services Association and the Worshipful Company of Launderers.

Retiring in 1996, Brian spent four most enjoyable years of his leisure time writing a 'magnum opus' on Wolfgang Mozart – his great passion and delight. In the event, the finished work was far too extensive for publication and therefore has remained abandoned in his word processor, awaiting resuscitation! In due course perhaps, sections of it will be edited and published separately. In the meantime, he started delving into his National Service diaries, which had been left discarded on his bookshelf for some fifty years.

Before long, he saw the possibility of re-writing the contents into a lasting record of his experiences for his children and grandchildren. By the end of 2002, much of *Recollections of Gunner Goodliffe* had emerged in draft form, and at this point, further encouragement came after contacting some of his erstwhile Army friends mentioned in these chapters. Not only were they most enthusiastic about the work, but before long, they had also sent some of their own remembrances which have now been included as a postscript.

Although *Recollections* was originally written entirely for the sake of his family, it was decided later to print additional copies of the finished book so that others might also have the opportunity of reading a slice of recent history, not often recorded so fully in this way.

Brian Goodliffe now lives in Beckenham with his wife Cynthia.

Chapters

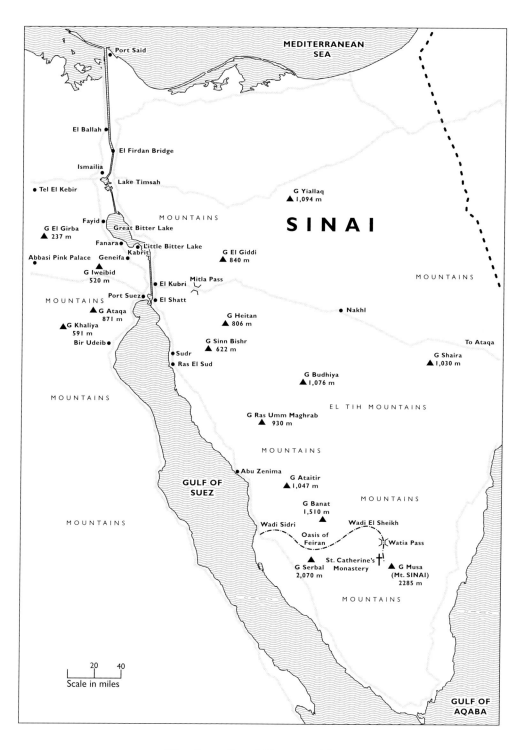

The Suez Canal Zone and Sinai
xiii

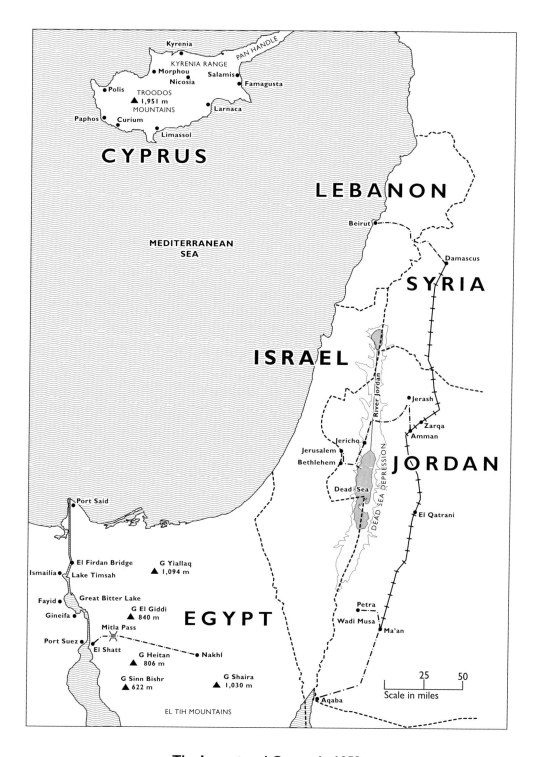

The Levant and Cyprus in 1953

Glossary

8 Battery	= Senior Battery in 29 Field Regt RA
79 Battery	= Second Battery in 29 Field Regt RA
145 Battery	= Third Battery in 29 Field Regt RA
25 pounder	= Field Gun that fires shells weighing 25 lb
2 I/C	= 2nd in Command

***

Able	= 'A' when used 'on the air'
Able Troop	= 8 Battery's 1st Troop of 4 x 25 pounder guns
ACC	= Army Catering Corps
Ack Ack	= Anti-Aircraft Guns
Adjutant	= Senior administrative officer
Baker	= 'B' when used 'on the air'
Baker Troop	= 8 Battery's 2nd Troop of 4 x 25 pounder guns
Barney	= Major Barney Brook-Fox (BC of 8 Battery)
Bdr	= Gunner Bombardier (equivalent to Corporal)
BC	= Battery Commander
BHQ	= Battery Head Quarters Company
BK	= Battery Captain (his 2 I/C)
BMH	= British Military Hospital
BOD	= Base Ordnance Depot
BSM	= Battery Sergeant Major
BTE	= British Troops of Egypt
Bty	= Gunner Battery of 8 x 25 pounder guns
Charlie	= 'C' when used 'on the air'
CO	= Commanding Officer
CPO	= Battery Command Post Officer
CRA	= Commander Royal Artillery
CSM	= Company Sergeant Major
Dhobi	= Laundry
Dog	= 'D' when used 'on the air'
Easy	= 'E' when used 'on the air'
Egyptian PT	= Slang for lying down or sleeping
Fox	= 'F' when used 'on the air'
George	= 'G' when used 'on the air'

Gebel	= Mountain (in Egyptian)
George Able	= GPO's truck of Able Troop, 8 Bty
George Baker	= GPO's truck of Baker Troop, 8 Bty
GPO	= Troop Gun Position Officer
IG	= Instructor of Gunnery
HAA	= Heavy Anti-Aircraft Guns
Khamseen	= the hot southern wind in Egypt
Lt	= Lieutenant/Subaltern
Maj`	= Major/Field Officer
MELF	= Middle East Land Forces
Miredahm	= our slang for the desert
NCO	= Non Commissioned Officer
NS	= National Service
OP	= Observation Post for directing fire for shoot
OP	= (also) The Officer directing the fire
ORs	= Other Ranks (i.e. Gunners)
QM	= Quarter Master (in charge of Stores/Armoury)
QMS	= Quarter Master Stores
RA	= Royal Artillery
RAC	= Royal Armoured Corps
RASC	= Royal Army Service Corps (all transport)
RCSigs	= Royal Corps of Signals
RE	= Royal Engineers
REME	= Royal Electrical and Mechanical Engineers
RHA	= Royal Horse Artillery
	(with 25 pounder guns mounted on tank chasses)
RHQ	= Regimental Head Quarters
ROO	= Regimental Orderly Officer
RSM	= Regimental Sergeant Major (i.e. RSM Brittain)
2nd Lt	= Second Lieutenant/Subaltern
TARA	= Technical Assistant RA
Tec Acc	= Technical Assistant RA
Toc L Baker	= Troop Leader's truck of Baker Troop
Tp	= Troop of 4 x 25 pdr field guns
Tp Com	= Troop Commander
Tp Leader	= GPO's 2 I/C (sometimes the TSM)
TSM	= Troop Sergeant Major
Wadi	= Dried up rivercourse in the desert
Wireless	= Now called radio
WO1 & WO2	= Warrant Officer Class 1 & 2

CHAPTER I

Aftermath of World War II

There is an old Chinese saying which goes: 'May you live in interesting times'. Although its origin is obscure, it could be deduced that this yearning for something new and interesting stems from those living in the countryside of ancient China, where life remained unchanging, unexciting and toilsome for generation upon generation.

This saying could never have come from more recent times, for since the start of the twentieth century, we have seen countless sociological and technological changes, many of which have resulted from the immense upheavals caused by World War I (1914-1918) followed quickly by World War II (1939-1945). Together, these two appalling tragedies have affected every country and every living person on the earth.

World War II ended in Europe after the fanatical Hitler finally shot himself, and Nazi Germany surrendered on 8 May 1945; but hostilities against Japan continued until the horrors of the atomic bombs dropped on Hiroshima and Nagasaki finally compelled its wicked leaders to surrender on 12 September.

There had been a massive bloodletting, and in contrast to the horrors of World War I, the casualty lists included huge numbers of civilians. Although total figures can never be ascertained, historians might agree that more than 60 million people perished in total, of which nearly half were Chinese and Russian.

Apart from all the devastation caused throughout the world, the *estimated* loss of life suffered by the main contenders could be put in the region of:

USSR: 13,600,000 armed forces and 10,000,000 civilians.
Germany: 3,500,000 armed forces and 500,000 civilians.
Japan: 2,600,000 armed forces and 600,000 civilians.

China:	2,200,000 armed forces and 20,000,000 civilians.
Philippines:	20,00 armed forces and 980,000 civilians.
Britain:	420,000 armed forces and 100,000 civilians.
Romania:	350,000 armed forces and 60,000 civilians.
Yugoslavia:	305,000 armed forces and 60,000 civilians.
USA:	300,000 armed forces and 6,000 civilians.
Italy:	279,000 armed forces and 150,000 civilians.
France:	213,000 armed forces and 320,000 civilians.
Hungary:	200,000 armed forces and 60,000 civilians.
Poland:	123,000 armed forces and 500,000 civilians.
Greece:	88,000 armed forces and 30,000 civilians.
Finland:	82,000 armed forces and 15,000 civilians.
Canada:	37,000 armed forces.
India:	24,000 armed forces.
Australia:	23,000 armed forces and a few civilians.
Belgium:	12,000 armed forces and many civilians.
Czechoslovakia:	20,000 armed forces and many civilians.
Bulgaria:	10,000 armed forces and many civilians.
New Zealand:	10,000 armed forces.
Netherlands:	8,000 armed forces and 15,000 civilians.
South Africa:	6,000 armed forces.
The Colonies	8,000 armed forces and 10,000 civilians.
Norway:	3,000 armed forces and some civilians.
Denmark:	1,800 armed forces and some civilians.
Brazil:	943 armed forces.

In addition to the above figures, some 6,000,000 Jews were murdered by the Nazis.

The after-effects of these appalling hostilities were widespread, lasting and far-reaching:

- The Soviet Union emerged as a world 'superpower' with enormous armed forces in place, and under the leadership of the evil Joseph Stalin (1879-1953), soon to be identified as a mass murderer. Stalin immediately annexed the countries of Eastern Europe to the USSR, and put them under Communist rule. In March 1946, Winston Churchill encapsulated the situation by remarking that 'the Iron Curtain of Communism has fallen across Europe' and from that time onwards, Stalin perpetrated the so-called 'Cold War', and promoted unrest and the spread of Communism throughout the world (aided and condoned by many left wing politicians of all countries, including Britain).

- China under Mao Tse-tung (1893-1976) proclaimed the 'People's Republic of China' in 1949, and he also did his best to make trouble and to promote the Chinese brand of Communism as widely as possible, causing bloodshed and unrest in the Far East – in countries such as Indo-China, Malaya and Korea.
- With all the destruction of the past five years, Britain and so many other countries were economically crippled by the conflict, and throughout Europe most commodities were rationed or in short supply for many years to come.
- After 1945, the class structure in British society would never be the same again, and women became far more liberated than before. They had made an important contribution during the war years, and the way was now clear for them to play a much greater role in the future, especially in the professions and in business.

Influenced by these huge pressures, the decade following the end of World War II saw many events which directly affected Britain both at home and abroad.

- In July 1945, the Labour Party under Clement Attlee ousted Winston Churchill, and won a landslide victory in the General Election in the UK.
- In September 1945 with the end of the war against Japan, the USSR received the surrender of Japanese troops in Korea north of the 38th parallel, whilst the USA did likewise south of that line. As a result of this division, the stage was set for the Korean War which started five years later, when North Korea invaded the south.
- In 1945, Britain was still administering Palestine under a 1919 Mandate from the League of Nations, but with thousands of displaced Jews now flocking into the country to create a new state of Israel, the British position soon became untenable
- In 1946, the newly elected Left-Wing Labour Government nationalised the Railways, Road Haulage, the Ports, and the Iron and Steel Industries in Britain.

3

- In July 1946, Jewish terrorists bombed the British Army H.Q. in the King David Hotel in Jerusalem, killing and injuring 147 persons. With the situation worsening still further Britain told the U.N. that it would be pulling out of the country.
- In 1947 the Coal Mines were nationalized in Britain, and that year also the Government introduced 'austerity cuts' and currency controls. In all parts of the country there were shortages and queues.
- Also in August 1947, India and Pakistan became independent, and this was followed by much violence and bloodshed between Hindus and Moslems.
- The first microwave oven was sold in the USA.
- In 1948, the state of Israel was established – after a war in which some 600,000 Palestinian Arabs were forced to leave their homes. There was lasting bitterness between Jews and Arabs, and Jerusalem was left divided in two parts; one Arab the other Jewish.
- During 1948 also, British troops were sent to Malaya, where guerrilla warfare had begun. It was not until 1960 that the communist rebels were finally suppressed.
- In June 1948 the Russians stepped up the Cold War by preventing supplies reaching West Berlin by road and rail. This resulted in the 'Berlin Airlift'.
- Also in 1948, the Gas and Electricity Industries were nationalized, and the 'Welfare State' and the National Health Service (NHS) were put into operation;
- And later in 1948, the Labour Party introduced three 'Comprehensive' Schools as their first move to abolish the Grammar Schools.
- The Olympics were held in London in 1948.
- In 1949 NATO was formed, and Eire left the British Commonwealth and became a Republic.
- Britain's trading position worsened during 1949 and more rationing had to be introduced. In September, Sterling was devalued by 30%.
- In June 1950 Communist North Korea invaded South Korea, and the United States bore the brunt of this attack by dispatching forces from Japan to support South Korea. The United Nations including Britain eventually supported the US-led UN force, and by the end of the Korean War (in May 1953) Britain and the British Commonwealth were providing an armoured Division. Many of the British troops were

National Servicemen.

- By the end of 1950, China started to intervene on the side of North Korea with vast numbers of ill equipped soldiers, and large numbers of these were slaughtered.
- In May 1950, petrol rationing in Britain finally ended.
- As a sign of things to come, in August 1950 Sainsbury's opened its first self-service grocery store.
- In September 1950, due mainly to Britain's involvement in the Korean War, National Service was extended from 18 months to 2 years.
- Five years after the war, large areas of London, and many other cities, were still devastated by the affects of 'Blitz', and it was not until 26 October 1950 that King George VI was able to open the restored House of Commons, which had been so badly damaged by German bombing.
- In January 1951, meat rationing in Britain was still in operation, whilst in May the Festival of Britain opened on London's South Bank, which included the building of Royal Festival Hall and the National Theatre.
- In October 1951, the British General Election returned the Conservatives to office under the leadership of the 77 year old Winston Churchill.
- It was also during the whole of 1951 that trouble continued to brew in the Middle East.
- In May 1951, there were riots in Iran where the government under Premier Mossadegh tried to nationalize all the British oil installations and properties at Abadan run by BP. British troops were sent to protect the installations, but two years later the Shah regained absolute power which he continued to hold for over two decades.
- The Suez Canal was still owned and operated by Britain after the war, but when there was unrest in Egypt and anti-British rioting in Cairo, more British troops were sent in to occupy the Zone in October 1951 to ensure the Canal's security.
- It was also during 1951 that the first two working business computers were launched – the LED in the UK, and the UNIVAC in the United States.
- On 6 December 1951, Gunner Goodliffe started his two years of National Service in the Royal Artillery Training Camp at Oswestry in Shropshire.
- In February 1952, King George VI died of lung cancer.
- In May 1952, British Overseas Airways Corporation (BOAC) inaugu-

rated the world's first regular scheduled airline service to be operated by a turbojet-powered aircraft – the de Havilland Comet.

- In July 1952, King Farouk of Egypt abdicated and the monarchy was replaced by a military regime under General Naguib. At the same time there was an upsurge of nationalist fervour in Egypt.
- Also in July of 1952, London said good-bye to its last tram.
- At the end of July 1952, Gunner Goodliffe received his Commission, and on 28 August 1952, 2nd Lieutenant Goodliffe flew out to the Suez Canal Zone to join 29 Field Regiment, Royal Artillery in Ava Camp, Geneifa.
- Unrest flared up in Kenya in October 1952, when Mau Mau terrorists started to murder white and black people indiscriminately with the ultimate objective of gaining independence from Britain. As a result of this, British troops from BTE and elsewhere (including many National Servicemen) were flown into the country to start a full-scale security operation.
- It was also during that year 1952, that the number of immigrants from the West Indies, India and Pakistan, were starting to increase sharply; and within the Labour Party, the left-wing supporters of Aneurin Bevan won 6 out of 7 Constituency seats on Labour's National Executive.
- On 2 June 1953, Queen Elizabeth II was crowned in Westminster Abbey, and the Service was broadcast on television to more than 600,000 sets throughout the UK.
- Appropriately, just before the Queen's Coronation, news was received that Edmund Hillary and Sherpa Tensing had succeeded in reaching the top of Mount Everest.
- Egypt became independent.
- Also in 1953, the number of people flying by air started to increase dramatically, and in April of that year, it was reported that air travel had risen by some 20% on the previous Easter. However, within a year all BOAC Comet jet-airliners were grounded after a series of crashes. It was later discovered that 'metal fatigue' had been the cause.
- The Armistace was signed in the Korean War in July 1953.
- In December 1953, 2nd Lt Goodliffe was demobilized and joined the Territorial Army – 298 Field Regiment (Surrey Yeomanry) RA., TA.
- On May 1954, Roger Bannister ran the mile in 3 minutes, 59.4 seconds;

- It was in July of that year that the Conservatives finally finished all rationing in Britain.
- Also on 27 July 1954, the Government agreed that all British troops would leave the Suez Canal Zone by 1956.
- On 18 December 1954, there were ominous signs of future trouble in Cyprus, when two Cypriots were shot dead during hostile and aggressive demonstrations outside a Police Station in Limassol.
- By November 1955, an aggressive campaign had gained support for 'Enosis' amongst the Greek-speaking Cypriots, and before long, indiscriminate acts of murder by the EOKA (led by the Greek, Grivas) were being perpetrated.
- This caused a State of Emergency, and many extra British troops (including National Servicemen) were sent to the Island.
- Before long, the Turkish-speaking minority (who were totally against any union with Greece) had also formed their own defensive militant organisation (called TMT), and the once peaceful population, became divided and antagonistic towards each other.
- The final batch of National Servicemen finished their service in 1962, and the British Army was then comprised of Regular soldiers only.

As can be seen from this partial résumé of events, the decades after the end of the World War II were a period of great change and strife. Communism, religion, nationalism, racism, tribalism and the fervent desire for independence, all contributed towards causing severe tensions and hostilities throughout the world; and the old colonial powers – Britain, France, the Netherlands, Portugal and Belgium – all had to cope with important disputes and discontents that had remained controlled and latent during the inter-war years.

In regions such as Korea, Indo-China, Algeria, Indonesia, Palestine, Malaya, the Congo and Kenya, there were serious wars, bloodshed or guerrilla activities, and during this time, many countries such as India, Pakistan, Sri Lanka, Egypt, Indonesia and the British Colonies in Africa all gained their independence, sometimes with turmoil. Also, serious unrest was beginning to brew in the oil-rich states of the Middle East, which saw the western powers controlling their countries' wealth.

After years of attrition, Britain had emerged victorious but virtually bankrupt. It retained its 'world power' status and responsibilities, but possessed insufficient funds to finance these roles. The British Empire and Commonwealth was still intact, but it was beginning to break up, and Britain, with its large Armed Forces – more than half of which were National Servicemen – was constantly committed to fighting wars, mini-wars and anti-terrorist activities throughout the world.

My two years of National Service from December 1951 until December 1953 fell in the midst of these tumultuous and 'interesting' times, and by delving liberally into the diaries which I wrote during those two years, I have attempted in the following chapters to faithfully describe an isolated aspect of those far off days.

CHAPTER 2

Prelude & First Fortnight at Oswestry

Looking back, it is quite clear that the world was in great turmoil in December 1951 – the starting month for my two years of National Service.

Conscription had been introduced in Britain with the outbreak of World War II in September 1939, and from that time, all men between the ages of 18 and 51 were liable to be called up for service in the Armed Forces. Shortly afterwards, women from 21 to 31 were also included. After the end of the War in 1945, conscription for women ceased immediately, and also many of the existing conscripted Forces were demobilised as soon as possible. It was decided however, that National Service for a period of 12 months would be introduced for all men reaching the age of eighteen and a half. Then in 1949, with the continuing threat from the Soviet Union and the formation of NATO, this period was increased to 18 months – and with the prospect of Britain's involvement in the Korean War, this was extended to 2 years in 1950.

So all young men had to attend a medical examination as soon as they reached the age of 18, and if they passed, had to register by filling in an Enlistment Form, stating their preference of Armed Force and choice of Regiment. Deferment was possible for those going onto University or for those wishing to study a profession like the Law, Medicine or Accountancy, but this was a difficult decision for the individuals to make, because, if they decided to complete their National Service first, they might later lose their urge for serious study; whereas if they joined up for two years after qualifying, they might well have forgotten much of what they learned by the time they were demobilised.

During the last year at school, there was naturally much discussion about the prospects and pitfalls of National Service, and those who had left a few Terms before were most helpful in passing on their advice and first-hand experiences. The first decision needed was to decide the choice of Arms, and we were advised by some, that it was much more difficult to obtain a Commission in the Royal Navy or the Royal Air Force, unless you joined up for three years instead of the normal two. So the choice seemed to be the Army if you wished to try for a Commission. But then, if it was to be the Army, which Regiment or Corps should be selected as the first choice?

My friend at school, Richard Davies, who had joined up a few weeks before me, had chosen the Royal Artillery, and he gave me some compelling reasons for following suit. He told me that the Gunners were normally transported about in motorized vehicles, and also, that during their two years they learned about the art of Gunnery, whereas the Infantry Regiments were far more involved in 'foot-slogging', manoeuvring in the field and firing rifles. Furthermore my elder brother Derek and my cousin David Cracknell had also chosen the Royal Artillery instead of the 'PBI' (the poor bloody infantry), and they both thoroughly recommended that I should do the same. So the Gunners it was to be.

I was young enough to have continued for another Term at school, but with National Service looming ahead, I decided to leave at the end of July 1951, and to learn about the family business by working a few months with it in London before joining the Army. After the end of the Summer Quarter also, I took part in a memorable school camping expedition in Corsica during August 1951. This is when I saw the Mediterranean Sea for the first time and toured round all parts of the island, much of which I considered very primitive at that time.

So by the end of the month, I was working in the big wide world. I put on my brown bib and brace overall, and joined Office Cleaning Services (OCS) as a 'day cleaner' working from 7 am until 4 pm in the City of London. OCS and its sister company New Century Window Cleaning Company were, at that time, by far the largest cleaning organisation in London, and even then, was employing several thousand early morning cleaners and several hundred window cleaners and supervisors, and had already started branching out around London and elsewhere in Britain.

For OCS, the whole of London was divided into a network of areas, and each was controlled by an Inspector with his own team of Supervisors and early morning cleaners – commonly called 'char' ladies in those days - as well as a back-up squad of day men cleaners like me!

The area I joined was in the City of London and consisted of cleaning contracts in buildings to the north and east of the Royal Exchange and the Bank of England, and north as far as City Road and east towards Spitalfields. This whole region was skilfully organised by a likeable Cockney Inspector named Dick Cooley. My little squad's various tasks included the periodic cleaning of floors, light fittings, grillwork to lift shafts, tiles to lavatories, high level dusting and the polishing of wood panelling - in fact any special cleaning jobs which could be done during the working day to supplement the cleaning work of the early morning 'chars'.

I travelled up to the City by bus each morning, and met up with my two colleagues in the 'bib-and-brace Brigade' - 'Dusty' Miller and 'Chalky' White - and it should be recorded, that during those three months, our little squad made quite an impact on the fight against grime within the Square Mile!

During 1951, very few new buildings existed in London, so most of the cleaning contracts consisted of premises which had missed the worst of the German bombing and had since been patched-up and repaired. At this time, large areas of the City and the East End were still completely devastated and flattened as a result of the German blitz. For instance, most of the areas stretching from the west of Moorgate to Smithfield Market, and southwards from Old Street to the Guildhall and St Paul's Cathedral remained bomb-sites; and all the roads crisscrossing these gaps were bordered by four foot high brick walls on both sides. This also applied to much of Shoreditch and Spitalfields towards the north and east of Finsbury Square and Liverpool Street Station.

The Eagle Star Insurance Building in No.1 Threadneedle Street was one of the many OCS contracts in the City, and I remember cleaning the white tiles in the two enormous washrooms (which must have had about forty washbasins and cubicles) serving all the office workers occupying the whole building - except for the seniors who each had keys to their own private loos on each floor! This was a typical design for large office buildings built in the Victorian Era. It is also interesting to note that this particular building at Number 1 Threadneedle Street has twice been demolished and rebuilt since I washed down those wall tiles so well in 1951!

In those days, hygiene standards were far lower than they are today, and the London air was badly polluted. During the early mornings for instance, it was quite common to see bread rolls being delivered in the streets to restaurants well before they opened for the day, whilst the women cleaners in adjoining buildings were liable to bang out their dusty coconut door mats in the street! Also, the buildings were far dustier than they are today, since many still had open fires for heating the offices, and most of the lifts were encased in open, dust-attracting grillwork, with hand-operated, concertina-type doors.

On one occasion during these weeks, I was given the floor cleaning job at one of our customers – the Imperial Bank of India – which occupied an ancient building in Old Broad Street not far from the site where the NatWest Tower Block now stands. I was quietly busy in mid morning, cleaning off the black build-up of wax-polish on the wooden parquet flooring surrounding the carpet squares, when suddenly I picked up an enormous splinter in my finger from the rotten wood on the skirting board! I went along to a local Chemist where the helpful young girl tried to pluck it out with a pair of tweezers – but this was to no avail. All she could say was one Cockney word: "Itaintarfard!" Without more ado, I walked to the nearby St Bartholomew's Hospital to receive some more expert treatment.

At that time St Bartholomew's Hospital was one of the top London Teaching Hospitals, and it turned out to be an excellent choice for my little injury. Within minutes a senior doctor had given me an anti tetanus injection and a local anaesthetic, and then deftly cut the splinter out. It must have been an interesting and unusual 'operation' because before long I had about twelve student doctors queuing up to inspect my outstretched, bloody finger, as I sat there in my brown, OCS bib-and-brace overall!

I immediately recognized one of the student doctors as he entered the room. He was a bulky Jamaican, called Arthur Wint, and he had won the 400 Metre Race at the London Olympics in 1948. When I was in the Athletics'

Team at Charterhouse School in 1951, he and a sprinter called McDonald Bailey – who came 6th in the final of the 100 Metre Race, just 0.3 of a second behind the winner! – came to give us a memorable demonstration on 'how to run'.

Anyway, sitting there in my brown bib-and-brace overall with my bloody finger outstretched, I said to Arthur Wint: 'I know who you are – we met each other a few months ago when you came to Charterhouse to give a demonstration to our Athletics' Team. Do you remember?' He of course did remember – and he was dumbfounded! Eventually, he was able to say: 'Gosh! You haven't done very well for yourself have you?'

Life is full of paradoxes....

The National Service Adventure

On 6 December 1951, I bid goodbye to my parents, and took the morning train to start my National Service adventure at Park Hall Camp, the Royal Artillery Training Centre near Oswestry in Shropshire. Many of my fellow passengers on the train were bound for the same destination and in those days, these trains stopped at a special Halt near the Camp, just after Oswestry.

The first observation I made whilst walking from the train was that very few of my fellow 'soldiers-to-be' carried any suitcases or grips of any kind. Most of them just had paper bags and cardboard boxes tied up with string to carry their few belongings. We must have looked like a crowd of homeless refugees as we trailed our way up the hill to the Camp! I was later told that the December in-take of recruits was normally much smaller than at other times of the year, and for some reason, it also included less than the average number of well-educated recruits. In due course, I certainly confirmed this opinion.

After our motley collection of some 300 recruits had eventually assembled at the Guard House of 67 Training Regiment Royal Artillery, we were put into some semblance of order after much swearing and shouts of: 'Get fell in!' by the NCOs in charge; and eventually, they had split us up into separate squads and had begun marching us round to the various barrack rooms which were to be our sleeping quarters for the next fortnight. They told us that after those two weeks, we would be put into different Squads again for the next three months of training. On the way round, they showed us the locations of our nearest NAAFI and YMCA canteen buildings, which were soon to become our favourite little haunts during our off-duty periods. As we unpacked our belongings, the Bombardier advised us not to stay up too long that night, because, he told us ominously that 'reveille will be at 6 o'clock in the morning and tomorrow will be a very busy day!' It was quite clear now that we had all started playing our part in the 'Army Game'!

In spite of this first squad being a real mixture of people, I remember that the others in this barrack room were a very good-natured bunch, and from that very first night, we were all most helpful to each other. I suppose this was not really surprising, because we were all rather apprehensive about the unknown before us, and many had never been away from their roots before.

My friends at school had warned me beforehand to take some spare basin-plugs in my sponge bag, and sure enough, when I went along to wash before going to bed, I found that there was not a single plug in any of the basins! I felt quite generous lending my precious plugs to some of the others – but I always made sure that they returned them to me! I came across this prob lem many times whilst in the Army and never learned what had happened to all those missing rubber plugs!

The other point that mildly surprised me in this first squad was how few of my fellow recruits had any pyjamas to change into when they first went to bed. In fact, some used to keep most of their outer clothes on, even in bed, which of course meant that they were not only warm on the cold nights but also had an unfair advantage when getting dressed and ready in the morning!

Park Hall Camp was another world, and for long periods, we were completely cut off from the rest of humanity. I suppose it was similar to being in prison!

The barrack room complexes where all the recruits slept and had their being, were called 'spiders', and this is exactly what they resembled in design: The body of the spider in the centre was where all the washbasins, showers, lavatories, boilers and drying rooms were situated, whilst the six legs were the long barrack rooms, each sleeping about thirty people. Park Hall Camp covered a very large area, and consisted of dozens and dozens of these 'spiders', as well as a number of large Parade Squares for each of the four Training Regiments on the site.

There were also various brick-built buildings scattered about the Camp:– there was the large Quartermasters' Stores for storing and issuing all the bedding, uniforms and other clothing and equipment required by the new recruits and the permanent staff. In addition to these buildings, there were the Cookhouses and Canteens, and the Vehicle Maintenance Buildings, and the many Sheds for housing the field guns and vehicles. Then, there was a Chapel, a Cinema, a Gymnasium and many Lecture Rooms, and also a number of much used NAAFIs and YMCAs canteens and leisure rooms for those off-duty. Surrounding all these buildings and tarmac roads were the many sports grounds and other sporting facilities for recreation. Park Hall Camp and its 50,000 or more inhabitants, was like a separated, self-contained island, virtually cut off from the rest of the community.

Those first two weeks were rightly considered to be the 'settling in period'. We were issued with our Army Numbers, and told to remember them 'until death' (which most soldiers do – mine was 22616387!) and we went to the Equipment Store to be issued with our own uniforms, as well as boots, belts, gaiters, berets and badges and all the other kit. When issued with ill-fitting clothes, some were told that it would shrink if it was too big – or conversely, would soon stretch if it was too small!

We also queued up for our first 'short back and sides' haircut, and it was when we reappeared after this drastic initial haircut that we all, for the first time, really started to resemble – 'a soldier'.

We marked up all our kit with our Army Numbers, and made a start at 'bulling up' our new boots, and blancoing and polishing the brass on our belts and gaiters. Those who had been in their Cadet Forces at school knew all about this, but it was surprising how many had no idea what to do.

Not only did we start to learn how to wear our uniforms properly, but we were also taught some of the basic rules in the 'Army Game'. After one of our first evening visits to the NAAFI, a group of us was innocently walking across the Parade Square back to our barrack room when suddenly the thunderous voice of a Sergeant Major rang out in the silence: 'Get off that Square!! You walk *round* the Square!! – Get off that Square! – And at the double!!' That was a lesson which none of us needed to learn again!

There were lectures and plenty of running and physical training and this was the time that many of us were introduced to the mysteries of drill on the Regimental Square. Here again, there were many who had never done this before and it took many sessions before, for instance, some of the recruits were able to turn correctly on the spot, or remember their left from their right, or (much more difficult) to carry out commands on the march.

It is easy to forget how young most of us were when we joined up for National Service after the war. Many had never been away from home before nor fended for themselves, and many had little or no knowledge about what happened outside their own village or town. Although I did not actually witness any serious bullying first-hand, I did hear the odd tale about simpletons being taken advantage of by their more streetwise comrades, but this was bound to happen on occasions. Nonetheless, I am quite sure that most NCOs would not have condoned this sort of behaviour.

The following true remembrance illustrates the callowness of some of the recruits in these initial squads. On one occasion, the Bombardier walked briskly into our barrack room and made a show about the untidiness of the place – one of our first introductions to the 'Army Game'! In his attempt to create a lasting impression (in which he succeeded!) he stomped around shouting and swearing and finding faults to criticize here and there – and then made his exit with the telling, rhetorical remark: 'and this f-ing barrack room smells like a f-ing brothel!' There was a stunned silence after his departure. The silence was eventually broken by someone's genuine query: 'What's a brothel?'

Perhaps during those initial two weeks, the fact that surprised and appalled me most was the number of illiterates we had amongst our thirty or so recruits. Similar to alcoholics, illiterates hide their frailties carefully; but nonetheless, I concluded that we had at least four illiterates (or near illiterates) in that first barrack room! I remember that we wrote letters for them, just to make sure that their families back home realised that they had arrived and how they were getting on.

This first squad was a real mixed bag of persons. Luckily I made some brief notes about some of them in my diary: There was, for instance, a dullard called Bell amongst these illiterates. He had formerly been a farm-hand in Norfolk and he told me quite frankly that he just hadn't paid much attention at school! The poor lad was right out of his depth for most of the time and I noticed that he seldom spoke to any of the others, or ever showed much interest in anything that was going on. He was an obvious recruit for the Royal Pioneer Corps, but nonetheless, he would hopefully have finished his National Service much better informed about life than if he had just stayed at home and on his farm for those two years. In my later experience, the Army took considerable time and trouble in providing additional instruction for the likes of Bell.

Another room-mate who could neither read nor write was a tractor driver from Dudley, called Greenfield. He said that he had never left his own 'map-square' before being called up and his excuse (or reason) for not learning to read was because he had missed so much of his schooling due to illnesses, as well as having to look after his sick mother for long periods. When I queried him, I noted that he had no idea which County he lived in nor who Winston Churchill was nor which Government was in power.

During my time with the Gunners, I came across many others like Greenfield who had previously worked on tractors in farms. I should imagine that whenever the words 'tractor driver' appeared on the Enlistment Form, this automatically channelled them into the Royal Artillery where they could use their skills on towing the guns instead of ploughing the furrows! Whatever the reason however, I noted in my diary that there were two other tractor drivers in that initial squad at Oswestry, although these other two showed much more potential and initiative than the poor young Greenfield.

The first of these was a likable and cheerful person called Charlie Taylor, who came from the Tunbridge Wells area, and the other was Des Cowell, who came from Worcestershire. Cowell was passionate about his farm tractors and he spoke at length on the subject, telling us how they operated and all the jobs they could do on the farm. I am quite certain that both these recruits would have made the most of their time in the Gunners and also that they would complete their two years with plenty of benefits. I met many others like these two when I later joined my Regiment in the Suez Canal Zone, and they were just the sort of person who made the British Army such a formidable force. Des Cowell told me that he had five brothers and that one of these was currently serving in Malaya and another was at the Royal Artillery Camp at Rhyl in North Wales.

There was also a Cockney called Collins, whom I considered to be a most disagreeable, street-wise character. He was very pleased with himself and told us without any shame or regret that he had previously spent two years in prison for car stealing. He also told us more than once that he was most accomplished with the boxing gloves!

Also amongst this mixed bag was a talented pianist called Reed, who told us that he had played with a jazz band before he had joined up. The night before our squad disbanded a fortnight later, he gave us a little demonstration on the NAAFI piano and his enthusiastic listeners gave him great acclamation. Someone in the Oswestry Camp must have noticed his abilities, because I saw that he was posted to 67 Training Regiment to ensure that he remained on the site for future entertainments!

Len Chapman, who came from Dover, was one of the most interesting and likable characters in this barrack room. He was boss-eyed and talked incessantly, telling us the most unlikely stories which most of us totally disbelieved! He told us (I can't understand how) that he had already been in the R.A.F. for a spell but that he had later switched to the Army. This previous experience of his made no sense whatsoever, because he was quite hopeless in all aspects of drill on the Square and if anyone was ever out of step in our squad, it was bound to be our Len! The other amusing incident about him that I luckily recorded, happened when we were all taken for the first time to practice rifle shooting on the small-arms ranges. Beforehand,

Len had been boasting about the number of times he had fired a rifle – but when we each came to fire our five rounds, Len was the only one who missed the target every time! Whatever the reason for this I don't know but I doubt if his squint did anything to improve his sharp shooting!

The last person I am able to mention in that initial squad was an electrician named Ginger Whitmore, who also came from the Dover area. He was another lively, well-educated individual, and by chance he and Len Chapman had attended the same local school so they knew each other really quite well. I noted in my diary that these two continually kept us amused by their friendly bantering during that first memorable fortnight.

With all the preliminaries now completed and with Christmas 1951 hard at our heels, the squad dispersed into the big pool of National Service recruits, and as far as I recorded, I never met any of these individuals again.

Without drawing breath, we were transferred to a completely new squad of recruits and we proceeded straightaway to the next memorable three months of our training.

Right Section "A" Troop, 149 Battery, 64th Regiment R.A. Oswestry, January 1952

Back:: Tony Opperman, Peter Glenister, Stan Love, 4, Jem Davies, Buz Collingwood, 8, Ian Lucas, Vernan Jolly, Rolly Parris, Brian Goodliffe
Middle: I, Bill Proctor, Jack Collett, 4,5, Bryan Trotter, Jerry Treherne-Thomas, 8, Ted Child, 10, 11, Bob Gonda
Front: 1,2, Mike Falconer-Flint, 4, Bdr Ayling, 'Gladys', Hugh Alexander, Barry Waters, Bob Bartlett, Cliff West, 11

CHAPTER 3

Basic Training with 64 Regiment in 1952

On 23 December 1951, I was transferred from 67 Training Regiment to another part of Park Hall Camp, and to a barrack room which was to house Able Troop, of 149 Battery, 64 Training Regiment Royal Artillery. Able Troop consisted of a new squad of people, and I soon learned that 24 of the 33 recruits in this Troop had aspirations to become officers. We very soon 'got fell in' again, and it really wasn't many days before we began to feel something like real soldiers!

Gunner Goodliffe

Before long, we were summoned to attend our USB (Unit Selection Board). This was the first hurdle to overcome before it was possible to progress to the much more difficult test, the WOSB (War Office Selection Board). If we passed both these examinations, the way was then clear for us to proceed to one of the two Officer Cadet Training Units (OCTUs) – either at Mons in Aldershot or Eaton Hall in Cheshire.

The objective of USB was for the officers in charge of the Training Batteries to appraise their new recruits and to decide whether or not they were possible material for officer training. The interviewing panel in our case consisted of our Commanding Officer (CO), the Battery Commander (BC), the Battery Captain (BK) and the National Service Second Lieutenant in charge of our Troop – and the judgment they made was absolutely crucial to us.

Naturally, this USB test was a topic frequently discussed amongst ourselves. As always in the Army, knowing 'the rules of the game' was absolutely essential. The fundamental advice here was to show self-confidence – and to make sure that you demonstrated 'loud and clear' that you were enthusiastic about the Army. Flippancy had no place whatsoever in this interview. Another cardinal rule was to give the right response to the proverbial question: 'Why do you wish to become an officer?' The correct answer was something along the lines: 'Because I believe I am capable of leading as well as following;' whilst the wrong answer was certainly: 'Because I want an easier life-style and better food in the Officers' Mess!' I do not entirely jest when I write this, because if any of these obvious guide-lines were not followed fairly closely in this initial interview, the odds are that the candidate would be rejected out of hand.

Therefore, 24 recruits from Able Troop went for their USB interviews on 31 December 1951, but in true Army fashion, it was not until after four days of waiting on tenterhooks, that we were eventually told whether or not we had passed. Eight disappointed recruits were eventually called into the Commanding Officer's office and told that they had failed – whilst the other 16 heaved a great sigh of relief. Shortly afterwards, the successful candidates were told that they would be taking their WOSB (pronounced 'Wozby') in about a month's time.

In retrospect, it is not surprising that some of the better educated recruits failed in this initial test, because most of us were merely eighteen and a half years old at the time, and many were still quite immature at that age. Furthermore, it could be said that most of those who *did* fail, would have been much happier at that age, to continue their training as Non-Commissioned Officers (NCOs) or in some other specialist activity, rather than trying to cope with the much wider responsibilities of becoming an officer.

In spite of this objective way of thinking, some of the applicants were naturally disappointed when they were turned down at this early stage – and I remember feeling very sorry for one of these in particular. He was an unsophisticated young boy, and he had previously told us that his father had been a Colonel in the Army during the war, and was most anxious to see his son receiving his Commission during his National Service. Sadly, he might well have passed through the system when he was several years older – but there was no way that he could have subsequently passed WOSB and OCTU in 1952.

This person was clearly worried about what his father would have to say about his failure at the USB test. I remember how he used to wince every time he received a letter from his censorious father, knowing that it would include a lecture, as well as a list of spelling mistakes which he had made in his last letter.

In any case, since the uncertainties of USB were now behind some of us, the successful recruits started focusing their attention during the next few weeks on that much more demanding hurdle – WOSB.

It was just before Christmas that the recruits in Able Troop were given their first TAB and anti-Tetanus injections, and for this, we had to queue up with our right hands on our hips, so that the Medical Officer and his Orderly could go down the line (with the *same* needle take note!) and give the injections to each one of us. We were all advised that this injection might well give us a sore arm and affect us badly afterwards, so we were told not to leave the Camp during the following week-end. In spite of this warning, one of our number who lived nearby (Stan Love by name) took no notice of this advice and went off home. On that Saturday afternoon, we heard that he had later collapsed on the Railway Station and had to be collected by a Regimental truck and returned to Camp!

Christmas had come and gone without much acknowledgement, and during the January that followed, Shropshire received a large quota of snow and frost, and at times it was really cold. At the end of January, I noted that the snow was lying 5 inches deep for several days, and that it was then when we had a good-natured snowball fight with the rival recruits in 17 Regiment – which we considered we had won convincingly, even though two windows were broken in the process! A large fall of snow inevitably meant an alteration in our normal training programme, but it also gave a good excuse for long sessions of energetic snow clearing on the Square!

Except on special parades, we normally wore our denim drill uniforms, and although this dress was made from quite thin cotton material, there was never any problem about keeping warm during the cold weather, because we always wore our pyjamas underneath, to act as an insulating layer!

Speaking to others serving during those years, it seems that this ploy was quite common practice in those days of initial training.

On the whole, I found my colleagues in Able Troop a most congenial group, and at the time, I was friendly with at least five of them, although sadly, I lost touch with all but one soon after the two years were over. Since they were such a large part of my life during this period, and since I often wrote about them in my diary, I am able to relate a few brief comments about them here.

To start with, there was my friend, the urbane Jerry Treherne-Thomas. He was a year or two older than I was, and he and I shared much of our leisure time together during those weeks. After we had finished our 'bulling' in the evenings, we often went up to the YMCA or NAAFI canteens together, or went out to see a film at the cinemas in the Garrison or in Oswestry. Jerry was always good company, and in preparation for WOSB, we both read the 'Opinion' Columns in the Daily Telegraph avidly each day, and helped each other by debating current affairs together. Since he was not a 'sweet eater', his friendship had the added bonus to me of receiving extra Sweet Ration Coupons each month!

Jerry Treherne-Thomas

During that February, Jerry and I both took and passed WOSB in the same batch, and later went on to Charlie Company at Mons Officer Cadet School together. After the first six weeks at Mons however, he decided to transfer from 'Field' to 'Ack Ack' for the second part of his training, so from then onwards we saw less of each other in the hurly-burly. His reason for changing to the Anti Aircraft branch was because he thought that this would give him an easier route through Mons, and all the 'Field Gunners' smugly agreed with this view, and considered that he was taking the soft option! (There was much regimental snobbery like this within the 'Army Game'.) Jerry spoke with a slight American accent, and had lived over there for some years, although he had come back to England for his schooling at Harrow and to serve his National Service. I heard later, that after Mons he had been posted to a Regiment in West Africa, and I expect he then returned to the USA after his two years were over.

Jack Collett was another particular friend of mine during those weeks we spent together in Oswestry during early 1952. Jack had been at school in Downside Abbey, and we always enjoyed each other's company. He was a congenial and cheerful companion and we had many laughs together. We were kindred spirits in some ways because we could both so readily see the funny side of some of those ridiculous antics we witnessed and took part in whilst performing the 'Army Game'. Unfortunately, although we both passed WOSB, we saw little of each other after leaving Oswestry, because he went on to Eaton Hall OCTU instead of Mons, and was then transferred to the Intelligence Corps due to his aptitude for languages. He spoke

Jack Collett & Stan Love

Spanish fluently, and after just 6 weeks at Eaton Hall, he went to Cambridge to learn Russian. I heard from him that he was later posted to Vienna, which was then one of the gateways between East and West. We met up and wrote a few letters to each other whilst we were still in the Army, but sadly, we soon lost touch after the two years were completed.

Rolly Parris

Rolly Parris was another congenial friend of mine at that time, and when we went to WOSB together, he stayed the night at my home in South London. I could see that he was going to be a doubtful candidate for WOSB, and in the event he failed the test, although he told me later that he was not particularly disappointed about this result. He came from Basingstoke, and was a brilliant artist. On one occasion he drew a very good pencil portrait-sketch of me, but sadly, this has since been mislaid. After leaving Oswestry, Rolly was posted to the Royal Artillery Radar Station in Southend-on-Sea, and although we wrote several times to each other, we failed to keep in touch for long.

Bob Bartlett, who was an Old Bancroftian, also passed WOSB and went onto Mons OCTU at the same time as me. We completed our first six weeks

Infantry training together, and as mentioned later, we continued into Fox Field Battery. Unfortunately, during one of the Schemes towards the end of the course, everything went wrong for Bob when he was in charge as GPO (Gun Position Officer), and he lost his cool and found himself relegated. I heard later that, after this great disappointment of being relegated only a few days before Passing Out in Fox Battery, he had recovered himself and had received his Commission just two months later. He was then posted to a Medium Regiment in Larkhill where re-joined Ian Lucas. After our National Service days when we all worked in the City of London, Bob, Ian and I used to meet up for lunch for a few years; but then, after we went onwards to live our young lives, we lost touch with each other.

The last person I should mention at this point is Ian Lucas, who was the one person who remained my companion during all my training, from Able Troop in Oswestry, right through to the end of our spell at Mons Officer Cadet School. I spent much of my time with Ian during those hectic six months up to the end of July 1952. Looking back, perhaps his most infuriating trait, was that he always managed to be the smartest recruit in the whole squad! At Mons OCTU we were also in the Athletics Team together,

Ian Lucas

and without a trace of modesty, it can be said that he and I were two of the very few persons in our Platoon or Troop (Jerry was another), who completed the whole course at Mons without receiving a 'warning', or being 'relegated' – or worse still, being 'RTU'd' (Returned to Unit).

Ian was an Old Whitgiftian and lived quite near to me at Purley in Surrey, so after we had completed our two years of National Service, it was logical that we should both join the same Territorial Unit together. This was the Surrey Yeomanry, 298 Field Regiment RA (TA), and subsequently we went on many summer camps together at the Artillery ranges at Sennybridge, and Larkhill. Ian originally worked for a re-insurance company in the City of London for a few years, but when he discovered that his conscientious hard work was going totally unnoticed – after two years he discovered that his immediate boss didn't even know who he was! – he left the company, and joined Scotland Yard to learn about finger-print interpretation. Later he became one of Britain's top finger-print experts. In about 1990, he retired to New Zealand, where his children and grandchildren had settled.

So back to life at Oswestry in January 1952: One of the most important maxims in the Services has always been, 'to keep the soldiers busy', and this is just how it was in Able Troop during those three months of initial training. Time was short, so the initial training had to be intensive and single-minded.

The day normally started with reveille at 6 o'clock, breakfast at 6.30 and then the first parade at 7.30 am. From then onwards, the morning programme would be split up between strenuous and sedentary periods, with a NAAFI break in the middle of the morning. We spent hours 'square bashing' and practicing rifle drill and 'gun drill' (on the 25 pounder guns), as well as physical training sessions in the Gymnasium, or runs on the roads around the Garrison Camp; and all this exercise would be interspersed with lectures and discussions on subjects like military history, Gunnery matters, aspects of the Army; or maybe maths or map reading. Then from time to time, there would be exams to make sure that all this information was going 'in', rather than 'through'! After lunch we might spend the whole afternoon on the target ranges, firing rifles or bren guns; or sometimes perhaps, sporting events like Soccer or Rugby; or fatigues in the Cookhouse, the Sergeants' Mess, or in the Garrison grounds.

At other times there were regular inspections to keep us busy, which meant that our uniforms had to be ironed frequently, and our boots 'bulled-up', and our belts and gaiters blankoed and polished every night. Our beds had to be laid out correctly each morning before parade, and the barrack rooms had weekly inspections to make sure that the floors were well polished and the washrooms kept in top condition. If on one of these inspections, the standard of the barrack room fell below the level set arbitrarily by the Sergeant or Bombardier on duty, then the whole Squad would be automatically penalized in some way, because this was the Army's way of ensuring that all the individuals pulled together as a team!

In addition to all this, individuals and groups were given extra duties as well, such as room orderly, or serving out breakfast, or doing Garrison

Guard Duty. With all this activity going on, there was certainly no reason for anyone to feel either bored or unfit!

From the very beginning at Park Hall Camp, it was clearly understood that swearing and coarse language was the order of the day – every day! It seemed that whenever a Sergeant or Bombardier commented, ordered, reacted, bollocked, praised, described, answered or questioned – his sentence or phrase had to be punctuated liberally with swear words, normally including that f–ing word! They swore between swearing! It is difficult to judge how necessary all this swearing was, but one thing is certain:– the methods they used (and swearing was an integral part of all this) did in fact prove most successful in speedily transforming a diverse and disorderly batch of civilians into a smart and disciplined squad of soldiers. It is true to say that after a few weeks of this concentrated square-bashing and inspections, we all soon started to look like soldiers; and furthermore, started to believe we were soldiers – and to act like soldiers. In today's parlance, 'we had been brainwashed'.

All this concentrated swearing was new to most of us, but in spite of its absurdity, it has to be admitted that some of this cursing and foul language did add a certain spice to the whole recipe of the 'Army Game'. On occasions perhaps, it did relieve some of the sameness and the boredom. For instance: 'take that f–in smirk off your f–in chops!' does tend to have a little more about it than just ordering someone to, 'Stop smiling!' But before I move on from this subject, another exchange which I dutifully recorded in my diary was made during one of our inspections. The Bombardier was heard to say: 'Lies, f–in lies!' To which the soldier replied: 'But I *did* blanco it last night Bombardier'. The NCO remained unconvinced: 'F–in 'ell! You're breaking my f–in'art!'

I suppose verbal abuse has always been in vogue in the Services, and to a certain extent, this has taken the place of other forms of physical abuse or punishment, which has of course been totally outlawed and forbidden in the British Army since 1868.

A friend of mine, Malcolm Unsworth, was enlisted in the Intelligence Corps during his National Service from 1949 to 1951, and he was selected for an unusual and little known role:– he acted as a National Service 'spy'. After the War, a few of the raw recruits were just unable to take the strain of life in the Army and as a result, there were an alarming number of suicides. The Government reacted to this by selecting a number of suitable recruits – who always worked in pairs, but were told not to be openly friendly with each other – and posted them several times for initial training at the different Army camps. As a reward for their efforts, they received Regular Sergeants' pay, with the additional balance being sent separately to a bank account at home.

Malcolm and his accomplice therefore, joined up on six separate occasions during the next two years, and were given a new Army Number each time. No on except the Commanding Officer and the Adjutant knew of their existence, and they were given free access at all times. He said that during his time, he witnessed a few instances of racial abuse and bribery; but to be specific about one particular case, he witnessed a Sergeant throw a 303 magazine at one recruit which hit him in the face, and wounded him slightly on the cheek. When Malcolm and his colleague subsequently reported this incident to the CO and the Adjutant, all the facts were given, Malcolm and his colleague were excluded from all the enquires that followed when all witnesses were being questioned, and the Sergeant involved was stripped of his stripes and disappeared from the scene immediately!

To illustrate some more aspects of life in Park Hall Camp, I have included a few extracts from my diary which I made at the time. First, Saturday, 5 January 1952:–

'There was no frost last night, so everywhere is very wet this morning. We had a barrack room inspection by Bombardier Collins before the customary morning parade. Up to 10 o'clock, the time was wasted by just cleaning up the dummy guns again, and also in idle chatter, but by 10.30 we were all changed and ready for the cross-country run. We joined the rest of the Regiment on the Square, and were marched off across Tinker's Halt railway line, and then lined up in the fields there. Our great-coats were left on the fence, and the race commenced. We all ran across this rough, squelchy field towards a tiny opening in the fence through which hundreds of us had to squash! I saw no point in racing, so I just went through the gap with the rest of the throng. We soon saw that the ground beyond was extremely muddy and our legs just sank into the mire above our ankles. Many lost their plimsolls in the mud and had to hunt around for them with their hands! The run also went over barbed wire fences and streams, so we came to the conclusion that the route chosen for this particular run hadn't been very well thought out! To Oswestry in the evening with Jerry (Trehearne-Thomas), Rolly (Parris), Tony (Opperman) and Bryan (Trotter) to see *Rich, Young and Pretty'*.

Then Wednesday, 16 January 1952:– 'We were woken up by a noisy Bombardier this morning. Sergeant White gave us a lecture about some different types of shells used (High Explosive, Delayed Explosive, Air-burst, Anti-tank, Smoke etc) and after that we had an hour of drill, followed by some films about the sten gun (we heard that it cost only 17 shillings and sixpence each to make – that's. $87\frac{1}{2}$ pence in today's currency), and we also heard about Directors (used for setting up for the guns). After some more drill before lunch, we were given a session of PT, and since this is our games afternoon, we thought that we had no further commitments today. Some are playing rugby for the Battery, and the remainder either went to watch the match or practiced with the Directors. After Tea, when we were all taking it easy, we were all suddenly told to get out and clean the guns again in readiness for the General's Inspection tomorrow! These extra inspections are really a nuisance! This evening, Jerry and I went to the NAAFI for a snack. Weather this evening is snowy and wet, after a lovely sunny day today.'

Finally, some notes on the subterfuge we witnessed during the General's inspection on the following day, which clearly illustrates the truth of that well known Army saying: 'bullshit baffles brains!' On Thursday, 17 January 1952, I wrote:

'There is snow on the ground today, but it isn't very deep. Extra trouble was taken in cleaning out the spider today, because of the annual visit by a General from the War Office, and we noticed that various new travel posters have now suddenly appeared on the walls of our barrack room – no doubt to make the place look more homely! The whole afternoon was then spent in a lecture room, waiting for the General to reach us. All the

Artillery Boards (used for plotting the guns and the targets) were set up and all the questions and answers rehearsed, so everyone knew exactly what they had to do! We then just sat there chatting amongst ourselves and with Bombardier Ayling and waited for near on 4 hours! Someone had been posted at the window on lookout, closely watching the General's movements round the camp, and after a few false alarms (when he unsportingly changed his direction!), we eventually received the definite warning that he was actually on his way to see us. When the General appeared in our lecture room, the pre-arranged questions were duly asked, and sure enough, we all knew the answers straightaway, which meant that the General continued his rounds with a satisfied smile on his face!'

Now what harm was there in all that deception and kiddology? The incident certainly showed us all beyond doubt, that bullshit *really does* baffle brains!

During those weeks we spent much of the time studying the 25-Pounder Field Gun, which had been one of Britain's mainstay Artillery pieces during World War II. It was explained to us how it worked and what its capabilities were; and then we were introduced to the ramifications of 'Gun Drill' and 'Fire Discipline' – two complicated subjects which needed much study. In future months, these two subjects in particular, were soon to be of prime importance to all of us going on to Mons OCTU as Field Gunners. For this reason, I shall quickly explain both these subjects in a little more detail:

Firstly, a 25-Pounder is manned by a team of six gunners: the No.1 (normally a sergeant) who is in charge of the gun; the No.2 who loads the gun; the No.3 who sets the sights; and the other three gunners who prepare the ammunition ready for loading. 'Gun Drill' explains the duties and responsibilities of each member of the gun team, whereas 'Fire Discipline' lays down the strict way in which all orders are passed to the guns during firing, and conversely, how all these orders are acknowledged and carried out at the guns.

As the weeks went by and WOSB came and went, we studied and revised many of the wider aspects of Gunnery, which are an extension of those two main disciplines. We learned about the different types of fire and barrages which could be given; and the different fuses which can be used (such as 'air-burst' 'time fuze' and 'smoke-screen'); how to compensate for the differing gun positions; how to choose and set up a gun position; how to direct the fire by plotting the gun position in relation to the target; and how to correct the fire using an observation point – and there were many more quite technical but interesting matters. There really was plenty of details about Gunnery to be learned and absorbed by the time we started at Mons.

Some of our colleagues in Able Troop quickly picked up the intricacies of this complicated subject, and they were a great help to some of the others who were eager to learn but slower on the uptake. One such bright pupil was Bob Gonda, who was an old Tonbridgian and obviously a good scholar and mathematician. He was a most amiable individual, and someone to whom I always turned if ever I wanted to clear up some specific point about Gunnery. Poor Bob was one of those academics, who probably wasted two years of his life in the Army. He failed his WOSB, and I believe he spent the rest of his time as a Tec Acc (RA Technical Assistant) at Larkhill, which was a job well below his capabilities.

Bob Gonda

There was of course no television for us to watch in Park Hall Camp in those days, so during the evenings after we had finished cleaning all our kit and the barrack room, we normally socialised in the NAAFI or the YMCA, where there was a very basic, unlicensed cafeteria (chocolate and sweets were of course in short supply due to rationing), a piano and also such games as darts and billiards. For alcoholic drinks, I expect the troops went out to the local pubs. There was a Garrison Cinema to go to and also a number of other Cinemas in Oswestry, and dances were sometimes organised on Saturday nights in the Camp.

Soccer and Rugby were often played in the afternoons, and I had at least four Soccer games during those weeks. In one of these matches, I found that the standard of play was exceptionally high, because, not only were some Physical Training Instructors (PTIs) playing, but I also noted in my diary that there were a few professional footballers in the teams as well. I see that I spoke to one of these professionals in my team. He was a likable young northerner called Woods, who told me that he had signed up for Everton before he joined up. In that particular game, I was playing on the right wing, so I was pleased to be kept well out of harm's way! There were many professional Soccer players doing their National Service during those years and they were much sought after by all the Regiments wishing to perform well in the Army Championships!

On another sports afternoon, the Rugby players in Able Troop, instigated by my friend Jack Collett, challenged the Soccer players to a Soccer match. This turned out to be a very amusing game because so few of the Rugby players had any idea about the rules of Soccer. The game was played in a good spirit, but nonetheless there were many free kicks and 'professional' fouls throughout the game, so the PTI referee's whistle was seldom idle. We had many laughs, and I am pleased to relate that according to my notes, the Soccer players won the game 11-0!

The Army was, of course, very keen on promoting all kinds of sport, so naturally, boxing appeared on the programme more than once. I boxed a number of times and I see that in those days I weighed in at just 11 stone 12 lb! One Saturday we had a competition that involved Able and Baker Troops, although the whole competition only lasted just about two hours. The Boxing Ring had been set up in the Gymnasium, so after a 2 mile run and some exercises in the open air, we marched down to start the contests. To give everyone a round, the fights lasted only

Jem Davies

one minute each, but even so, I noted in my diary that poor Bob Gonda (who was not a sporty type), Jem Davies and Rolly Parris all had a very hard time in the ring and came out battered and bruised. To them, those 60 seconds must have seemed more like a quarter of an hour!

To my mind, the most unpleasant task in the Army was Guard Duty, and everyone in our Troop was allocated his dose at least four times during his stay at Oswestry. Guard Duty lasted from 6 o'clock in the evening until 6 o'clock the next morning, but in addition to this there was also a special procedure for taking over from the day guards as well as handing over to the new guards in the morning. The duty Orderly Sergeant was in charge and he had six soldiers detailed each night, divided into pairs. Each pair did 2 hours on duty and 4 hours off, and the two hourly shifts started from 6 o'clock onwards throughout the night. To add to the fun, the Orderly Officer would sometimes turn-out the guard during the small hours, so if the off duty guards were able to drop off to sleep after their spell, they might well be woken up again! But not only did this Guard Duty mean a badly inter-rupted night's sleep, those 12 hours were also so very, very boring!

On the day following a night on Guard Duty, there was of course no recog-nition whatsoever to the individuals involved. There were no compensa-tions or time off in lieu – everything just went on as usual. This attitude is entirely understandable, because the real Army life can never be a 'nine to five' job, with set times for sleeping, and set times for duty. We were soon to find, that on schemes (and I should imagine during wartime as well) the involvement alternates between periods of intense activity, and long peri-ods of extreme boredom. In fact, very similar to Guard Duty!

One morning, after we had just finished a spell on Guard, the six of us were detailed again to stay on duty until 7 o'clock in the evening as Regimental Police, so that we could look after three prisoners who were locked up in the Guard House. They really were a pathetic trio, and all they did the whole day long was to sit about looking miserable. We were told that all three were deserters who had overstayed their leave (AWOL), but one in particular had to be watched very closely, because he had pre-viously been in prison for robbery with violence. That really was a memo-rably boring day!

On one Saturday towards the end of January, we were all given our sec-ond batch of injections, and some of us were very badly affected again this time. I wrote pathetically in my diary:– 'We had our jabs at 2 o'clock. This injection hurt much more than last time. I went to bed early, and it was snowing quite hard when I went to sleep. My arm is extremely sore. I took two Aspros.'

The next day, Sunday 27 January, I wrote:– 'I had a horrible night. I was woken up by the draught from an open window about 2 o'clock and had to get out about 4 o'clock to shut it. I was very hot and felt feverish. I heard from the others that Cliff (West) had been delirious last night about 10.30, and had said some very peculiar and amusing things. He was quite convinced that he was going to die! I didn't bother to get up today, and most of the others are also feeling pretty bad. Since we have been jabbed we are excused other duties such as serving at breakfast, and also sweeping the snow off the square. I didn't get up or get dressed for the whole day. I wrote a letter home. I am not feeling at all well. I hope I am better tomorrow. Rolly (Parris) brought me some cakes and orange squash from the NAAFI, and Cliff (West) blancoed my belt etc. Everyone went to bed early tonight. I took two more Aspros.'

Cliff West

Surprisingly enough, I read in my diary that we had a third tetanus jab on 14 February, but this one didn't hurt much, and afterwards it caused us all minimal reaction.

One part of the forthcoming WOSB which I was really dreading was having to give my 5 minute lecturette. I practiced it frequently but I never felt really confident about the way I delivered it, although Jerry (Treherne-Thomas) did his best to reassure me. I always practiced the same little talk about my visit to Corsica in 1951 and I repeated this dozens and dozens of times before the fateful day.

I met at least seven other Old Carthusians during my time at Oswestry, and it is true to say that we invariably established an instant rapport and were always willing to help each other as much as possible. One of my school friends I met at this time was Richard Davies, who had started his National Service about a month before my own draft. Since he was ahead of me, he was able to give me some invaluable first-hand advice. He must have passed WOSB in early December, because he moved on for his training at Mons OCTU on 25 January. During our leisure time before he left,

Peter Glenister

we often met up for a reassuring chat in the YMCA, and we also later saw each other regularly at Mons to my great advantage. He was an extremely competent and able soldier and I could see that he was bound to sail through all the hazards with flying colours – and so it proved.

January was coming to an end and WOSB was looming ahead. On 5 February, the first batch from Able Troop, 8 other candidates and myself, were to start their journey towards Andover. My fellow applicants were to be:

Bryan Trotter

Jem Davies
Peter Glenister
Vernon Jolly
Ian Lucas
Jerry Treherne-Thomas
Rolly Parris
Bryan Trotter
Barry Waters

The day before our departure I wrote in my diary: 'practiced my lecturette and finished bulling my kit for tomorrow. Went to see the film *Walk in the Sun*. I wonder what WOSB will bring forth?'

In the event, just four of us were to pass.

Vernon Jolly

CHAPTER 4

WOSB and Last Weeks
At Oswestry

After parade on Tuesday 5 February 1952, the 9 candidates from Able Troop taking the War Office Selection Board Examination (WOSB), handed their kit into the stores, were given their group travel warrant and then took two taxis to Gobowen station in time for the 10.10 am train to Paddington. When we arrived in London at 2.30, we went our separate ways and arranged to meet again at Waterloo station on the following morning at 8.30. Rolly Parris was staying the night with me at Streatham, so we made our way home and before long my mother had produced a plate full of eggs and bacon, which we soon demolished. We decided to go down to the Streatham Odeon that afternoon to see an early programme with a film called '*the Magic Box*', and soon went to bed that night, mindful of the importance of tomorrow.....

Next morning, we learned sadly, that King George VI had died in the night – but then I had other matters to think about today!

When we met together at Waterloo, we had a slight panic on the platform, because Barry Waters, who was the person entrusted with our Travel Warrant, arrived just in time to catch the train as it was pulling out at 9 o'clock! Anyway, all was OK and on arrival in Andover, we were picked up by a 3 ton Army truck and driven at break-neck speed to Drayton Camp, Barton Stacey, near Winchester.

After registration, we were put into teams of eight and each of us was issued with a coloured

Barry Waters

37

tabard with an individual number front and back, which we had to wear at all times during the days, so that all the supervisors could watch our every move! My team's colour was yellow, and my special number was 74. There must have been at least a hundred others included in this particular group of candidates.

After lunch, a Captain came and spoke to us all and briefly explained the arrangements for the next two days. In short, he told us that this first afternoon would consist of various written examinations, whilst tomorrow and the next day would be some practical tests in the field and some interviews. The papers after lunch were obviously set out to test our aptitude for words and numbers, as well as our ability for solving puzzles and intelligence tests. After we had completed these tests, we had a break for tea and then returned to the examination room and given a choice of subjects from which to write an essay. I see from my diary that I chose 'Youth Clubs' for my subject, though Heavens knows what I wrote about on this topic!

I felt fairly happy after completing these initial tests, but it was quite clear that tomorrow would be the most crucial day of WOSB, since that was when the supervisor of our little group would be judging our leadership qualities, and observing how we conducted ourselves under stress. I ended my diary entry for that first day· 'practiced lecturctte.'

The second day started at 7 o'clock, and after breakfast we divided into our different colour teams, in which we were to remain for the rest of our two days at Barton Stacey. We had a short introductory talk from the Colonel in charge of the Yellow Board and he handed us over to the smooth-talking Captain, who was to be our team's supervisor for the rest of the time. He explained the programme of the day to us – and then we were off....

The first session was a team discussion and here I began rather badly, because the first topic was 'Rugby Football', which meant that my own contribution was fairly lightweight! Anyway, before long we were discussing current affairs and here I made sure that I scored a few telling points!

Next we went out into the grounds, where we walked past various obstacles and tests spread out between the trees over a wide area. These were constructed from a variety of different objects, such as planks, trenches, ladders, brick walls, ropes dangling from trees and so on. As we walked past some of these, we eyed them warily, but eventually, we reached the obstacles selected for the Yellow Team. The first few tasks we had to solve and tackle as a team and as we were sorting ourselves out, the Captain in charge gave the odd comment and advice and kept the time. I also noted that he was watching us all like a hawk! This took us up to lunchtime.

In the afternoon we went out into the grounds again, and this time each person in turn was put in charge of the team and given an obstacle to overcome. The leader then had to explain the problem, and organize the others over the obstacle. We were told that the object of the exercise was not necessarily to solve the problem (some obstacles were apparently insoluble!) but the objective was to find out how we took control, how we reacted and the way we handled the others in the team.

When my turn came, the obstacle given to me was like this: There was a trench with a small 'island' half way across; a plank which reached the island, and some sand bags. I had to take the team and the sand bags across the trench. Luckily, this seemed to be one of the easier tasks. I brought the team together, explained the task, and told them how we were going to get across. The plank was put onto the island in the middle and I then went across to the island. After that, I told the first person to pick up a sand bag and to join me on the island. I then put the plank across to the far bank, and sent the first person across. The rest of the team crossed similarly and then I joined them on the far bank.

The rest of the Yellow Team completed their various tasks, and I noted in my diary that some of them made a real hash of their few minutes in charge! After this, we all went into the main building to give our lecturettes. My little talk on 'Corsica' was trotted out again, and I considered that it went down as well as I could have hoped. I remember that I heaved a great sigh of relief after this uncertainty had been completed!

This crucial second day ended with two important interviews, the first with the Colonel of our panel, and the second with the Major, both of which seemed to go quite well. And so to bed at 9.30 pm.

On Friday 8 February 1952, I wrote in my diary: 'Woken up at 7 o'clock, after a rather bad night. I am very worried about the result which we shall be given today.'

On the final morning, our supervising Captain first took us to another obstacle course out in the grounds and there we had our individual agility tests. We were each given 90 seconds to complete as many of the seven obstacles as possible and for every obstacle completed, a certain number of points were awarded. I managed to cope with all of these obstacles except for the rope climbing, so this must have been quite a satisfactory result. Anyway, as a final test before lunch, we all returned to the lecture room, where we were given a fairly searching written quiz on current affairs. Thus ended the formal testing. Now all we had to do was to wait for those decisive judgments about us....

After lunch, we all went along to a large waiting room and there we had to wait for at least 45 excruciating minutes. We were then each called in at 5 minute intervals. We had to march in, stand in front of the Yellow Team panel, and to state: 'Sir, – Candidate Number 74, Gunner Goodliffe, 64 Regiment Royal Artillery; choice of Arms: Royal Artillery, Royal Army Service Corps, and Infantry'. Then back to the waiting room.

After another wait, we were told to line up and receive our Certificates. The Captain walked down the line and deliberately handed each of us our Certificate. We knew that if the top part of the paper was crossed off, it meant a failure....But if the bottom part was crossed off, it meant that you had passed....I looked at mine....The bottom half had been crossed off....I HAD PASSED!!!! I wrote in my diary that night: 'I am feeling inexpressibly relieved and joyous'.

When I later saw the others from Oswestry, I learned that only four out of the nine had passed, namely: Ian Lucas, Jerry Treherne-Thomas, Bryan Trotter and myself; whereas the other five had all failed: Jem Davies, Peter Glenister, Vernon Jolly, Rolly Parris and Barry Waters.

In retrospect, it is very easy for some people to belittle or dismiss the difficulty of passing WOSB, but for those involved *at the time*, it was certainly no pushover because the outcome from those three days could never be taken for granted. All that was needed for a crucial rejection was: just one bad slip up; or one important mistake; or perhaps too much cockiness; or maybe over-confidence; or otherwise appearing too flippant. Some mistakes in the judgements were inevitably made, because I met many Other Ranks in the Services whom I considered would have made satisfactory officers, whereas there were also the odd few officers whom I thought should never have been Commissioned in a month of Sundays!

However, there is always a certain amount of good luck and bad luck involved when taking any type of exam, although regarding WOSB in particular, it seems to me that the selection procedure evolved by the Army does and did produce a very high percentage of correct judgments at the time on peoples' capabilities. Furthermore, on that crucial piece of paper handed round to each candidate at the end of WOSB, there are three possibilities stated:

- (a) Recommended for OCS Training.
- (b) Not recommended at present, but your C.O. will be called upon for a report in three months' time or if in the meantime you have been posted to a Service Unit, three months after such posting. (The term used in the Army for this recommendation was: 'Failed Watch'.)
- (c) Not recommended.

Before I leave the WOSB scene completely, I recorded a little anecdote which was told to me during my time at Drayton Camp. Although we had little time to socialise with the other candidates during those hectic days, I did record a conversation I had with another member of the Yellow Team. He was a friendly young Scottish National Serviceman who was wearing the kilt of the Argyll and Sutherland Highlanders. He told me quite seriously that they definitely do not wear any pants under their Regimental kilt. In fact, he said that during inspection, the sergeants often made use of up-turned mirrors to ensure that there was no cheating going on! Whether or not his remarks were true, I have never confirmed, but when it is remembered that I am writing about far off 1952; and also, that in my opinion at the time, he was telling me the truth, then I really do believe what he said.

After WOSB, we were back in Park Hall Camp on 9 February, and life continued to move at quite a pace, because in ten day's time Able, Baker and Charlie Troops were scheduled for their 'Passing Out Parade' (i.e. the end of their Initial Training Course). In the 'Army Game', this always meant extra 'bulling' and extra inspections to make it a memorable occasion for all!

I noted that during the build-up days, we were scrubbing floors, distempering the beams and painting our boxes, whilst on the day before Passing Out, we had several hours of drill on the Square in preparation and I also recorded: 'this evening the bulling began in earnest. We scraped the brooms, painted the red line, and repainted the beams amongst other things. It was 11.45 before I managed to get to sleep.'

After Passing out, our Able Troop NCOs had completed the training, so many of our colleagues were now posted onto their future Units, whilst the remainder moved all their kit to another barrack room. This meant that our old spider was vacated and could be prepared for the next new intake of untrained recruits. Thus the conveyor belt was able to move on.....

It is interesting to note that not all the NCOs connected with Able Troop had the 'thumbs down' from us. Our Bombardier Ayling was really quite a sensible and helpful instructor, and we all considered that he had looked after us very well during our training period. We were discerning enough to realise this, and as a result, before we passed out, we clubbed together and bought him an engraved tankard, costing £3, as a token of our thanks. He was really quite taken aback by this present!

Bombardier Ayling

On the other hand, the pompous little National Service Subaltern in charge of Able Troop was never very popular with us, so we always referred to him as 'Gladys'! We didn't see much of him – only from afar on parades, or during his barrack room inspections, or when he gave us lectures. He was a dumpy little man, who seemed to relish his all-powerful position over us – but then, I suppose that was his job in a Training Regiment. He never showed any friend-liness towards us, even after we had passed WOSB and were about to be moving on to OCTU. At the time, I always considered this a foolish way for him to act, because after all, we were all just playing at soldiers for a couple of years, and it was only a few months ago that he himself had progressed from being a raw recruit at Oswestry!

"Gladys"

At this stage, I had been in the 'Army Game' for merely three months, so I was progressing into the unknown and had no idea where I should eventually end up. However, I thought to myself at the time, that if ever I should get through the hazards of Mons, the posting I should least relish would be similar to that of Gladys at a Training Regiment.

The week before Able Troop disbanded and we all went our separate ways, a group photograph was taken, and with the help of this and with notes that I made at the time, I have listed below, the names of most of the 33 persons who completed their initial training with me. Where pos-sible, I have also mentioned how they faired. All in all, they were a very friendly and good-natured bunch to be with, and I can't remember us ever having any unpleasantness during all those weeks we spent and worked together.

Hugh Alexander	Failed USB
Bob Bartlett	Mons and Medium Regt. RA, Larkhill.
Michael Berks	Failed WOSB, became a Tec Acc.

Jack Collett	Eaton Hall, and Intelligence Corps.
Ted Child	Failed WOSB, became a PTI.
John Clymie	Failed USB.
Buz Collingwood	Failed WOSB, posted to Larkhill.
Mike Collier	Failed USB, became a PTI.
Jem Davies	Failed WOSB, posted to Larkhill.
Mike Falconer-Flint	Failed WOSB.
Peter Glenister	Failed WOSB, to Larkhill as Surveyor.
Bob Gonda	Failed WOSB, posted to Larkhill.
Dave Holland	Failed USB.
Vernon Jolly	Failed WOSB, to Military Police.
Stan Love	Didn't take USB, posted to MELF.
Ian Lucas	Mons and Medium Regt. RA, Larkhill.
Tony Opperman	Failed WOSB, posted to MELF.
Rolly Parris	Failed WOSB, posted to Radar, Southend.
Phil Price	Failed USB, became a PTI.
Bill Proctor	Eaton Hall, transferred to RAOC.
Colin Tetlow	Failed USB, became a Tec Acc.
Jerry Treherne-Thomas	Mons and AA Regt RA in West Africa.
Bryan Trotter	Mons and Medium Regt. RA, Larkhill.
Barry Waters	Failed WOSB, Regimental Clerk.
Cliff West	Failed USB, became a Tec Acc.
Dave Weldon	Failed USB, became a Tec Acc.

MELF	= Middle East Land Forces.
PTI	= Physical Training Instructor.
RAOC	= Royal Army Ordnance Corps.
Tec Acc or TARA	= Technical Assistant Royal Artillery.
USB	= Unit Selection Board.
WOSB	= War Office Selection Board

To put some more meat on the bone, here are some random comments about four of those mentioned above:

Firstly, Tony Opperman: He left Oswestry on the day after Passing Out Parade and was posted – together with Stan Love – to 41 Field Regiment RA in the Suez Canal Zone. Tony was a real comedian, and kept us all laughing in the barrack room with his jokes and witticisms. He was a personable and intelligent person but strangely enough, he failed WOSB. This must have been due to his apparent flippancy at the time, although I feel quite sure that he could have passed the test if he had taken it again. I saw Tony and Stan Love a few times in the Middle East, when I met them both in the Athletics Championships. Tony was then a Lance-Bombardier and a Troop Technical Assistant, and he told me that he was quite happy with life in MELF. I met him again when I was by chance acting as Safety Officer for his Troop in 41 Field, and suddenly heard his jolly voice coming out of their Command Post.

Tony Opperman

Mike Falconer-Flint was probably the most surprising colleague in Able Troop who failed WOSB. He was a few years older than most of us, and had a moustache, which made him look like a military man. He had previously

started to train as a doctor, but had failed his exams or quit before finishing his training. Mike was brimful of confidence which bordered on the arrogant, and he had obviously 'seen life'. He pulled his weight in the Troop, but he was a person whose company I never sought. We all thought he would be certain to pass WOSB (and so did he) – but not so. I remember him being much deflated on 1 March after he had returned a failed candidate. I expect that the examiners considered him too cocky and pleased with himself. I never learned what happened to him after leaving Park Hall Camp, but I expect that he subsequently took WOSB again and passed.

Mike Falconer-Flint

Bill Proctor was another person I liked less than the others. I believe he intended to enter the Church after his National Service,

Bill Proctor

though I personally would never have seconded his application form! For some reason he opted to transfer to the RAOC after passing WOSB, and we all thought that this was a very strange decision to make. Perhaps he wanted to keep away from 'real soldiering' during his two years. After celebrating our Passing Out, Bill and a few others returned late at night to our barrack room very drunk, and by shouting and banging the boxes, purposely woke us all up. We all told him off but he took no notice, so I got out of bed and quickly went alongside him.

I was obviously at a great disadvantage because he tried to tread on my toes; but he was very drunk, and I knew a ju-jitsu 'throw' which I had often used in the past. Without him suspecting anything, I got him in my special grip, and in a trice, he had landed heavily on his back with a great thud. In his surprise he was completely non-plussed, and everyone jeered and laughed at him as he was lying there on the floor. No; on further consideration, Bill Proctor was certainly not one of my favourite colleagues in Able Troop!

Finally, I must make a small mention about Buz Collingwood, who was a most jovial character, and possessed not a wicked bone in his body. Most of us in Able Troop would fondly remember Buz lying in bed after reveille, and lighting up his pipe, whilst still reclining in his bed! After a good few deep puffs, he would be finally ready for his morning ablutions! When I sent these recollections to my friend Ian Lucas in New Zealand, this was one of the lasting memories that he had retained clearly in his mind after all those years! What happened to all that thick smoke which he puffed out into the barrack room I have no idea. Perhaps it just wafted away through the rafters! Buz Collingwood failed WOSB, and I believe that he was another one to be posted to Larkhill.

Buz Collingwood

Those of us who had passed WOSB were told that we would not be going to Mons until the end of March at the earliest, so 64 Regiment made good use of us during those last six weeks. We were all promoted to acting, unpaid Lance-Bombardiers, and attached to one of the new Training Troops. This was important to the other NCOs, because it meant that we were available for camp duties such as BONCO (Battery Orderly Non Commissioned Officer). As a result, Ian Lucas, Bob Bartlett, Jack Collett, Jerry Treherne-Thomas, Bryan Trotter, Bill Proctor and myself were all given this duty more than once.

I was BONCO during my last three weeks at Oswestry, and the duties included waking up the whole Battery in the morning, unlocking the Gun Sheds, then writing out the sick list in the Battery Office. After breakfast, most of the day was spent taking round the mail, or sitting in the Battery Office and dealing with any messages or queries, or just reading a book to fill up the time. The duties ended at about 6 o'clock after taking the roll-call, and supervising the cleaning of the Battery Office.

Bob Bartlett

Regular Dances were held in the Camp to which many of the nurses from the local hospital were invited to brighten up our lives. On one occasion when Bryan Trotter was BONCO, he was delegated to look after the door, take the money, and ensure that everyone entering bought a ticket. When the Sergeant in charge gave him his instructions, he ended up by saying, 'and when my wife comes in, you let her in free – OK?' There was a pause – 'Just a minute Sergeant' queried Bryan, 'how shall I know which one your wife is?' There was another pause. The Sergeant looked him straight in the eyes: 'Listen to me laddie! – I'm telling you – she's the ugliest f–ing bitch that comes through that door!' I didn't make a note in my diary, whether or not the Sergeant was correct in his judgment about his wife, but as we discovered on many other occasions, Sergeants were never particularly well known for their accuracy, nor indeed, for their moderate turn of phrase!

In early March, Bill Proctor, Ted Child and I had a trip away from the camp for one week-end, when we volunteered to guard some prisoners in the Detention Ward of the Military Hospital in Chester. After being driven to Chester in a 15 cwt truck, we mounted the guard outside the locked door in two-hour shifts, from midday Friday until midday Saturday, and I don't believe we ever actually saw the prisoners during that time! Although this guard duty was as boring as usual, the trip to Chester did have its compensations.

Ted Child

It was the first time that I had ever seen this lovely old city, and we had a chance on the Saturday afternoon to have a good look round. I noted that we had a meal at one of the pubs in Foregate Street, and saw the unusual two-storey medieval shopping galleries called 'The Rows'. I also noted that 'we walked round the old Roman walls, and saw the Castle and Military Museum, as well as the Cathedral with its square tower and with some of its old sections dating back to the 11th century. The oldest house I saw had the date 1497 painted on the wall'.

The guard duty was as boring as usual, but according to my diary, I had a heart to heart talk with Ted Child to wile away the time during the week-end. Ted was one of those who had failed WOSB and was now waiting to start his training as a PTI. I noted that he was 'a great talker and he told me his life history!' Unfortunately, I ran out of space in my diary so I failed to record very much of his indiscretions; but one piece of information that did intrigue me at the time was the disclosure that he had been something of a burglar before his call-up! We met so many colourful characters during those two years of National Service that I only wish that I had been more sensible, and recorded far more details of these conversations.

During those last few weeks at Oswestry, we paraded with the PS (Permanent Staff), who included all those running Park Hall Camp and the NCOs attached to the Training Troops. This arrangement was not entirely without some antipathy towards the 'WOSB boys'. The following little episode partly illustrates this slight resentment. During a big Regimental Parade on one Saturday morning, the Major inspecting us all, singled me out to compliment me on the standard of my boots; 'Excellent!' he said as he looked me up and down. Later, when we were told to 'Stand Easy!' all the Regular NCOs immediately turned round and looked at my 'excellent' boots, and to a man they commented: "F–ing hell! Those boots are f–ing rotten!" (or words to that effect!) We all had a good laugh about that trivial incident afterwards.

Whilst I was in the Army, I met at least a dozen survivors from the Japanese Prisoner-of-War Camps, and all of them had sadly been permanently damaged and scarred by the terrible treatment they had received at the hands of those cruel and uncivilized fiends. Whenever you saw these poor, luckless survivors, you could immediately identify them from a distance of some 20 yards, by their gaunt and haunted appearance and their deep sunken eyes. They also had a personality defect that caused them to 'fly off the handle' at the least provocation caused by their horrific ordeal.

We had one such unfortunate Sergeant at Park Hall Camp, and heartlessly (though very aptly) we universally nicknamed him 'the screaming skull'. Now and again, it would be his turn (or maybe he volunteered!) to wake up all the Battery in the morning, and the noise that he made during these sessions was not only deafening, it was also terrifying!

There are six barrack rooms in each 'spider' and the spiders in the camp were spread over a wide area, so when the duty NCO came to wake up the troops in the mornings, he would normally make his rounds using a particular route. Those sleeping in the furthest spiders therefore, could stay in their warm beds for a minute or so longer than those nearer to the start of the rounds. Likewise, those sleeping in the 6th barrack room of the spider, could easily remain lying in bed for a few seconds longer than those sleeping in the 1st barrack room, and so on. With most NCOs it was only necessary to sit up in bed and show that you were awake, but when the 'screaming skull' was on duty, the reaction of the troops was quite different. His loud shouting, and his bangs with his big stick on the boxes, could be identified as soon as he started his rounds in the furthest spiders. Even so, as he made his progress from spider to spider, everyone remained motionless in their beds, apparently fast asleep – although in fact, they were all listening intently to the progress of his shouts and bangs as he approached closer and closer. Then, just as his hand was on the door handle of their own barrack room – everyone suddenly leapt out of bed in one movement, with both feet firmly on the floor! Nobody wanted to get on the wrong side of the 'screaming skull'!

Life and war can be so very unkind and unfair. In 1952, when I saw these ex-prisoners of war like the 'screaming skull', the Japanese War had ended barely six years before, so these young men must have been in their twenties. At that age, they ought to have been in the prime of life, but instead, those evil Japanese soldiers had purposely scarred and damaged them mentally for the rest of their lives. Thankfully, the Atomic Bomb was available to the Allies just in time to prevent even more atrocities being perpetrated by those wicked, unscrupulous and inhuman fanatics.

One evening, towards the end of my time at Oswestry, I felt the need for a little culture (in addition to the large dose of films we constantly saw at all the cinemas!) so I went along to investigate the 'Music Circle', which held its meetings in the Educational Centre on the other side of Park Hall Camp. I found a small gathering there on the evening, but they were a knowledgeable group of people, and there was a good gramophone and plenty of long-playing, 33⅓ records. On that particular night they were playing and discussing Gustav Mahler's 4th Symphony. This was the first time that I had ever heard any of Mahler's music and I was most impressed by what I heard. However, when I openly admitted that I had never heard any of his symphonies before, I noted in my diary that my fellow music-lovers were horrified – and from then onwards treated me with great disdain! I was definitely placed at the very bottom of the class!

Another Old Carthusian I saw frequently at Oswestry was Jo Hills, who had been in the same House as me at school, and was stationed at Park Hall Camp during all the time that I was there. We often met up in the NAAFI during the evenings, and he proved to be a great help in showing me all the ropes. He had 'Failed Watch' on his first attempt at WOSB, so he was obliged to wait at Oswestry for a further 3 months before he was allowed to take the test again. On the last occasion that we met before I went to Mons, he told me happily that he would shortly be taking WOSB again, so we discussed all the tests fully together. I never heard later how he fared, but I did comment in my diary on 26 March 1952: 'In spite of all my warnings, he seems to be a little over-confident to me....'

Our time at Oswestry was fast running out. Most of our former colleagues had now left either for Eaton Hall or to their other postings, and those of us going to Mons OCTU were just marking time. During March we were given a few days welcome Home Leave, and when we returned to Oswestry again, we were told at last that we should be starting at Mons on 28 March.

This news encouraged the five of us to intensify our efforts at revising all those Gunnery details together, as well as improving the standard of our boots. We used to spend hours and hours shining up our boots together with 'spit and polish'! Doesn't that now seem quite ridiculous?

By now, Richard Davies was well established at Mons, and he continued to give me plenty of useful hints and advice. He also told me that standards there are very high – as I was soon to learn.

If Oswestry had seemed like a different world to me in December 1951, then Mons Officer Cadet School was shortly to be an even greater shock. It would seem rather like dismounting a work horse - and then suddenly re-mounting a racing steed!

25 Pounder Field Gun, on Firing Platform and Ammunition Limber

Vicky Sau narez

CHAPTER 5

Infantry Training at Mons OCTU

For the past few weeks at Oswestry, Bob Bartlett, Ian Lucas, Jerry Treherne-Thomas, Bryan Trotter, and myself had all been impatiently kicking our heels, waiting for the big day to arrive – Friday 28 March 1952. When it did eventually come, the weather was icy cold.

After the usual kerfuffle at the disorganized Battery Office waiting for the necessary Travel Warrant to be signed, we took two taxis down to Gobowen station and caught the train to Reading in the nick of time. To make the journey more eventful, after the train had started, poor Bob Bartlett suddenly realised that he had left some of his luggage on the platform at Gobowen, and so had to jump out of the train at Shrewsbury and quickly make a telephone call. Unfortunately, his time ran out before the message got through, and so the train pulled out of the station without him! I forgot to record in my diary how this episode eventually ended, but I am quite sure that Bob will still clearly remember that first journey to Mons Officer Cadet School!

After changing stations at Reading and catching the train south, we arrived at Aldershot in darkness and in the freezing cold. We must have found the cost of all this incidental travelling very expensive on our Army pay of just £1 per week, because when we learned that the taxi fare from the station would be an outrageous 2/6 each (12½ pence), we all immediately decided to take a bus instead, and then to hike it. When we eventually reached Mons Barracks, we were all tired out, and absolutely frozen!

Gunner Goodliffe (now Officer Cadet)

Sergeant F. Snaith (Green Howards)

Soon after our arrival, my ever thoughtful friend Richard Davies came over to welcome me and to have a reassuring chat. He also brought me over some items that he knew would be needed from now on:– some white gorgets for my uniform, a white back-plate for my beret, some of the special coloured blanco as used at Mons, and also, a very necessary white paint brush! Before we went to bed, our Platoon Sergeant, a little Yorkshireman from the Green Howards called Sgt Snaith, came in to introduce himself and to say a few words to us. I won't say 'to welcome us', because his little introductory talk consisted of a series of warnings and threats about what was going to happen to us if 14 Platoon didn't come up to scratch during the next six weeks! We now fully appreciated that we had arrived at Mons – and tomorrow the fun would really commence!

C.S.M. G. Wilkinson (Welsh Guards)

The next morning, Saturday, we woke up to find it snowing hard outside. After breakfast, we paraded at 8 o'clock in the blinding snow, and then doubled off to the lecture room where our Company Sergeant Major, CSM Wilkinson of the Welsh Guards, started proceedings by giving us a short talk about drill on the Square. This was followed by our Company Commander, who told us something about the Course; and then each Platoon Commander introduced himself and also said a few words. We learned that, for the first six weeks, we shall be concentrating mainly on 'Infantry' training, and after this initial period, the successful cadets would be proceeding to their chosen specialist arm for the rest of their training.

They warned us that we were about to start a very concentrated Course, and they made it quite clear that if any of us ever fell behind, or showed himself unsuitable in any way, then he would be instantly 'warned', or 'relegated', or RTU'd (Returned to Unit) – and indeed, I had already spoken to a number of my colleagues in 14 Platoon who had been relegated down to us from a previous Course.

Edward (Greg) Peck

There must have been over a hundred cadets in the Platoons for our intake, and they certainly came from a wide variety of different Units. These included the RAC (Royal Armoured Corps), the Royal Corps of Signals, the REME (Royal Electrical and Mechanical Engineers), the RE (Royal Engineers), the RASC (Royal Army Service Corps), RAPC (Royal Army Pay Corps) as well as a few others; and in addition to this, there was of course, a large contingent from the Gunners (sub-divided into 'Field' Gunners and 'Ack Ack' Gunners). I met and spoke to, two other Old Carthusians I recognized at this gathering (neither of whom I knew very well): they were Ronald Harrison (RAC) and Edward (Greg) Peck – another Gunner, who later Passed Out with me in Fox (Field) Battery.

R.S.M. Brittain MBE (Coldstream Guards)

After their talks, the officers left the room, and we started chatting amongst ourselves. We heard some noise at the back of the room, and suddenly the loud command came: "Sit to attention!" followed quickly by the appearance of the massive frame of RSM Brittain. All this was transparently planned to give the maximum effect, and to

A Passing Out Parade at Mons OCTU

be sure, we all found the build-up most impressive and memorable. He spoke to us about drill for a few minutes in his distinctive, high-pitched voice, and then made his exit.

The bulk of Regimental Sergeant Major Ronald Brittain of the Coldstream Guards stood 6 feet 4 inches high, weighed twenty stone, and (we are told) had a neck size of 19 inches and a chest of 47 inches! Brittain was reputed to have the loudest voice in the British Army, and it was claimed that when he was drilling troops at Chelsea Barracks, his crystal clear, high pitched command 'parade.. shun!' could be heard in Victoria Station! He had omnipresence on the Mons' Parade Ground, and clearly relished his reverential role in the 'Army Game'; and there were many on parade who felt the sharp end of his tongue. To be sure, no one who passed through Mons during his reign will ever forget RSM Brittain.

Out in the snow once again, Sgt Snaith called 14 Platoon together and then marched us off at double quick time round to the cinema, where we saw an instructional film about the Army to round off the morning. Making us march so quickly through the blizzard and thick snow, was not only ridiculous, we also thought that it was very comical. In spite of all our efforts, no one could possibly keep in step with anybody else, so all our heads were just bobbing up and down. I made a note in my diary: 'we looked just like the horsemen's heads in the film of the 1937 Coronation!' We soon realised however, that this was just another part of the 'Army Game' we were playing!

The next day was a Sunday (30 March), so after the Church Parade at 10 o'clock, it turned out to be a day of rest and preparation. We were soon to find out that for most week-ends from now on, we would be allowed to change into civvies after Saturday lunchtime, leave camp, and not return until the Sunday evening. This was a great bonus for us to hear about, and particularly lucky and beneficial to all those living within easy reach of Aldershot.

On this last point, I was told that at least 75% of all the officers in the British Army at that time emanated from south of a line drawn from the Wash to the Severn. Furthermore, a large proportion of the remaining 25% came from Scotland. I never tried to substantiate that statement, but it was certainly borne out by my own observations in the Army, and I am here just passing on the bare facts as related to me.

After preparing all my kit for tomorrow and writing a few letters, I received a welcome visit from a great friend of mine at school, Patrick (d'Aguilar) Cleland. He was in the RAC, and had started his National Service a few weeks ahead of me. He had now finished his Infantry training and had moved onto Tournai Barracks, a short distance down the road where the Armoured Corps Officer Cadets received their specialist training. Luckily, the 'bush telegraph' had been working well, so he had come down to see how I was and to have a helpful chat with me. On our way down to the NAAFI, he told me that he had unfortunately just been relegated for four weeks!

The following little example will indicate just how very helpful this sort of meeting was to new arrivals at Mons like myself. We had just sat down for a coffee and a cake together, when he looked up and said firmly to me: 'Listen Brian; you're not a Gunner any more – from now on, when you take your beret off, you never put it tucked into your shoulder flap! OK?' Now that may seem a very trivial point today, but at Mons in 1952, this was just the sort of custom to be aware of, sooner rather than later.

Pat was an outstanding sportsman and racquets player, and although we were very special friends during our last few years at school, after that meeting in the NAAFI, our paths crossed just a few more times in all the hurly-burly at Aldershot. We went out together on Maundy Thursday in London during our week's leave, and I also later met him in the NAAFI with Richard Davies on 21 April, when he informed us that he had just been given 3 extra drills during the previous week! Poor Pat was so often in trouble during all the years that I knew him!

At the beginning of May, just a day before he Passed Out, I went over to Tournai Barracks to meet him again for the last time to say our final good-byes. He told me that he had been posted to Kenya where he would be join-ing the 3 Hussars (in Army snobbery terms, considered one of the 'top' Regiments), and that he was seriously thinking of signing on as a Regular for an extra year or two.

Later, during his Passing Out Parade on 8 May, I saw him slow marching up the steps (from my position in the ranks!), and I noted in my diary that the Inspecting Officer on that occasion was no less than Field-Marshal Alanbrooke. I wonder if I fully realised his significance at the time? Pat and I never met again after that. In 1979, I sadly learned that he had died when he was just 46 years old.

On our first Monday we started our training in earnest. After a most amus-ing lecture about 'the Qualities required in an Officer', we had our first drill period under the supervision of CSM Wilkinson. Since there was still some snow on the ground, the period was held inside a large hall, so every time we stamped our boots, the whole building shook! As might be expected, all the drill movements and timings at Mons were very much faster than any of us had ever experienced hitherto, so we always found these sessions par-ticularly intense and tiring. On this first occasion, whilst we were all stand-ing to attention, the huge bulk of RSM.Brittain MBE entered the room again and walked around the ranks scaring us all, and shouting out the odd terse, proverbial remark, such as:– 'Look up there!' and 'Look to the front!' On a later occasion on parade, he once shouted out:– 'That man in the front rank there; stop looking at me – if you want to see me, go to Madame Tussaud's!' This and other similar episodes, again emphasized to us all, that in spite of all the seriousness of our situations, life here was really just a game to achieve an end!

Thus our first week proceeded. The pace was always extremely fast, and we mostly found ourselves running or quick marching between periods. However, one point stood out straightaway: whichever instructor or lecturer we had at Mons, the standard was always exceptionally high; every one was clearly of the best. During those first days, I noted in my diary that we had lectures on a wide range of subjects including: 'Military Law and Administration', 'How to give a Lecture', 'The Need for Religion in the Army', 'Map Reading', 'Telecommunication', and 'Physical Training for Soldiers', 'Field Kitchens'; – and on the physical side, we had exercise sessions in the Gym, instruction on boxing, running, football, and of course, many long periods of Marching and Rifle Drill!

Our Sgt Snaith mainly took us for these drill periods, and we soon learned that he was really quite a slave driver. He kept us quick marching for much of the time at about 180 paces to the minute (which was the pace used by the so-called Light Infantry Battalions) and this speed is particularly difficult and tiring to the taller brethren like myself! I noted on the Friday: 'We were tearing about the Square at a cracking pace: 'left turn', 'right turn', 'right turn' and 'about turn' etc on the march, and at double quick time'. We then had another period on 'Military Law', which I found very interesting, and I came out thinking that this was a subject in particular, that will be of great importance in the future. After lunch we had yet another drill period, which was a replica of the morning one, so when we went on to a lecture about 'Organising a Range', we were again equally tired and sweaty.

It was Sgt Snaith's responsibility also, to ensure that our Platoon's barrack rooms were up to scratch, and during this first week, we were surprised to find ourselves having to scrape all the chairs ready for repainting, as well as cleaning up the floors and the rest of the room, in readiness for our first room inspection on the Saturday morning. I wrote the terse comment: 'Oh for a Dixon machine!' (which was the floor scrubbing and polishing machine which I had used at Office Cleaning Services)! A week later, I noted in my diary that I brought back a large tin of 'Waxol' (a special high-gloss wax floor polish), which my father had given me from OCS. The others in my room most gratefully received this valuable presentation!

The admonitions we heard at Mons from the NCOs and WOs were also something different again; for a start, the Officer Cadets were normally referred to as, 'Gentlemen' or 'Sir', so on the Parade Ground the frequent comment rang out; 'That was just f-ing horrible Gentlemen!' Nonetheless, swearing was generally at a much lower-key. On one occasion early on, when we were shouting out the times between drill movements, Sgt Snaith rebuked us in his thick Yorkshire accent: 'Come along Gentlemen! The Charterhouse CCF can make more noise than that!' But his favourite remark in these early days was: 'What ya harve bin dooin gentlemon, in th' larst six weeks – Ah doo not knoow – but ah shall find out in th' next six weeks!' He really worked us very hard during those first few weeks, but one thing was certain – he knew his craft as well as anyone else at Mons.

One of our cadets in 14 Platoon was much older than the others – he was called Jim Penton. He was one of the nine other persons in my barrack room and we all liked him very much and found him a most competent sol-dier and always helpful and friendly towards us youngsters. He had been in the Army for much of the War, and had finished up as a Captain – but after the war he had then resigned his Commission. We could never under-stand why it had taken him so long to get back to OCTU again. He was then 34 years old and although this doesn't seem much of an age to us now, he really did find the pace at Mons (especially the long periods of drill) almost too much to cope with. Jim was not included in the 14 Platoon group pho-tograph at the end of the Course, because he left Mons just before we fin-ished in early May. We were all very pleased when we heard that the CO had granted him a Commission with immediate effect, and also learned that he would start off as a Lieutenant. I often wondered how he finished up in the Army. One thing is quite certain – after all Sgt Snaith's tuition on the Square, Jim started off his second term as an Officer with complete expertise in drilling!

For our first full rehearsal of the Passing Out Parade on 1 April, Charlie Company was sensibly allowed to observe the whole spectacle from the ter-race. This included the Royal Artillery Band and the slow marching up the steps to the strains of 'Auld Lang Syne' – and we were all greatly impressed. A few months later, after we had participated regularly in this ceremonial, I suppose we became rather more blasé about the event (except for our own POP of course!), but when we saw the thousand Officer Cadets drilling so superbly for the first time, we really found it quite electrifying. I saw Richard Davies during and after this Parade, and I was very pleased to see that he had now been selected as Junior Under Officer for his Battery, which was very much to his credit. Richard was 3 months younger than me, so at that time, he was just 18 years and 5 months old!

On Thursday of this first week, we heard that 14 Platoon had to provide the Guard for next Sunday, so we drew lots out of a hat to see who would be involved. Luckily, I pulled out a blank, so I knew that I would be able to enjoy a welcome break at home for the week-end. Thus finished our first hectic week at OCTU.

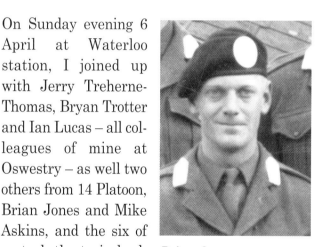

On Sunday evening 6 April at Waterloo station, I joined up with Jerry Treherne-Thomas, Bryan Trotter and Ian Lucas – all colleagues of mine at Oswestry – as well two others from 14 Platoon, Brian Jones and Mike Askins, and the six of us took the train back to Aldershot together.

Brian Jones

Brian Jones and I became firm friends in the Companies, and we often swapped notes about the lectures, and spent much of our leisure time together. Brian had been RTU'd last November 'for mucking up a Scheme', and had spent the last few months at Larkhill. He had now worked his way back to Mons OCS again, but this time he had decided to transfer from Field Royal

Mike Askins

Jerry Treherne-Thomas

Artillery to RASC, because he thought that this would give him an easier route through to a Commission.

Easter was fast coming up, so we were lucky enough to have the prospect of another week's holiday at home. Needless to say, at Mons, those three and a half days up to Maundy Thursday were packed full of action! The whole of Monday was taken up by a most informative map-reading exercise in the field, organized by our Platoon Commander Captain Rich, which took us over many miles around Frensham Ponds and Hankley Common – an area near Godalming well known to me since my schooldays. At mid-day we were also shown exactly how a mobile kitchen operates in the field, and given an excellent lunch. In the afternoon, we had our map reading test, for which I was paired off with Jerry Treherne-Thomas. We were taken 'blind' to a remote spot and told to find our position, and to make our way back to the truck as quickly as possible. With my local knowledge, I knew exactly where we were on the map straightaway, so Jerry and I arrived back well in front of all the others, and scored maximum points!

Captain A.G. Rich

Denis Waymouth

Denis Waymouth was a colleague of mine in 14 Platoon who slept in the same barrack room as me. During the night following that map reading scheme, he had a bad nightmare in the small hours of the night and woke us all up. We had a laugh about the incident afterwards, but at the time it was really quite frightening. When we were all fast asleep, Denis suddenly sat up in his bed - with the room eerily lit up by the full moon outside – and shouted out: 'who's that?' – 'What are you doing over there?' He then got out of his bed, still muttering – then, just as suddenly, got back into his bed again and went fast asleep. By this time, Denis was the only one in the barrack room who was asleep. All the rest of us were now wide-awake!

The next two days (Tuesday and Wednesday) were spent either doubling around or sitting down! We had many long sessions of drill on the Square; and between times we doubled off to the cinema to watch an excellent film on 'Aspects of Infantry Work', and had an energetic PT session consisting of relay races and boxing instruction; then a map reading quiz from our Platoon Commander Captain Rich; a lecture on 'the Organization of the Battalion'; followed by a talk about 'Arrest'; then a film on 'Field Craft'; and then, off to the range where we saw some impressive demonstrations, first-ly on the fire power of a Platoon using tracer bullets, and then showing a Platoon in the attack. On the Wednesday, after all the activities on that sec-ond day, we were back in the lecture room again preparing to write an important essay on the subject: 'the Relationship between Officers and Men', which was one of the many tests which would score points for our assess-ments at the end of the Course.

I mention all this in some detail, because these were all actual events recorded in my diary during those two typical days, and therefore, by relating them specifically, it gives a clearer understanding about the intensity and diversi-ty of this six weeks' Infantry Course. All the time, Captain Rich and Sgt Snaith were watch-ing us closely, and looking out for any inade-quacies. On this point, I noted in my diary on Tuesday 8 April, that a Yorkshireman named Dave Bottomley had joined 14 Platoon, after being relegated from the Platoon ahead of us.

Dave Bottomley

Before we were allowed to go home on Maundy Thursday 10 April 1952, the whole School was involved in an hour long rehearsal of the full Passing Out Parade. As usual, the Adjutant, closely assisted by RSM Brittain and all the other Warrant Officers, took the Parade and on this occasion he made it quite clear that he was not at all satisfied with our 'slack efforts' – no doubt to ensure that we all didn't feel too complacent before our Easter break! This was, no doubt, just another example of the 'Army Game' in operation!

After this parade was over, Sgt Snaith marched us off to take our rifles to the Guard Room, and then onto the tailors to collect our best Battle Dress Uniforms, which had been altered as necessary. I noted that, 'Sgt Snaith was in a particularly frantic mood this morning, and kept us marching back and forth at quick time because he said we weren't keeping up with the ridiculously quick pace he called out. As a result, we all arrived at the tailor's tired out and sticky – but also laughing at Snaith for being so foolish.'

In spite of all the hold-ups, I still arrived home in good time to start my Easter break – and I see that I really made the most of those seven days leave.

My father had thoughtfully and kindly provided me with a small car so that I could move around more freely. I drove up to Richard Davies who gave a party at his home in Barnet; and I went out with Pat Cleland in London, and also with my friend from Oswestry, Jack Collett, who was also on leave from Eaton Hall. I was also very keen to see my girlfriend Jennifer Chisholm again and we arranged to go out together more than once during the week. Jennifer and I were quite sweet on each other at the time – but I should not elaborate on this delightful relationship, in case I am guilty of gross deviation!

I was interested to read in my diary that during those few days at home from Mons, I saw four films: 'Viva Zapata', 'Quo Vadis', 'The Card' and 'A Streetcar Named Desire'; and also at the theatre, Alec Guinness in 'Under the Sycamore Tree', and then Jo Stafford at the London Palladium, with my family! I clearly had a most relaxing break!

Arriving back at Mons Barracks on the evening of Thursday 17 April, I soon had to get myself back into gear. I saw that I was to be Orderly Sergeant on the following day, so I had to arrange an early call at the Guard House. Being Orderly Sergeant was no great deal, but it did mean that I had to be up early to take the names of all those 'on sick', and to open up the Company Office; and then in the evening, to march out the Guard.

The weather had now turned quite warm, so towards the end of our furious morning drill session with rifles and fixed bayonets, I noted that one or two of us – including Bob Gerard and Ian Lucas – started to feel faint, and had to ask permission to stand to one side for a time. To the uninitiated, this may seem to be a weak and surprising attitude for the Army to take, but it has to be realised that if a soldier faints during arms drill with fixed bayonet, this is not only dangerous, but it can also be fatal. The session of course continued unabated, with RSM Brittain supervising us all closely by

Bob (Peter) Gerard

marching round the ranks making the odd caustic comment, interspersed with the proverbial command: 'Look up there!' 'Keep your eyes to the front!' and 'Take that man's name – damned idle!'

At this stage, wc had only been in 14 Platoon for just over two full weeks, but it seemed to us more like a couple of months! I can see from my diary comments that some of us were now beginning feel the strain. On that Saturday I wrote; 'Jerry (Treherne-Thomas) and I felt we must get out of this hole. We caught a bus down to the town and had a drink together. Poor Jerry had his name taken for having a dirty bayonet yesterday, so I expect that he will be given an extra drill before long.' On the next day I summarized my feelings again: 'We are all getting pretty fed up with this place. The best part of it, is that we can now dress in civvies and get home most weekends; also, the food is better, the other blokes are good company, and the state of the wash-house is better!' (I can't understand the significance of that last remark, but I believe that we had baths at Mons instead of the normal showers).

In retrospect, I can now see how the syllabus of this initial Infantry Course had been decided upon:– For the first few weeks we were given instruction on all the theories and background knowledge behind organizing an Army, coupled with the role of the Infantry within the Army– most of which was quite new to us at this stage. Then for the rest of the time, we were made to put all those theories into practice and to convince the instructors that we had fully understood them all.

In the meantime, we were tuned up physically, inspected regularly to ensure that our uniforms and rooms were bulled up to the highest standards, as well as introduced to most of the duties we should need to know about as officers in a Regiment. Lastly of course, we were subjected to all this continual, intensive drilling, which eventually made us every bit as polished up and as sharp as our more senior brethren in the Batteries and the Squadrons at Mons. Every working day was jam-packed full, so all the time we were gradually widening our knowledge and understanding about the Army and its organisation.

Whatever the faults of the system, those first six weeks at Mons certainly had the ability, in the shortest possible time, of pointing most of us in the right direction for the future!

During these busy weeks, they still managed to put aside some time for sporting activities, and these must have helped in the final gradings for those who participated. We had both a swimming and a boxing competition between the Platoons, and I was included in both of these. Boxing was often included during the Gym sessions, and this was a skill that I had often practiced in the past, although I was never particularly interested in the sport. In the Boxing Competition, I see from my diary that I fought as a light-heavy weight, and weighed in at just 12 stone and $2\frac{1}{2}$ lb! I also noted on 22 April that I went to bed with a sore nose as a result of one of these bouts, but I could find no more references to any other fights, so it seems that I competed without much success!

Much more to my liking however, was athletics, which was just beginning to happen now that spring was in the air. Ian Lucas, Hugh Knowles Mike

John Morley

Ian Lucas

Hugh Knowles

Mike Goodburn

Goodburn and John Morley were all good athletes and the five of us made a start by training together on the running track before we left the Companies. It wasn't until we later moved on to the Batteries however, that we all started to compete in this more seriously. On a good day, both Mike Goodburn and I could run the half mile in 'even time' (that's a minute for each lap) so when we ran together, our relay team was normally successful.

I ought to mention the Guard Duty we had on 23 April. The weather had now broken, and during most of the afternoon and evening it thundered and poured. When the Guard paraded at 6.30 it was still raining, so we were marched into the drill shed for our inspection. Unfortunately for me, when we were shouldering arms, my wet rifle slipped out of my grasp, and fell to the ground with a great clatter – 'Take that man's name!' came the call.

Anyway, when we started our Guard Duty, I was paired off with Jerry (Treherne-Thomas), and we drew out the times 7.30 to 9.30, and then 1.30 to 3.30, and thus we started our first boring stint. At 11.30, the Orderly Officer came along and called out the Guard, so we all dutifully mustered as quickly as we could. But about an hour later, after some of us had settled down again to catch some sleep, we were surprised to be called out for a second time. This time the Officer gave us all a real bollocking, firstly for being too slow in falling in, and secondly, for not guarding the Gun sheds closely enough. After he had walked away, still fuming about our inadequacies, we all agreed that he was 'the nastiest little sh-t we had come across since our arrival at Mons!'

It was not until a day or two later, that we had all come to the conclusion that we had been the victims of a great hoaxer – the second inspection had been made by one of the RAC Officer Cadets from the Squadrons, who was just about to pass out on the following day! That incident may seem amusing now, but at the time, none of us was at all inclined to see the funny side of *that* prank!

After the first three weeks, those of us in 14 Platoon started to notice a gradual change in Sgt Snaith. He seemed to be treating us with just a *little* more consideration. For instance, after a day of schemes in the field, 14 Platoon would be the first Platoon to get away, so that we were the first ones back in barracks and the first to commandeer the hot baths. And if there was only one TCV (Troop Carrying Vehicle), he would ensure that we were the Platoon who had that vehicle because it had the best seats. We also noticed that the pace and intensity of his drill periods began to decrease *just a little* These examples may seem trivial, but at the time, we all noticed the change. At this stage in the Course perhaps, he felt that he had now 'broken us all in', and therefore could start giving us a few privileges!

On 25 April, the day after that episode on Guard Duty, I noted in my diary: 'There is quite a turmoil this morning, since everyone is making final preparations for the barrack room inspection. We were on parade for drill at 8.15, and had the usual energetic period. We have all now changed our opinions about Sgt Snaith, because we have found him being far more considerate towards us, and we now see him often looking after our best interests. He told us today for instance, that the four of us in 14 Platoon who had recently had their names taken (including myself!), would now be let off, so there would be no need for them to report to the Adjutant.'

Regarding the coming room inspection, I continued in my diary by making the jocular (though perfectly serious) remark: 'After the drill period, we tiptoed into our bulled up barrack room (i.e. making sure we didn't disturb anything), put our packs on, and left our bayonets on our beds. We then got into the trucks, and went to the same ground as Wednesday, to watch another tip top demonstration of a platoon in the attack.'

Before I leave the subject of Sgt Snaith, it is relevant to mention at this stage, that in the inter-Platoon Drill Competition on 9 May at the end of the Course, 14 Platoon was judged to be the best, and so we became the Champion Platoon. Once again, Sgt Snaith's know-how and calculated methods had been completely vindicated!

I always found much of the Infantry training we practiced in the field most irksome and not at all to my liking. As a result, I became more and more convinced that I had made the right choice by joining the Royal Artillery. When it was my turn to take over the Platoon to be attacked on one of these schemes, I found that the most difficult part was to discover the exact location of the enemy firing at you. This was quite a disadvantage, because if you had no idea where the enemy was, it was quite tricky to decide in which direction to lead your attack! (I partly jest!)

We had many all day exercises to practice all the different Infantry tactics in the field, and then towards the end of the Course, we finished off by having a two day exercise on Hankley Common, after which we also slept out on the Hog's Back. We did the whole works, including night and day patrols, digging trenches and setting up defensive positions, as well as all the attacking and defensive tactics. I noted that when Hugh Knowles (Royal Signals) took over during this exercise, he made a terrible hash of it all, and Captain Rich was absolutely furious with him. We all thought that he would be warned or relegated after this, but luckily nothing happened.

Our Captain Rich had a reputation for being very tough about relegating Officer Cadets, but with just another week to go on this Course, he had still said nothing to us one way or the other. In the meantime, we heard the ominous news that no less than seven had just been relegated in 13 Platoon. Next day (8 May), we heard from 11 Platoon that everyone had just been given the all clear; yet still Captain Rich had told us nothing!

One of the many Passing Out Parades at Mons OCTU

Eventually, on 12 May, just three days before Passing Out, he told us that he had decided to pass everyone in 14 Platoon! What wonderful news that was for us all. The devastating prospect of having to repeat the Course from 'square one' was just too horrible to contemplate. In this connection, Brian Jones always told me how very difficult it was for him, to pick himself up again after being RTU'd from Mons last November. I always gave him very high marks for recovering himself after that disappointment.

After the Charlie Company Passing Out Parade early on 15 May, the Company Commander gave us a little pep talk and wished us well, and we then went into the Platoon lecture room to receive our reports and grading. Luckily, I made a few quick notes about these, although, judging by the wide variations, some may or may not have been completely accurate. I found that I myself had managed to pass right in the middle of the field, and certainly not one of Rich's favourites! Brian Jones (with minus 6) had obviously just about scraped through at the bottom of the grades! It seemed to me that if anyone had a grade of minus 10 points or worse, this would mean relegation.

I saw that Rich had awarded me the score of plus 3 made up as follows: Will-power, plus 1, Turnout, plus 1, Paper, plus 1, Sense of Humour, nil (!),

Oral and Written, nil, Maturity, nil, (there may have been more categories because I end with a comma in my diary, and left space for writing more).

The few other grades I noted were:

Jerry Treherne-Thomas	plus 8.
Ian Lucas	plus 8.
Bob Bartlett	minus 6 (in 12 Platoon).
Bryan Trotter	plus 4 (in 12 Platoon)
Peter Gerard	plus 7
Denis Waymouth	minus 5
Hugh Knowles	minus 6 (Royal Signals)
Brian Jones	minus 6 (RASC)

On 13 May, Charlie Company arranged an End of Course Celebration which we held at a local pub called *the Swan*. Most of the Platoon Commanders and NCOs made the effort to appear, and plenty of drinking, talking and conviviality went on from about 8 o'clock until 10.30. I noted in my diary that RSM Brittain had declined our invitation because we had not provided any transport for him!

I also noted that Sgt Snaith was in very good form at the start of the party, but after a couple of hours he became more and more pickled! This was not really surprising because I also noted that 'he was drinking quantities of beer mixed with rum all evening!' I barely drank at all in those days, so the notes in my diary are always rather critical when I make reference to all the heavy drinking I saw so regularly in the Army. For instance, I noted censoriously that my friend Jerry (Treherne-Thomas) 'was drinking double whiskeys all evening, which must have cost him no less than £3'. I went on to comment that this was, 'an awful waste of money!' .

The final comments in my diary on 13 May went on: 'At 10.30 Sgt Snaith was 'as tight as a drum' (this was one of my uncle Tom Goodliffe's favourite similes), so Denis (Waymouth) and I took him home in a taxi to make sure that he came to no harm!' The next day I also recorded that: 'I saw Snaith first thing on this morning, and he was 'as sober as a judge' (another of my uncle Tom's favourite expressions) and apparently, he was feeling no ill effects from the previous night's binge!'

Now that those first six weeks of intense Infantry training at Mons had been completed, the assortment of Officer Cadets in the various specialist arms were deemed ready for transfer to their chosen branch of the Army for further training.

The Gunners were duly split up into 'Field' and 'Ack Ack', and transferred to their two separate Troops in Fox Battery at Mons, whilst those in the RAC went to Tournai Barracks, and the Royal Corps of Signals, the RASC and all the other Corps went on to their own respective training barracks. The only person I was particularly sorry to see move away, was my friend Brian Jones who was transferred to Buller Barracks which took the RASC Officer Cadets. I tried in vain to meet up with him again in later months, but his commonplace name didn't help, and although I believe that he eventually received his Commission and was posted to somewhere in the West Country, we never met up again after we had said our farewells on 15 May 1952. This situation happened so often during National Service.

Time was short and we had to move on. Another chapter of experience was about to begin....

Vicky Saumarez

Morris Quad (or Tractor) for pulling 25 Pounder Field Gun and for carrying Gun Team

CHAPTER 6

Training in Fox Field Battery at Mons OCTU

All the Gunners who had been in Charlie Company were now well known to me, and these mostly joined me in Fox Battery on 16 May 1952, although the Field and Ack Ack Gunners were separated into two different Troops for their specialist training. My friend Jerry Treherne-Thomas had opted to transfer to Ack Ack, so from now on we would meet less frequently, although we came together now and again socially and also whenever the Battery paraded as a whole. We had been good companions for over four months now, but nothing stays the same for very long, and this saying certainly applies to National Service relationships.

Nonetheless, I did start off in Fox 90 (Field) Troop with many people I knew well. These were Ian Lucas, Bob Bartlett and Bryan Trotter, all of whom I had been with since Oswestry days; and there was David Story, David Bottomley, John Morley, and Dusty Foster (a Regular) from 14 Platoon.

Back Row: Bryan Trotter, Dusty Foster, John Morley,
Front Row: Brian Goodliffe, David Story, Mike Goodburn

John Moore

Then there were some others from the other Platoons in Charlie Company I knew quite well – Edward

Mike Gibbon and Ian Lucas

(Greg) Peck (an Old Carthusian), John Moore, Mike Gibbon, and Mike Goodburn (one of the other athletes). As far as my other future colleagues were concerned, two were Regulars who had transferred from the Royal Engineers to the Gunners, whilst the rest were unknown to me since they had been relegated to Fox 90 (Field) Troop at the start of the Course, or else joined later due to relegation!

There were four Troops in each Battery at Mons in those days, normally two Field and two Ack Ack, – consisting of two senior Troops and two junior Troops. The senior Field and Ack Ack Troops were always four weeks ahead in training, so when they Passed Out at the end of each month, the junior Troops automatically moved into the senior Troop's barrack rooms, to make way for the new junior Troops coming in – and so the Officer 'sausage-machine' progressed.

Our first day in the Batteries was a Friday (16 May), so we had the prospect of soon having a weekend, during which we could settle down into our new surroundings and start preparing for a return to Gunnery matters again.

Our drill Sergeant was CSM J. Bennett MM of the Coldstream Guards, and he was the one who normally took our parades as a Battery. He was a forceful character 'of the old school', and it is worth noting that the Military Medal which he held, is not just one of those medals which 'comes up with the rations' – it is awarded for conspicuous gallantry in action. Anyway, we had been warned that he was especially keen on 'shiny boots and faultless cap badges', so on the previous night, we all paid attention to bulling up these articles in particular!

As he inspected us for the first time, he asked our names and made a few caustic comments and sometimes criticized our turn-out as he went down the ranks. He had obviously looked up the list of names beforehand because he clearly came well primed. I noted two of his exchanges with cadets from the Ack Ack Troop:– "What's your name?" "Barren Sergeant." "Pity your mother wasn't! Mr Barren, your boots are just not good enough; do you understand?" "Yes Sergeant." – then later: "What's your name?" "Angell

C.S.M. Bennett M.M.
(Coldstream Guards)

Sergeant." "Mr Angell! If you turn out like this again, you'll end up in the other place!" He then put us through our paces for the next half hour, and by the end, we could see that the next two months with him were certainly going to be fun and games!

I was told that it was whilst CSM Bennett was taking an earlier Church Parade one Sunday that he gave the order to his squad: 'C of E on the left, other Denominations on the right!' After the Troop had split up, there was just one Officer Cadet standing to attention in the middle. 'Yes, Mr Butler – and what are you?' 'I'm an atheist Sergeant.' There was a pregnant pause of about half a minute whilst this information was sinking in. Eventually, Bennett had worked out his rejoinder: 'Mr Butler – 'Ow do yer think the f-ing trees and the f-ing flowers grow? Fall in over there with the others!' Appropriately enough, it was Mr Butler who was later selected to go round with the collection bowl!

CSM Wilkinson was another Drill Instructor to show his religious streak. Whilst forming up in readiness for a Church Parade, he told us: "You're goin' to Church this mornin' gentlemen – so for Christ's sake SING!"

After the Parade on that first morning, we were marched off to the Battery lecture room where we met and heard from our future Battery and Troop Commanders for the first time. These were Major K.S.Hamilton MBE, the Fox Battery Commander, and Major M.A.Tice, our Field Troop Commander – and some of us had reservations about both! After this first meeting I wrote about Hamilton: 'although he appeared to be a most intelligent man, he seemed to me to be rather dreamy and lethargic'. Tice, at this stage remained an unknown quantity, but he was a strange, thin, little man with fierce, deep-sunken eyes, and I believe we learned later that he had, in fact, spent some of his time in a Japanese prisoner-of-war camp.

Major M.A. Tice and Major K.S. Hamilton M.B.E.

Anyway, these were the two persons who would shortly have a crucial influence upon our future progress, so it was in our best interests to keep in their good books.

After this first introduction, we had talks for the remainder of the day on various Gunnery matters, both general and specific, which were given to us by a very 'switched-on' IG (Instructor of Gunnery). To some of us, after having had our dose of Infantry training during the past six weeks, it was really quite satisfying to start coming to grips again with Gunnery, even though it was obvious that we all had much to learn.

That evening, after cleaning the floors and windows of our room (!), Ian Lucas and I walked down to Charlie Company lines, to find out if we knew anyone amongst the new intake which had just arrived. The journey was worthwhile, because I did meet three more Old Carthusians, all of whom I knew quite well at the time, Peter Bunker, Paddy Spence and James Bogle, and we were therefore able to pass on some useful hints about the Infantry Course which they were about to begin. I had also spoken to both Peter and Paddy last March, just after they had arrived in Oswestry.

Our second day in the Batteries was a Saturday, and the first part of the morning was spent in frantic preparations for a room and kit inspection, which was carried out without much incident by CSM Bennett. The rest of the morning was spent with Major Tice, who spoke to us about the future Course, and also about gunnery matters in general; and it soon became obvious to us that he possessed little depth of knowledge in the whole subject – and this initial opinion was borne out increasingly as the Course progressed! He even began his talk by telling us that he had begun in the Indian Army as an infantryman; and also made excuses about his being an 'Ack Ack' Gunner rather than a 'Field' Gunner! He was just about the only instructor we came across at Mons who was not up to his job; but we all now knew exactly where we stood, and there would be many other instructors we could turn to whenever we needed to learn about the finer points in Gunnery!

That first Saturday morning was a lovely hot day, and Major Tice was keen to leave for the Goodwood Horse Racing, so he made sure that he finished the morning session early, and then we watched as he drove off speedily in his Allard car – a racy, sports car with a powerful Ford engine, which was much admired and sought after in those early days after the war.

**"C-O-M-P-A-N-Y – 'shun! —
Don't look at me; I'm not Marilyn
Monroe**

For the next two nights of the weekend, Fox Battery had to mount the Guard, and on the Saturday night I was involved. I was paired off with Ian Lucas and our stint was from 11.30 to 1.30, so the last one was from 5.45 until 8 o'clock. After we had dismounted in the morning, we went straight up to the canteen for some welcome egg and bacon, and spent the rest of the morning dozing on our beds to catch up with our sleep. In the afternoon I wrote: 'Ian and I went off to Aldershot by bus, and had some tea, and then went to see a really rotten film – but anything to get away from this barrack room!' Tomorrow the Course would really begin.

It was now mid-May and the weather was glorious (though perhaps rather too glorious for drill at Mons), so we were now dressed in denims and in 'shirt-sleeve order' rather than the thick khaki battle-dress. We got off to a bad start on our Monday morning parade, because Bennett immediately started to berate us about the standard of those on Guard Duty last night. He said that he had received bad reports about slackness, and threatened to give us all some extra Guard Duties if there were no improvements. We heard later that there had been some complaints about the Ack Ack Troop Guard who had mounted a few minutes late last night. I only mention this little detail, because it may possibly illustrate more fully, the way things were at Mons.

Thus the first week in Fox Battery started, and the whole of that Monday was spent recapitulating or introducing us to a wide-range of Gunnery matters: Tice started the morning by speaking about 'Elementary Gunnery', which he managed to cope with adequately! Then an IG told us about 'Basic Ordnance'; and later we had our first 'Gun Drill' and 'Gun Laying' period, and for this we were split up into gun teams of six persons, with each team and each 25 pounder gun having its own individual instructor. Our Sergeant for this was quite brilliant, and we came away thinking that we had really learned something. The day finished with the IG explaining the details of 'Fire Discipline'. Most of us who had trained previously in Oswestry, had at least touched on all these subjects before, but for all those of us (like the two Engineers) who were beginning from scratch with Gunnery, they must have found these early days most complicated and confusing – and probably wondered what they had let themselves in for!

I met Richard Davies in the NAAFI for the first time for some weeks, and he told me that he had just returned from the End of Course Camp at Sennybridge, and confirmed that he would be passing out as top RA Officer Cadet next Thursday 22 May – what excellent news! He told me that he had been posted to Germany and would be joining 3 Royal Horse Artillery – considered one of the senior RA Field Regiments. I told him that I would certainly have my beady eyes on him from my vantage point in the ranks next Thursday!

According to the Adjutant, Captain Webb-Bowen, the Tuesday rehearsals for this next Passing Out Parade were quite unsatisfactory, so the drilling on the Square went on much longer than usual, and since we were now in shirt-sleeve order, by lunchtime, marching for so long with rifles at the slope became most uncomfortable for us all. Next day however, when we had another rehearsal, everything went off much better and in the ceremony, when Richard Davies was 'presented with the baton', he performed his special drill for this ceremony much better than his counterpart from the RAC Squadrons – and he was publicly commended for this, both by the Adjutant and RSM Brittain.

As far as Fox Troop training was concerned during those two days, we learned more about 'Fire Discipline' and the various methods used for directing and controlling the fire from the guns. Luckily the IG gave most of this technical tuition to us rather than our would-be mentor, Major Tice!

Soon after midnight on the morning before Richard's Passing Out Parade, Fox Battery lines were invaded by some of the high-spirited Officer Cadets from the RAC Squadron who were also Passing Out today. They threw smoke canisters into some of our rooms whilst we were asleep, which naturally caught us completely unawares, but nonetheless, before the assault had finished we luckily managed to recover ourselves sufficiently to make sure that at least some of the invaders were sent back soaked to the skin!

That morning, we were given a session on 'Troop Deployment', before it was time for us to parade in readiness for the Passing Out Parade at 11 o'clock. The weather was fairly hot by the time we marched onto the Square to start proceedings with the Royal Artillery Band, and it was then RSM Brittain's task to see that all the ranks were formed up in proper order, so that the Parade could be handed over to the Adjutant, mounted on his horse. This he did as usual with much shouting in his high pitch, crystal clear voice and with the assistance of all his Sergeant Majors. The Inspecting General arrived in due course and the Parade 'Presented Arms' in the General Salute, and thus the Parade went on for over an hour, with various formalities, presentations, ceremonies and lengthy inspections.

As far as the Officer Cadets in the ranks were concerned, there was an awful lot of standing about to be done before the order for the march past was eventually given, and this order came as a great relief, because the marching would at last 'allow the blood to circulate again' after all that waiting!

I write about all this, because faintings are always a very real possibility on these occasions, and the Passing Out Parade which I am mentioning here, did not finish without some incidents in this respect. Earlier on, I had already heard some commotion in the back ranks which indicated that someone had fainted, so I did my best to take my mind off this possibility happening to me, by closely watching all the ceremonies going on – but suddenly, the cadet standing just next to me on the left, crumpled up!!! This had never happened so near to me before, so I really wasn't sure how I should react. I therefore remained standing rigidly to attention. Luckily, a Sergeant Major, CSM Sheldon, was close at hand, and he quickly took the hapless Cadet out of sight – and the show went on! I heard later that this Cadet had in fact cut his chin rather badly on his bayonet as he fell!

This whole incident was dutifully recorded in my diary, and I also noted that Richard Davies again performed all his duties faultlessly when he was 'presented with the baton' as the best Cadet. After the Parade had finished, I made sure that I acknowledged Richard's parents who were amongst the spectators, as well as one of his friends, who was the outstanding Art Master at Charterhouse at that time, Ian Fleming-Williams.

Our training continued fairly intensely for the rest of that

Richard Davies being presented with the 'Stick of Honour'

The RAC Senior Cadet & Richard Davies slow marching up the steps

week, and we also did some useful practical work with the 25 pounder guns, when we brought them into action for the first time. On the Saturday however, I noted that 'we all had another example of Major Tice's lack of knowledge in Gunnery matters, when we spent the whole of Saturday morning in the lecture room with him. He first gave us a quite sensible and adequate talk about the various duties of a GPO (Gun Position Officer) – which is probably the job most of us will be asked to do when we join our Regiments as Subalterns. However, for the second part of this session, he then went on to explain the tricky subject of 'Crest Clearance' (this is quite a complex point, where the guns are firing at a target, and there is a hill in between occupied by your own troops). Tice obviously didn't fully understand this matter, because in attempting to answer our queries, he found himself hopelessly confused and out of his depth. Finally, by discussing the question amongst ourselves, we all worked out exactly how it should be done, so at the finish, the only person in the whole class who was still baffled by the problem, was Tice himself!'

However humorous or otherwise this factual story may appear when it is read now over fifty years later, this situation at the time could have become quite a serious matter for us, because we were all now completely in his sway, and it was therefore most important for us to keep on the right side of him, and therefore to be as tactful as possible about his shortcomings. He had the absolute power to relegate or RTU any one of us instantly, so we all needed to be very careful – and furthermore, we soon found out that Tice (probably due to his insecurity) could quite easily 'fly off the handle' at a moment's notice! A few days later (28 May) I noted: 'Tice was rather annoyed during the lesson on revision today, because some of us didn't remember about 'Ballistic Angles' (a detail now quite forgotten!). We shall certainly have to watch our step with him; otherwise he could turn rather nasty'.

Having started to experience life in the Batteries after life in the Companies, we found that it was rather like moving from the lower school into the senior school. Although 'sense of urgency' – that great monster at Mons – continued to be ever present, as well as the importance of kit and room inspections, there was more emphasis now on learning about Gunnery, rather than running round at the double or learning how to present arms properly. Relegation or being RTU'd however, continued to be a constant threat, but even so, we began to get the feeling that the instructors were starting to treat us much more like *senior* cadets – or even possible future officers!

This natural progression was definitely necessary at this stage, because the Officer Cadets were an intelligent bunch, and after those six brim-full weeks in the Companies, they could have learned little more from being given any extra weeks of the same recipe, so they were quite ready to move forward. In any case, after completing the concentrated drill periods given in the Companies, it was quite noticeable how much more polished and crisp were the more senior Officer Cadets in the Batteries and the Squadrons as compared to all those who had newly arrived in the Companies. CSM Bennett was however, a real master of his craft, and if he detected any slackness or falling off in standards or effort, he was onto it immediately and was quite prepared to start 'turning the screw' again at any time.

In the Batteries, even though we were ever mindful of the amount of learning we had to do, we did seem to have more spare time now for relaxation and recreation. A few of the Officer Cadets now also had cars, and Glynn Jenkins (one of the athletes) was one who had a motorbike. Jerry Treherne-Thomas had a little MG, and I recorded that four of us all crammed into it on the evening of 11 June, and went off to the Hog's Back Hotel for a very pleasant dinner, which cost each of us the princely sum of 10 shillings (50 pence).

It came as a stroke of good fortune to some of us, that on 26 May, the Commandant of Mons OCS pronounced that Athletics was to be treated as a priority activity, and therefore that training for athletics on Mondays, Tuesdays and Thursdays would be considered equivalent to a Parade.

This ruling was really quite significant to all the athletes at Mons, because I noted on the very next day that I was told I was excused Guard Inspection due to our athletics training, and as a result I was allowed to join the rest of our guard in my own time! Another immediate result of this ruling was that all the athletes were now thankfully excluded from a big National Military Exercise about to take place all over Britain at that time, which involved all the other cadets for a number of days and nights. In future also, athletics training would take precedence over the need for all athletes to attend any of the regular Physical Training sessions. This was all very good news for us, and it showed us quite clearly that there are no half measures in the Army when sport and the prestige of the unit are at stake. A few weeks later indeed, we athletes were even told we should be allowed to travel back in the middle of our crucial End-of-Course Camp so that we could compete in the Southern Command Championships at Aldershot!

Ian Lucas

Some of us had already been training for athletics spasmodically whilst in the Companies, but from now on, five of us in Fox Field Battery trained together on a much more consistent basis. These were, Ian Lucas, a hurdler and high jumper, Glynn Jenkins, a pole vaulter, John Morley, a 3 miler, and Mike Goodburn and myself, who both ran the 880 and 440 yards – in those days in Britain, we always competed in yards rather than metres. Another significant stroke of luck for us athletes was that Major Tice was particularly keen on the sport himself, and so he always showed great interest in our results, and referred to us as his 'Gladiators'. In spite of commitments for our intensive Gunnery Course, I see that during those weeks in the Batteries at Mons OCS, we competed successfully on six occasions, including against Reading University, and a close match with Eaton Hall OCS (when we romped away with both the 440 and 880 yards relays), in the Southern Command Championships when we came third, and the Aldershot District Athletics Championship which we won.

Glynn Jenkins

Mike Goodburn finishing well ahead in the 880 yards relay against Eaton Hall OCTU

By the beginning of June, after just two weeks in the Batteries, I see that the pace started to quicken for us. On 2 June, Whit Monday, I wrote in my diary: 'Certainly no red-letter day for us! We were rushed from pillar to post for the whole day, and we seemed unable to put a foot right with those in charge. Bennett bollocked us for being too late on parade, and told us that in future we shall be marching everywhere; the IG told us we were being too slow at Gun Drill; and Tice flew into one of his frequent tempers over some other trivial matter. So on the whole, we didn't have a very success-ful day! Spent the evening doing amendments which need to be checked for tomorrow; and also working on some questions from Tice.'

The following day was 'another rushed day. Marched everywhere. Exam results 57%. Suffice it to say that we are all rather browned off with this place. Bed at 11 o'clock. Up early tomorrow'.

Next morning, we had 'an early parade to practice for the Passing Out Parade today and for the big Parade tomorrow. Bennett wasn't satisfied with our turnout again and harangued us for several minutes and warned us with a thorough inspection tomorrow before the Queen's Birthday

Parade'. This was the day when our senior Troop in Fox Battery completed their Course, and had their Passing Out Parade. During the afternoon therefore, whilst our Troop toiled on with our training Course, our senior colleagues (who we scarcely knew and never mixed with) made their jubilant departure. This meant that we were now ourselves the Senior two Troops in Fox Battery, so during the evening we moved into our new accommodation which had been vacated by them. This made way for the next two junior Troops joining the Batteries and coming up from the Companies. Thus the training process continued.

Instead of having a barrack room which we had as the junior Troops, we were now accommodated in smaller rooms for three persons and the rooms also had additional furniture including a chair, a bedside table and light and a large wardrobe. What luxury, we thought! I was now sharing the room with just Bob Bartlett and a newly relegated arrival, Bryan Ingham.

Our new room mate, Bryan Ingham came from Macclesfield, near Manchester, and he was a most convivial, even-tempered and laid-back individual. It is one of my lasting memories of Bryan, seeing him in charge as Gun Position Officer during one of our schemes, when everything seemed to be working against him, and also with Tice breathing down his

Back Row: Mike Nightingale, John Marshall, Bryan Ingham
Front Row: John Moore, Greg Peck, Dave Bottomley. Pat Daniel

neck. Yet there was Bryan, cool-headed as always, calmly sorting out the problems as they occurred! By this time, Bryan was quite experienced as GPO, because when he joined us in Fox Battery, he had already managed to get himself relegated on two separate occasions in the Batteries!

He told me quite frankly in his matter of fact Northern accent, that he was lucky not to have been RTU'd on the first occasion, when he did very badly on a scheme, whereas his second relegation was mainly because he got on the wrong side of Major Palmer, who was in charge of Dog Battery. Like the rest of us, Bryan was astonished when he discovered Tice's lack of Gunnery knowledge, but he immediately told me that this could be to our advantage, as long as we didn't antagonise him in any way! He was probably quite correct in this assessment.

Bryan and I soon became close friends and he was also one of the few cadets in the Batteries who had his own car, so we often drove out in it together, whenever we had any spare time. His car was one of the oldest, clapped out Fords you could ever see and it was really in a most appalling state of disrepair. Its one great advantage however, was that it actually kept working! One of its most hazardous failings was that whilst driving along, the passenger door might suddenly fly open without warning, so constant vigilance of the passenger was essential! In later years, I met Bryan several times when I went up to Manchester on business, but I am sorry to relate that he was never very successful in his business life as an Estate Agent. Perhaps he was just a little *too* laid-back for that!

During those two short months, there was plenty of knowledge about the intricacies of Field Gunnery for all of us to assimilate. We had to learn:

- Signalling procedures and how to operate the temperamental wireless sets.
- All the correct procedures for passing orders to the guns and receiving them – Gun Drill and Fire Discipline.
- How to quickly choose and lay out a suitable gun position for the four guns.
- The many ways used in setting up the guns on the correct line (both by day and night) so that they were ready to fire on a given target as soon as possible.

- The different types of fire used – ranging, Troop fire, Battery fire, Mike fire, barrages, salvo ranging and fire, air-burst, smoke screens, anti-tank procedures, and others.
- How to give and receive ranging corrections from the OP (Observation Point) and AOP (an observer aircraft).

There were many other details related to these topics which needed to be absorbed, but the above remarks should give some idea of the scope and complexity of the subject being taught. It is no wonder that that some of the cadets on the Course were relegated along the way and told to re-learn some of the finer points, due to lack of understanding or application.

From 16 May until the beginning of Camp on 12 July, we were feverishly learning all these aspects of Field Gunnery, and more important, putting them into practice. We frequently went out on day schemes with the guns; and we practiced manning the guns, and acting as Technical Assistant and GPO (the Gun Position Officer) and Troop Leader (his 2 I/C and assistant) and TSM (his Troop Sergeant Major).

The first time that I was told to take over as GPO in the middle of one of these exercises, I was not a great success. I went over to Tice with my map to receive the orders for the next gun position and was just writing down details on my proformer when Tice suddenly hit the pencil out of my hand, and with flaring eyes said that I should be putting all the data straight onto the map! Not a very helpful start! Anyway, having received my orders I hurriedly left in my truck without completely orientating myself on the map, so I went off in the wrong direction! Eventually I did sort myself out, and quickly doubled back, and found the correct spot for the guns, and pre-pared the position in the nick of time, just as the guns were driving onto the site! Phew!! The guns very nearly arrived at the gun position before I had!

Although I was not very pleased with myself after that display, when some of the others took over for the first time on 12 June, I noted in my diary that, 'the GPO's didn't get on all that well, which gave me heart after my shambles the other day. Tice again flew off the handle a few times for little or no reason with the others. He really is a silly little man; you can't tell what he'll do from one minute to the next. And his attitude is so counter-productive and unhelpful. To sum him up:– he really acts like a petulant spoilt child!'

As time passed and we had more practice and saw more gun positions occupied by others, most of us became quite proficient and began to feel more confident at facing the trials of Practice Camp at the end of the Course. Some however, found it more difficult to cope with the pressures, and I noted on 19 June, that Bob Bartlett, David Reeves, Dave Sorbie and Bob Jopling all received a verbal warning from Tice. In due course, all four of those were relegated.

A week later on 26 June, we had an examination and this was followed shortly afterwards by an interview with Hamilton, when he told us all how we were progressing. Encouragingly, he said to me that I was on course for passing and then gave me my grading, which didn't seem very good to me. They had put me down for minus 1! Tice's report stated: 'Started badly, but doing better now. Reserved, but has a pleasant personality'.

Unfortunately, I made no notes about anyone else's results – not even Bryan Ingham, with whom I went out later that day to celebrate at a café near Odiham. There, to set us up for the evening, we both had a slap up meal of eggs, fried bread, sausages, spam and chips, costing just 1/9d (8¾ pence)! We then went back to do some revising. I noted that poor Bob Bartlett was not feeling too happy as he got into bed that night.

A fortnight before Camp, we went to the Larkhill Ranges to fire the 25 pounder guns for the first time. I wrote in my diary: 'The noise that the guns make when firing is really quite considerable, and it's much louder than I had expected'. It seems incredible to us now, but I can't recall ever seeing anyone use any form of ear protection whilst firing the guns in those days!

An incident happened at Larkhill which showed us all how dangerous it can always be when firing live ammunition on the ranges. During the last shoot of the day, whilst I was acting as the first Tec Acc and Bob Bartlett was GPO at the gun position, one of the shells landed short, and might well have hit those observing and directing the shoot from the OP. There are four charges which can be used in the cartridges when firing 25 pdrs, and all our cartridges for that day should have been primed with Charge 2. In the enquiry afterwards, it was thought that this rogue shell must have been fired with just a Charge 1 by mistake. There are of course many safeguards to prevent this sort of error from happening, but in this particular case, it seems that the mistake was caused by our inexperience at the guns, coupled with a large dose of 'Sod's Law'!

Just before Camp, we were given our options for postings at the end of the Course (if we passed!), and we were asked to put down our first three choices. The possibilities were: one for Korea, two for FELF (Far East), three for MELF (Middle East), five for BAOR (West Germany), five for Oswestry, three for Larkhill, two for Woolwich, and I think a few other Home postings.

It seemed that most of the Cadets chose BAOR, but I opted for (i) MELF (Field), (ii) BAOR (Field), (iii) BAOR (Locating Battery). I heard afterwards that none of us had volunteered for Korea, so I suppose some one had to be delegated for that posting! On this point, I wrote in my diary: 'As for being posted to Korea; I shouldn't volunteer for it, but if I was posted, I shouldn't mind going. The reason is that if anything happened to me, I should feel that it had been my own fault.' I ask the reader: 'What do you think you would have decided to put down in similar circumstances?'

On 10 July Major Hamilton told us about our postings (subject to alteration of course!): I was extremely pleased to find that I had been given my first choice of MELF (Field). I was really keen to visit that part of the world at the government's expense and I should have been most disappointed if I had been sent to anywhere in the UK – particularly, one of the training Regiments at Oswestry (like my brother). Some of other people's postings I noted were: Bryan Ingham to Woolwich, Ian Lucas and Bob Bartlett to Larkhill, and Mike Goodburn and Glynn Jenkins, both to the Far East.

In July 1952, the Korean War was raging critically, and it was primarily due to the implications of this War, National Service in Britain had been extended from eighteen months to two years. The Chinese Communist Army had intervened massively more than a year before, and as a result, the South Koreans, the US and the United Nations forces had been pushed back to the 38th parallel, and the bloody conflict had come to a near stalemate. The casualties for the UN forces were considerable, and before I left school, I heard of at least three Carthusians who had been badly wounded in the Commonwealth Brigade or Division.

Our time at Mons was hopefully drawing to a close, and eventually the date for the End-of-Course Camp at Sennybridge arrived. On 12 July we took the train from Aldershot, with changes at Hereford and Brecon. We had to wait two hours at Hereford for our connection, so we had a chance to look round this interesting little City. I visited the Cathedral and Castle, and walked round some of the streets with all their Tudor timber-framed houses, and I was most impressed. I wrote in my diary that 'it is rather like a smaller version of Chester'. After a whole day's travelling, we arrived in time for dinner in the Officers' Mess, and we soon went to bed that night.

Next day was a Sunday, and we spent the time testing all the equipment in preparation for tomorrow and then loading up enough ammunition for a whole day's shooting.

The Sennybridge Gunnery Range is in a lovely part of Wales, and many of us later became quite familiar with those hills and features during our time in the Territorials. Much of the range is 1,200 feet above sea level, and on

On the Sennybridge Ranges

that Monday morning in July, we found ourselves frozen to the core by the cold crosswind. Up to mid-day, Tice sent the five athletes (the 'gladiators') to the observation post to direct some shoots, and then we swapped with some of the others at the gun position. During the afternoon, we were all given various tasks to perform during the shoots, and most of this seemed to pass off without much incident, although I did note that, 'Hamilton can be just as petulant as Tice and is very apt to suddenly start shouting at the GPO or some one else about some trivial mistake.' When we returned to camp, we had to clean the guns, and then we all had a discussion about the day's shooting.

For the next two and a half days of this Sennybridge Camp, the 'gladiators' really did benefit from their privileged status, because we were permitted to leave on Tuesday morning and to travel back in preparation for the Southern Command Championships taking place at Aldershot on the Wednesday (16 July). This absence from the fray was a great advantage for us, because it kept the five of us completely out of harm's way during that very testing period.

Salvo Ranging with 25 pounder field guns on Sennybridge Ranges

End of firing at Sennybridge

At the championships, the Mons team performed moderately well, since we ended just a point behind the School of Artillery, to come third. In the 4 x 880 yards, we were disappointed to just lose to the Royal Engineers' quartet again, who beat us the last time we ran against them in the Aldershot District Championships a month ago. Also Ian Lucas, who normally scores a few points for us, had some bad luck and fell at one of the hurdles, and came fourth.

In true Army fashion, we had to travel back to Sennybridge on the first available trains over night, so we found ourselves in Reading at midnight, and ravenously hungry. We managed to find a late night café open, before catching our train westward, and eventually we joined the rest of the Troop at the gun position about midday on Thursday 17 July. The weather was wet and horrible, so we soon returned to camp and cleaned up the guns in readiness for tomorrow. When we arrived back, we heard that Bob Bartlett and Bob Jopling had both done badly today, and so they will both be relegated to Easy Battery when we return.

Friday was the last day of End-of-Course Camp, and although I

Returning to Camp

**Final Inspection of Passing Out "F" Battery by Major-General Nigel Duncan
Front Row:- Pat Daniel, Brian Goodliffe, David Story, Mike Goodburn, Ian Lucas**

was chosen to be the third GPO on the list, the weather was so bad that Hamilton and Tice decided to return early – so thankfully, I was not put to the test!

But next day, we didn't leave Sennybridge until we had taken the CI's Exam and the final practical Test. The Exams proved to be more difficult than we expected, so waiting for the results put us all on tenterhooks once again.

Back at Mons on the afternoon of Monday 21 July, *just three days* before our Passing Out Parade, Major Hamilton called us into the Battery lecture room and read out the names (very slowly) of all those who would be relegated:– 'Bob Bartlett – John Cruikshank (a Regular, previously with RE) – Glynn Jenkins (one of the Athletes) – Bob Jopling – Mike Orford – Dave Rose (who I later met in MELF) – David Reeves – and David Sorbie (another Regular who had transferred originally from RE)'.

The relief felt by the other 20 of us who had actually passed, was indescribable – and in our relief, I hope that we were able to spare a thought, and some sympathy, for those other 8 who had stumbled at the last hurdles and now would have to go back a few squares and start again. Nonetheless, I expect that they all eventually passed out as officers after that extra dose of training.

Our own Passing Out Parade on Thursday 24 July went off without much incident. We were inspected by Major-General Nigel Duncan CB, CBE, DSO, and my mother and father were there to witness the impressive ceremony. At the end of proceedings, I had the memorable experience of slow marching up the steps whilst the Royal Artillery Mounted Band played 'Auld Lang Syne', and I thanked my lucky stars that all the uncertainties were over at last!

I was really overjoyed to see that chapter at Mons Officer Cadet School finally draw to a close, and equally excited at the prospect of going to the Middle East. I was eagerly awaiting the start of the next chapter...

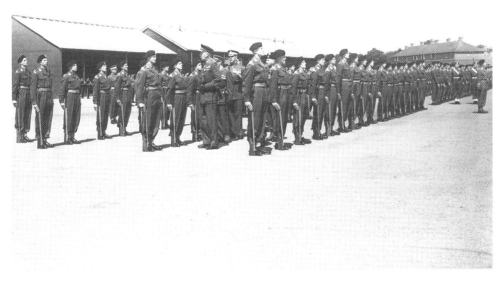

The General (with help from RSM Brittain) inspecting 'F' Battery at a Passing Out Parade at Mons O.C.T.U

Bryan Ingham and John Morley (and others!) slow marching up the steps.

Vicky Saumarez

25 Pounder Field Gun, Limber and Morris Quad

CHAPTER 7

And so to
MELF 27

It was a commendable Gunner tradition in 1952, that all the newly Commissioned National Servicemen from Mons Officer Cadet School were entertained for their first night at Woolwich, the 'home' of the Royal Artillery. This would be the first time that they wore their officers' hats and put their pips up; and also, the first time they received and returned salutes as officers. After the frantic months at Mons, all this seemed very strange at the time, but the circumstances also made the occasion most memorable to those involved.

That evening (25 July) we were given a slap-up dinner in the main Dining Hall at Woolwich, with all the Regimental Silver displayed on the table, with Toasts and with speeches of congratulation and encouragement. Afterwards, we were all entertained convivially in the Officers' Mess before retiring to bed. We were all in the right frame of mind for celebrating at that stage, and I remember that after imbibing liberally, the room was spinning round and round when I eventually went up to bed that night!

The next morning, we said our farewells to our friends and colleagues from Mons before we all went our separate ways, and from all those I knew so well at the time, the only two I ever met up with again, were Bryan Ingham and Ian Lucas.

It was the responsibility of the secretariat at Woolwich to make all the necessary arrangements for the Gunner postings, and they were also most helpful in giving advice to those going abroad. They told me that I should not be flying out to the Suez Canal Zone until about 22 August, but that I should keep in touch with them in case there was a change of plans. I had already arranged a holiday with family and friends in Cornwall, so in two days time, I was driving westwards in my little Standard Eight.

After a wonderful restful week at Perranporth in North Cornwall, during which I celebrated my nineteenth birthday, I then made my way back to London, stopping on the way to see the beautiful Cathedrals at Wells, Salisbury and Winchester, and also by making a diversion northwards to Oswestry so that I could see a school friend of mine who I heard was just starting his Basic Training there.

It was a Sunday when I arrived at Park Hall Camp, so I knew that my friend would be off duty, and it seemed very strange to see this old stamping ground again. I avoided meeting any of the Officers or NCOs I might have known, but instead went straight to the lines of the 67 Regiment and was lucky enough to find the correct barrack room without too much trouble. I was just having a helpful chat with my friend, when a Bombardier came stomping into the room and started throwing his weight around.

I kept a low profile, but eventually, he came up to me and said with an officious voice: 'And what are you doing here?' I looked at him evenly, and replied quietly but firmly: 'Just be careful who you are speaking to Bombardier!' This took him aback and he just replied: 'Oh! Sorry sir!' and walked on. I learned an important lesson for life from that little incident. No matter how important you are in your own domain, remember: there's always a boss out there somewhere!

On 22 August, I took all my baggage up to the Goodge Street Deep Shelter off Tottenham Court Road, but after waiting around with the 'Middle East' contingent for a few hours, we heard that there would be a delay due to maintenance problems with our Hermes aircraft at Blackbushe Airport. We were therefore told to return home again, and to await further instructions. Three days later we heard that another Hermes on its way to Khartoum had just crashed in the sea off Sicily and that all those on board had been killed! (At the time, I am sure that I didn't fully realise the significance to me of that horrible tragedy.)

As a result of this disaster, all Hermes aircraft were grounded, and we were told that we should be flying out instead in a York aircraft (a converted Lancaster bomber). We finally left Blackbushe at 5 pm on 27 August 1952, and after a flight of some 6 hours, we touched down at Malta to refuel. Here we were allowed to stretch our legs, and I noted in my diary: 'We had a dreadful meal in a brand new building at the airport, and I noticed that they had the usual filthy Continental lavatories'. (I made this last remark after remembering the appalling standard of most public lavatories in France and Corsica which I had seen during our visits there in 1950 and 1951).

After arriving at Fayid in the late morning, I was surprised to find a complete lack of organization at the Military Airport. There seemed to be no reception, no one in charge and no one to help all those arriving. We just had to fend for ourselves, and to use our own initiative!

29 Field Regiment RA was situated some 20 miles to the south of Fayid at Geneifa (or Gineifa), but when I telephoned the Regimental office, nobody seemed to be aware that I was even arriving that day. The communications between Woolwich and MELF had obviously broken down! The temperature was 97° and waiting in the Airport Building was like sitting in a furnace! Eventually at 3 o'clock, a 15 cwt truck arrived to take me on to Ava Camp.

There were two roads running southwards from Fayid: the Canal Road which ran down beside the Suez Canal and the lakes; and the Treaty Road

Egyptian Street Scene

which took a route further inland. My driver took the Treaty Road, and I found the journey quite fascinating, because all the sights were so completely new to me.

We started by driving past the so-called 'Sweet-Water Canal' with its cultivated fields nearby and some horrible, smelly, mud-hut villages. This was the first time that I had ever seen anything so squalid and filthy in my life, so it was a real eye-opener to me. The muddy water in the 'sweet water' canals seemed to be used not only for irrigating the crops, but also as drinking water for humans and cattle alike – and in addition, as a convenient lavatory for the Egyptians! There was muck and rubbish everywhere, and the shops we passed had all the merchandise and food (including fruit and whole hanging carcasses) displayed in the open and quite unprotected from the glaring sun and the myriads of flies. It seemed to me no wonder that most of the Egyptians I saw looked skinny and disease-ridden. On the other hand, I wrote in my diary that some of the young girls I saw looking out from these horrible little hovels were really quite beautiful.

The road ran due south through the desert, and this was not at all as I had imagined it to be. There were no sand dunes to be seen, but to the west-

Treaty Road and Coca Cola Stall

ward, just a flat stony wilderness covered with dry, thorny vegetation and low hills in the distance; whilst to the eastward, a similar flat stony wilderness towards the Suez Canal and Bitter Lakes about a mile away with its many ships passing through. Across the canal, there were more dry stony hills in the distance. We passed by several Regimental and RAF camps on the way, as well as some isolated huts by the side of the road where the locals were selling the occasional bottle of Coca Cola to the infrequent Egyptian traveller passing by. In the dry, stony desert, the only movement to be seen was some thorny shrubs rolling in the wind, and the occasional little whirlwind (or 'sand-devil'). I had certainly arrived in another world!

Ava Camp at Geneifa stood on its own about 200 yards to the west of the Treaty Road and surrounded by the wilderness on all sides but with a range of dry flat hills about half a mile to the westward towards Cairo. The camp had a few brick-built buildings and a water-tower, but it mainly consisted of lines of bell-tents with concrete floors, and some larger ridge-tents. To stop intruders, the camp was surrounded by a perimeter fence consisting of three coils of barbed-wire.

Ava Camp through the wire

On the other side of the Treaty Road to Ava Camp was 10 BOD (a large Base Ordnance Depot), which stood on a large site and stored all kinds of Army equipment, from clothing, sheets and blankets, to paint, ammunition, chemicals, jerry cans and petrol. Also within the compounds of 10 BOD was a good-sized Swimming Pool, some hard stony football pitches, a Chapel and an Open-Air Cinema.

About 30 miles to the south of Geneifa was the southern end of the Suez Canal at the town of Port Suez, and northwards the road went some 80 miles up to the northern end of the Canal at Port Said on the Mediterranean Sea.

Ava Camp was about a mile west of the Suez Canal itself, so we only saw the shipping moving up and down when we drove eastwards to places like Kabrit on the Little Bitter Lake. The Suez Canal was always busy with shipping in those days, and when we were there in 1952 and 1953, about 8 or 9 ships out of every 10 passing through, were flying a British Flag! That was during the years before all those 'flags of convenience' annihilated the British Merchant Fleets.

Entrance to Ava Camp, Gineifa, Suez Canal Zone

For over six months before I joined 29 Field at the end of August 1952, there had been a steady build up of British troops in the Middle East. Although the units were well under their correct 'strength', I believe that the force by then consisted of 1 Infantry Division (with its three Brigades), and another Brigade, the 3rd Armoured, backed up by a number of RAF and Colonial Guard and Pioneer Units. The number of troops in the Suez Canal Zone at that time was probably in excess of 100,000.

The political situation in the whole region continued to be most unstable, and in October 1951, after some anti-British rioting in Cairo, Britain had occupied the Zone with additional troops to safeguard the efficient operation of the Suez Canal. At that time also, Egyptian army officers had overthrown King Farouk (the playboy King of Egypt) and had installed General Naguib as President of the new Republic. Before this coup d'état, Egypt had virtually been a British puppet State.

The rise in Egyptian nationalism meant that the Egyptian Government now wanted to nationalise the Suez Canal Company, which was an enterprise wholly owned and controlled by Britain. From that time onwards therefore, the British Army was increasingly *persona non grata*, and during my whole time in the Zone during 1952 and 1953, it was quite common in Moascar and Fayid to see the Egyptian inhabitants pointedly spitting in the streets as we walked by!

It was because of all this animosity, that when I arrived in Fayid, all the British units in MELF were on a '24 hour alert', and prepared to take up belligerent positions round Cairo! This of course never happened, but later, when General Naguib was replaced by Nasser, the situation became even more unsettled. It was not until later in 1956 that Britain eventually agreed to pull out its troops from the Zone. I was not fully aware of all these matters when I arrived on the scene, but it is now quite clear that this was a most 'interesting' period!

During that first month in the Middle East I started to acclimatise myself to my new surroundings; and there was plenty for me to assimilate. I had arrived in late summer, so the weather was still very hot, and at this time of year it was normal to have sunny, cloudless skies every day. The only

At Ava Camp

uncertainty was whether the temperature would be 95° or 110° – and during my first few days the temperature did reach 108°. But in addition to all this heat, the air was also extremely dry – and it was actually so dry, that the fire buckets full of water would virtually evaporate after a day or two in the open air!

It was always simple to pick out the new arrivals from Britain by the colour of their knees, and although we were continually warned about not exposing our skin too quickly to the fierce rays of the sun, some foolishly took no notice, and as a result paid a merci-less price. However, after a sensible conditioning period, there was no problem for most of us to go without shirts – although the one proviso was that hats needed to be worn, and many also wore thin neck-scarves. It was interesting to see those returning after a long scheme out in the desert; some were so brown, they were nearly black.

Although many would not agree with this advice, our Regimental doctor Bill Cattell advised us not to wear sunglasses unless we wore them *always* during day-time. He said that it was bad for the eyesight to wear them spasmodically, although the one exception was for those driving long distances in the glaring sun. Certainly, I followed this advice during my time in Egypt, and so did many of the others.

Ogden Nash in his succinct phraseology, once aptly wrote: 'God in his wis-dom made the fly, and then forgot to tell us why' – and the flies in Egypt

were one of the notable curses of the country. They were much more difficult to swat, twenty times more irritating and persistent, and at least a
hundred thousand times more numerous than those in England! They were
everywhere; and due to the flies it was also essential to sleep under netting
at night to prevent being woken up at first light. There was a slight respite
from these flies during the cooler months of December, January and
February, but otherwise, they were ever-present.

Hygiene was always a top priority in Ava Camp, and spraying with insec-
ticides and disinfectants was a continual activity. The latrines were disin-
fected every day, and the canteens and dining areas were sprayed extensively before all meals. Nonetheless, within an hour or two, the flies had
returned again in their droves. Ever since my time spent in the Suez Canal
Zone, I have never been able to regard flies in any other way except with
caution and extreme antagonism.

Whether or not it was due to the affect of these flies, or to the different
water, or maybe to some other unknown Egyptian phenomenon in the air,
but almost everyone visiting the Suez Canal Zone suffered from the curse
of 'Gyppy tummy' sooner or later. I see from my diary that I had my first
bout on 8 September, just eleven days after my arrival. Dr Bill Cattell
always had his tried and tested remedy at the ready. This was a dose of
some 35 'special' pills to be taken with water within 24 hours. Heavens
knows what these pills contained, but they certainly did the trick by the
end of the day!

I don't know how many Regiments had their own doctor, but Bill Cattell
was the National Service one attached to us during my first year in the
Middle East. He was never run off his feet in the job, because, after all, he
was only administering to the medical needs of some 700 healthy young
men. Furthermore, he always told us that the climate in the Canal Zone
was, on the whole, fairly healthy so long as the hygiene rules were strictly
adhered to.

When Bill wasn't reading Medical Journals to keep up to date, he spent
much of his time in the Regiment giving talks on health and hygiene matters. Otherwise, the only ailments he needed to treat were stomach trou-

bles, or skin problems such as boils and rashes, or wounds such as cuts and grazes. In the dry atmosphere, even the slightest cut or graze could take months to heal completely; and in the meantime it had to be cleaned thoroughly, and protected from the flies to prevent any festering.

I noted on 17 February 1953:– 'My knee, which I grazed playing hockey yesterday needs watching. These wounds go septic very quickly. I have washed it in Dettol several times. Tom Keeble – another affable National Serviceman who was demobbed in September 1953 – has been badly affected by septic wounds which he received playing rugby recently. He told me that he will *never* play the game again out here!'

In this connection, I remember thinking that this healing difficulty must have been the main reason why (I had read somewhere) more soldiers died of their wounds *after* battles in the Middle East, rather than those being killed *during* the battle itself.

Ava Camp, Gineifa

The most prevalent skin problem with the ORs in 29 Field was 'foot rot' (or 'athletes' foot'), and it was during that first month that I was told to organize a foot inspection in 8 Battery. I went along to Bill Cattell's surgery for some advice, and he told me – according to my diary:– that 'the things to look for are ring worm and foot rot; both of which can be prevented by washing the feet regularly, by drying them thoroughly after washing, by using the special foot powder regularly and by only wearing clean, darned socks.'

When I later carried out this first foot inspection, I soon concluded that most of the ORs were totally disregarding Bill's simple advice. Virtually every person I inspected had foot rot to a lesser or greater extent! As I went round, I talked to them all like a (very young) 'Dutch uncle', and came away feeling complacently that I might well have saved 8 Battery from a very severe epidemic!

We had a really excellent device in Egypt for keeping the drinking water cool at all times; locally, this was called a 'chuggle'. These chuggles were earthenware pitchers, which were slightly porous, and this chemical process somehow caused the water inside the vessel to be cooled down to just the right

Water Tower and Shower House at Ava Camp

temperature for drinking. Nowadays, with refrigerators widely used, perhaps these chuggles are less necessary, because I have never seen any being used since that time. In those days, most of our tents in Ava Camp had a chuggle placed by the entrance. I expect the idea dates back to ancient Egyptian times, but the British Army in the Suez Canal Zone also issued modern versions of these containers made from some type of canvas material which reacted in the same way as the porous pottery. In 1952, whenever we went out into the hot desert on schemes, these canvas chuggles were normally to be seen on the front of most vehicles.

Apart from acclimatizing myself to the elements and the environment, my main task during those first weeks was to learn all my Regimental duties, brush up on my knowledge of Gunnery matters and to get to know my colleagues. I happened to arrive at Ava Camp on a Thursday, and this was usually when the Officers' Mess held its weekly Dinner Night. On these occasions, instead of wearing the usual civilian shirt and tie for the evening meal, we all dressed up in our Regimental Blues Uniforms.

Dinner Nights in most Officers' Messes were rather special events: not only did we dress accordingly, but the meal was always of the best available, and guests from other Regiments were often invited. At the appropriate time, the Loyal Toast: 'The Queen, our Captain General' was proposed and the port and the Madeira wine were passed round freely to the left. This was the one occasion, when British officers, wherever they were stationed, kept up their standards and pretended that they were dining at Woolwich or at their club in London! I always thoroughly agreed with this civilised tradition, even though it meant higher Mess bills all round!

The conviviality and friendliness throughout those evenings, and the sing-songs, I always thoroughly enjoyed – but what I was never so keen on were those puerile games we so often played, such as: 'Are you there Moriarty?' and 'High Cockalorum' and 'Battery Rowing' (or was it 'tug-of-war'?) in which everyone (including myself!) participated with great verve! Perhaps my lack of enthusiasm at that time was due to my low alcohol intake, but I always disliked those ridiculous, childish games right from that first Thursday night.

In spite of these disparaging remarks, I did find my fellow officers in 29 Field a most congenial bunch – varied and most friendly and convivial, and they all seemed to accept me, the newcomer, without any reservations. Almost everyone, whatever his rank, made a point of speaking to me during that first evening, and also in wishing me well.

The Officers' Mess in 29 Field consisted of some 40 officers:– the CO who was a Lieutenant-Colonel, some 20 Majors and Captains, 10 Regular Subalterns and about 8 National Service Subalterns.

Gunner Regiments were split up into four parts:– the Regimental HQ, and 3 Batteries, each with 2 Troops of 4 x 25 pounder guns. I joined 8 (Alma) Battery, with its 2 Troops called Able and Baker. The other two 'junior'

8 Battery Lines, Ava Camp

Batteries in the Regiment were 79 Battery with Charlie and Dog Troops, and 145 Battery with Easy and Fox Troops. (In the Army, all letters of the alphabet had a distinct connotation to avoid misinterpretations when sent over the radio.) This sort of Regimental organization was ideal for stimulating competition and 'esprit de corps' between the Batteries, as well as sharpening up all gunnery skills.

After I arrived at Ava Camp to join in all the fun, my first tasks were to get to know my colleagues in 8 Battery and then to learn all my Battery and Regimental duties; and to brush up my Gunnery knowledge. There was plenty for me to learn, although I was given every support from Mike Martin and the others, and I found it all very interesting and also within my scope.

The Battery Commander of 8 Battery was away on leave when I arrived, but those in charge at Battery HQ were Major Rex King (Battery Captain), Capt Peter Nicholson (who soon moved on), Lt Ted Burgess and 2/Lt John Gilmour (all Regulars).

In the two Troops:– Able Troop Commander was Capt Peter Brereton and his Gun Position Officer (GPO), 2/Lt John Stansfield (a National Serviceman). In Baker Troop, Capt (Mac) MacKenzie was the Troop Commander, with 2/Lt Mike Martin (a Regular) as his GPO. I was detailed to be Mike's assistant (his Troop Leader), and as a 'new-boy', I always found him to be a most helpful and considerate colleague to introduce me into Regimental life. I remember that the word 'splendid' was one of his favourite comments.

On one of my first parades with 8 Battery, I made the unwitting faux pas of turning up in black shoes instead of brown! (Officers never wear black shoes on parade). Mac was very quick to notice – and was absolutely appalled. He sent me back immediately to my tent to change into brown shoes at once. I felt just like the man in Stanley Holloway's classic song! Anyway, I never made that mistake again!

I soon found that there was much activity in preparing for the Regimental Athletics Competition which was to take place in a month's time. In fact this was one of the first questions that my colleagues in 8 Battery had asked me on that first dinner night, and they were well pleased when I told them that I had run in the Mons Athletics Team. Ted Burgess was in the middle of training all the Battery athletes, so I was able to help him immediately in this. There was a good running track just a mile or two to the east at Kabrit and this is where the 8 Battery athletes often went for their training sessions after morning parade.

Ted Burgess was one of the 8 Battery athletic stars and on the first occasion we went to Kabrit, one of the Bombardiers bet me two pints that I couldn't beat Ted in the first practice 880 yard race we ran together. I was really very fit at that stage and I have to say (without a hint of modesty) that I won the bet really quite easily. From then onwards, they all thought that I was a budding Roger Bannister!

Kabrit was on the Canal Road on the west bank of the Little Bitter Lake, and after athletics training we often had a swim in the lake, in spite of the water being unpleasantly salty. The link road between Ava Camp and Kabrit took a route through some mud-brick houses and some cultivated

Little Bitter Lake near Kabrit

land, and I noticed at one point that there were some demolished areas by the side of the road. When I asked what had happened here, I was told that in this section, our Army vehicles had been continually subjected to stone-throwing from the local inhabitants, and after many warnings had been given, the Royal Engineers eventually went in and flattened all the buildings to within 50 yards of the road! There was no messing in those days!

In fact, the British forces were always liable to have trouble in the Suez Canal Zone during those years, so we needed to be ever watchful, especially when we had to stop the vehicles. We always had a soldier sitting in the back of the trucks to prevent intruders jumping in; and we always went out of camp with loaded weapons. Whenever vehicles were left unattended, such as at night, it was general practice to disable the engines by removing the distributor arms.

With only about twenty Subalterns in the Regiment, we regularly found ourselves detailed for ROO (Regimental Orderly Officer), and this meant being confined to Camp for the 24 hours, and being responsible for various other duties. When the Regiment was on 'Full Alert' (which was for much of the time) the ROO or some other Officer had to be near the Regimental telephone for 24 hours a day in case some action was needed. Otherwise, his main duty was to be readily available to look after any Regimental matters which had to be dealt with.

The ROO took over from the previous one before breakfast, and always made a tour of the Camp during the morning with the Orderly Sergeant, and checked on the cleanliness of all the washrooms and the latrines, and went into the Dining Room at Lunchtime to ask if there were any grumbles about the food. Every day, the ROO also checked the Regimental Armoury where all the ammunition was kept and the rifles and other weapons were chained up. He mounted the new Guard at 6 o'clock in the evening, wrote his report and then turned out the Guard again during the night hours. Also during the night, the ROO normally went out to check that the prowler guards were challenging correctly.

One of the ROO's tasks during the Camp inspections was to thoroughly inspect the perimeter barbed wire fence to ensure that there were no obvious 'holes' which would allow some wily 'westernised oriental gentlemen' to get through. This was something that never ceased to amaze me. Although the wire was checked carefully every day like this, it was still sometimes possible to find another slight gap which needed a little more attention! Also, in spite of all this checking and rechecking, intrusions through the wire still did occur. It was on 18 January 1953 that I wrote: 'This morning, Major George Warren woke up to find a 'westernised oriental gentleman' in his tent, piling up his clothes, ready for departure! George said that he 'bellowed like a bull', and the startled intruder ran off empty-handed and went out through the wire again before anyone could stop him.' I don't think any other incidents happened like this, but we were never able to be complacent about being completely secure within Ava Camp.

I see that I was very busy during those first few weeks with 29 Field:– I helped the others to measure out and construct a rifle range by the row of hills at the back of the camp and then helped to organise a number of rifle shooting competitions there – went out with 8 Battery into the desert as Mike Martin's assistant on some practice schemes – and had my first session as Safety Officer with one of our sister Regiments, 26 Field – and started to learn all the names of the ORs in our Battery. In fact, I was really beginning to settle into Regimental life, when I was told about the possibility of a most extraordinary diversion which I could never fully understand:– I was told by the Adjutant that my name had been put forward by Colonel Chris Hutt for consideration as aide-de-camp to the Governor-General of Cyprus!!!

I had first been told about this amazing possibility when the Adjutant Peter Roberts spoke to me after lunch on 7 September, just ten days after I had joined the Regiment. He told me that the current ADC to the Governor had been obliged to start an Army Course two months earlier than the arranged finishing date of his appointment at Government House. As a result, a number of BTE Regiments, including 29 Field, had been asked to submit a name for consideration and the CO and he had decided to put my name forward. The Adjutant told me that this decision had been taken due to no particular merit on my part, but because the Regiment was on 'full alert' and 'was short of officers', and therefore 'wouldn't miss a new arrival like me' (or words to that effect)!

After that conversation, I had heard nothing more about this possibility for three weeks and had rather discounted the whole matter, when the Adjutant again confirmed with me that the appointment was still very much alive and that it was a real possibility. Then on Friday 26 September, definite news came through that I was to leave by boat from Port Said on 29 September and take up the appointment on Tuesday, 30 September, at Government House in Cyprus! I had been with 29 Field for just 31 days! The wheel of Fortune sometimes makes some unusual turns. At this early stage in the episode, there was no knowing whether or not this particular turn of Fate was for good or for ill!

Having said my farewells at 29 Field, I set off somewhat apprehensively, on my way to Port Said and *HMS Empire Peacemaker*, which was bound for Farmagusta, in Cyprus.

The 80 miles up the Canal, was once again a most fascinating journey. Beyond Fayid we passed round the Great Bitter Lake and Lake Timsah in the middle of the Canal and then through the central town of Ismailiya, and onwards into the Northern Canal Zone. The Sweet Water Canal, which brings water from the Nile, runs along most stretches of the salty

Some Nile Sailing Boats (Dahabiyehs)

Suez Canal and irrigates the cultivated fields along the west bank, so there were plenty of palms and habitation, with the usual clusters of dirty mud huts.

There were fairly healthy looking cattle, sheep and goats in the fields tended by the women and children only and there were some unfortunate blindfolded camels and oxen which spent most of their days walking round and round, operating the ancient circular irrigation pumps. We also saw some old, dilapidated ferries which the inhabitants moved across the little branch canals by tugging on chains, and some of the distinctive flat-bottomed Nile sailing craft (called dahabiyehs) with their diagonal cross beams, moored by the banks. Some of these I also saw being dragged along the canal banks by just two weedy-looking Egyptians!

The last 40 miles of the Suez Canal run as straight as a die right up to the northern end at Port Said on the Mediterranean. These trips to and fro Cyprus, were the only times that I ever saw this northern part of the Canal Zone during the whole of my time in MELF.

Study in Perspective. The northern stretch of the Suez Canal

The Corvette, *HMS Empire Peacemaker*, was taking a large batch of servicemen to Cyprus on leave, and before long I had joined them on board with my luggage. When dusk came, we sailed off into the night – and for me, into the unknown.

The troop ship "Charlton Star" docked at Port Said

The Corvette HMS "Empire Peacemaker" waiting to take me to Famagusta

CHAPTER 8

Spell at Government House, Cyprus

By the 1950s, it was clear to all thinking people that the great British Empire had passed its zenith and was beginning to decline. India, Pakistan, Sri Lanka and Burma had all recently gained their independence, and there was unrest in many British Colonies such as Kenya and Malaya. All the other colonial powers, such as France, Belgium, Portugal and the Netherlands, were also having serious problems and unrest in their own colonies throughout the world. This infectious rise of nationalist fervour, stoked up by communistic agitations, was a worldwide phenomenon, and it continued to grow as the decade progressed.

Although Britain was struggling economically to maintain its world-power image and had recently lost much of its sway over Egypt with the rise of Naguib, British influence in the Middle East by September 1952 remained strong and widespread. King Hussein in Jordan for instance, was a firm Anglophile. Not only had he been educated at Harrow School and Sandhurst College, but also his Jordanian Army – the Arab Legion – was organised along British lines under its Commanding Officer, a British national, named John Glubb Pasha. The adjoining kingdom of Iraq, with King Faisal II on the throne, was similarly well-disposed towards Britain; and so was Iran, under the firm control of the Shah and with its large oil installations at Abadan being protected by British Army units.

Added to this, Britain had its forces well established in the Suez Canal Zone, as well as in nearby Cyprus, and also in Aqaba, Aden and British Somaliland to the south. Then southwards into Africa:– the Sudan was a puppet state under British influence, as were the adjoining British colonies from Uganda and Kenya right down to the Union of South Africa. As we have seen, the only exception in this whole region was now Egypt itself, which was currently in the grip of nationalist fervour, which caused turmoil and unrest in the country.

On the road between Nicosia and Famagusta

Small and large contingents of British troops were stationed in most of these countries and since he was the Queen's representative in the region, the Governor-General of Cyprus was the most senior General of all the British forces in the Middle East.

The Corvette, *HMS Empire Peacemaker* arrived off Famagusta in mid-morning of Tuesday 30 September 1952 and there we waited till midday for launches to take us ashore. After landing on the quay, I personally, was given top priority treatment. A government official came to meet me and then whisk me away to a glistening new Vanguard staff car and off we drove without delay.

We left the walled city of Famagusta and made for the open road westward towards the capital, Nicosia. Looking round with great interest at all the new sights, I soon noticed that the Cypriots appeared much more prosperous than the Egyptians I had just left behind in all their squalor. Everywhere I could see well stocked shops and an abundance of food, fruit and vegetables, many of which I had never seen before in the Britain of

1952:– there were all sorts of high-class groceries; and bananas, figs, grapes, dates, citrus fruits, pomegranates, olives, melon, beans, okra, carobs and a wide variety of other vegetables.

Some Fat-Tailed Sheep

The surface of the main road between Famagusta and Nicosia was surprisingly well-maintained compared to those in the Canal Zone and then, whilst driving across the parched central plain I could see that all the riverbeds were dry, and that the whole countryside was eagerly awaiting the winter rains after the long hot summer. I also saw herds of fat-tailed sheep for the first time waddling beside the road with their large, heavy tails flopping behind them. I learned later that the fat tails on this breed of sheep act in the same way as the humps on camels, and that these sheep are to be seen throughout the Middle East.

When we reached Nicosia in the centre of the island, I was most impressed by the orderly appearance of the place and the old circular Venetian walls round the city which I saw, and also by the number of smart new buildings. On the other hand, the continuous noise of car hooters coming from the city streets had to be heard to be believed! We saw little of the capital however, but drove straight up to Government House, which is a modern, impressive building situated on some high ground to the southwest of the city. As we drove up to the front entrance, the Guard turned out and 'Presented Arms' to us. Before long, the out-going ADC, Captain Bill Rawlings, came hurrying out to welcome me.

He soon introduced me to His Excellency the Governor, Sir Andrew Wright, – always referred to as 'HE' – and to his wife Lady Wright and their seventeen-year-old daughter Jill, who were all most welcoming towards me. Bill then told me a few basic pointers on the ADC's duties, but I thought that he was not particularly helpful in what he said, and he really gave me very little of his time. He soon excused himself and disappeared upstairs to pack his things for the morning. He did however tell me 'reassuringly' before he left, that he felt quite sure that I would soon pick up all there was to know about the job – and as a parting remark, went on to say: 'Oh, by the way Brian, you will soon need to get yourself ready for the party tonight. It is being hosted by the Colonial Secretary at his residence down the road, and it starts at 7.30!'

After these brief preliminaries, the doorman and porter, Aghabios, showed me up to my bedroom, which was situated in a prime position at the centre of the house, overlooking the garden at the back. I had little time to contemplate my present predicament. I took my first hot bath since leaving home (a 'supreme luxury' as I recorded in my diary at the time!), and then, before long, changed into my best uniform in readiness for the party down the road!

The big black Daimler (similar to the Queen's), with flags flying, arrived at 7.30, and after I had opened the back door for HE, Lady Wright, and Jill (as Bill had told me to do) I jumped into the front seat myself, and off we sped down the driveway in a great flurry, escorted by a detachment of police motorcycles! The party was already underway when we arrived, and after our hosts had welcomed us, I soon found myself being introduced as their new ADC to countless other guests. The host, John Fletcher-Cooke, was the Colonial Secretary of Cyprus and the Governor's right-hand man. He was an intelligent and friendly man, and by the end of my time at Government House he was a person I greatly admired. I noted in my diary that we had supper after returning from the party, and that I was very late to bed that night (1.30 a.m. I recorded!) Thus ended my first few hours at Government House in Cyprus!

From my bedroom window at Goverment House

I was up for breakfast at 7.30 next morning, and said my goodbyes to Bill Rawlings who was rushing off to his Army Staff Course in Britain – and there I was, 'left holding the baby'. I looked forward to my next few weeks as ADC with a certain amount of uneasiness!

I went along to my new office which was situated on a wing of Government House and met the Governor's English female Secretary and also the Greek-Cypriot Chief Clerk, a person called Costackis, who controlled the small staff in the secretariat and was the person responsible for all the general correspondence, the petty cash for purchasing the victuals and other provisions for Government House and kept the household accounts. All this was not the direct responsibility of the ADC, but he had to check the figures and make sure that he understood how the office systems were controlled. I was soon reassured enough to discern that Costackis appeared to be a most competent and helpful individual and that he was also the sort of person who appeared to have everything well organized and at his fingertips (and also, as I've implied, *appeared* transparently trustworthy!) He showed me the appointments diary which I should need to write up from now on and explained some of the office routines to me.

The ADC's office was adjacent to the Governor's suite, so all visitors had to see the ADC first and be vetted by him and then wait in his office, whilst being cleared with HE. Then if convenient, they could be ushered through into HE's Office. I always had to be very circumspect when some of these visitors arrived, because on occasions people came at the wrong time or without any appointments and I soon learned that not all visitors were welcome without prior appointments. For instance, many of the Cypriot mayors in Cyprus had 'Communistic' leanings at that time, so these persons were not always welcome unless preparations had been made beforehand.

One of the most difficult parts of my duties during those first few days and weeks, was to remember the names of all the people telephoning during the day, especially the names of all the Greek and Turkish officials. Costackis helped me here and I soon made a short-list which I kept on my desk, to act as my speedy aide-mémoire.

I also discovered that some of the Staff Officers at Army HQ in Nicosia were not the easiest of people for me to deal with. No – I must be quite frank – I thought that some of them on occasions, acted in a most pompous and unhelpful way towards me! It was quite clear that some of them considered *all* ADCs were jumped-up little whippersnappers, sitting in elevated positions, well above their rank and station! However right from the start I made absolutely certain that I acted with all due deference whenever I spoke to any of them – the correct term might even be 'sycophantic' (may I be forgiven!).

Being so very new to the 'Army Game' and to the whole set up of the Army Secretariat at that time, I found great difficulty in assimilating the Staff Officers' titles, seniorities and responsibilities when they first introduced themselves on the telephone by giving me a string of letters and numbers (such as GSO 2 etc), which they assumed I would immediately understand! To the initiated of course, these titles were quite clear and explicit in indicating their positions and ranks, but these titles were all gibberish to me at first and I had to ask for explanations (which, at times, may have seemed somewhat facetious)! Before long however, I made arrangements to visit the Adjutant of the nearby Gunner Regiment, 49 Field who was most helpful and gave me a print-out of the structure and titles of all the staff officers at the Cyprus Army HQ. Thus, my problem was *partly* solved.

Up to this point, I have mainly touched upon some of the ADC's administrative tasks (about which I shall say more in due course), but there were also two other important aspects to the job:– firstly, to accompany the Governor on his engagements and to deal with any details during the visit – and secondly, to look after the needs of all the visitors to Government House.

There was a continual stream of important guests and visitors to Government House and it was the ADC's task to ensure that these were received with all due decorum, and that all the arrangements for their stay were attended to without any fuss or bother. For instance, whenever there was a dinner or luncheon party, arrangements had to be prepared and supervised and the guests received properly and introduced, and then suitably looked after. Those who stayed overnight had to be 'told the form' and advised for instance, about the normal level of tipping for the servants – which the ADC would take care of, and later distribute to the staff through Costackis.

One of the many lessons I had to learn, was how to mix the various drinks required by the guests before dinner – an art quite unknown to me at that time. As a result, I soon arranged to have a crash course with the Head

Steward Kyriacos. From then onwards, mixing pink gins, gin and orange, dry martinis and all the other peculiar concoctions became one of my strongest suits! Having mentioned these details however, in practice much of the ADC's job was to be attentive to the needs of the guests and to use plenty of common sense. The most appropriate job description was:– the Governor's personal 'gofer' and 'lackey'!

Since I had been given little hand-over period or really worthwhile advice from Bill Rawlings, I had to learn all these matters very fast, although I was also fortunate enough to have help and understanding right from the start. Nonetheless, when I look back on those two hectic months there is no doubt about it – I was definitely 'thrown in at the deep end!'

Before I go further, I should mention more about the Wright family, because they were very much the central figures in this episode:–

The Governor-General and Commander-in-Chief, Sir Andrew Wright KCMG, CBE, MC, MA., was a smallish, tough-looking man, with a warm personality, and with a certain presence about him. Although he was right-ly conscious of the dignity of his high office and was at times a stickler for maintaining standards, yet he was not pompous in the least, and often showed a delightful sense of humour. He had fought in World War I and World War II, when he had been awarded the MC with a bar and during his Colonial service, he had spent much of his time in Cyprus and in Trinidad; and then later in Gambia, where he had been appointed Governor. He was 57 years old when I first met him and he was the Governor and C-in-C in Cyprus from 1949 until 1954. Sir Robert Armitage took over for a year after him, and then as the situation deteriorated and the EOKA crisis became more critical, Armitage was followed by the sol-dier, Field-Marshal Sir John Harding, who took over from 1955 until November 1957.

Lady Wright was a great support and foil to Sir Andrew in his position. She was a most courteous and warm-hearted person and gave much of her time in Cyprus to supporting charitable works. She was also a good Greek-speaker, which proved an important asset to Sir Andrew in his appoint-ment. Sadly, she suffered very badly from rheumatoid arthritis, which made her life very difficult, though I never remember her complaining about it. On one occasion when speaking to a hard-bitten Staff Officer, he made some snide, unkind remarks to me about her disabilities. Ignoring his callous comments I just said evenly to him, 'as a matter of fact sir, I find Lady Wright a very kind and generous lady'. And that was exactly how I found her.

Their seventeen year old daughter Jill was on holiday in Cyprus during my time there, and she was a most natural and pleasant girl, and not in the least snobbish or self-important (an attitude so frequently found in the *élite* during the 1950s). In later years when I visited the Wright family at their home in Horsham, England I was very pleased that I was able to introduce Jill to her future husband David Mace, an Old Carthusian I played Football with, and whose parents I met in Cyprus at Government House. In fact two weeks before the end of my tenure there, Sir Andrew Wright thoughtfully arranged a special 'Old Carthusian' dinner party as a parting 'thank you' to me, when Mr and Mrs Clive Mace and the Rev and Mrs Edmund Probyn were all invited.

During some of my time as ADC Jill had two of her school friends, Gillian Wiseman-Clark and Jean Birnie (both very pleasant girls as well) staying at Government House during their holidays and I am quite sure that their presence in the 'household' made the situation much easier and more relaxed for myself, especially since I was barely a year or two older than they were. As time went by, I was also able to take them out on trips in my little Austin car and to chaperone them with other young people and this must have scored a few points in my favour, and perhaps counteracted some of my inadequacies. It does occur to me in retrospect, that perhaps my young age had originally been a decisive factor in Sir Andrew selecting me as ADC in preference to the others on the list of possibles, most of whom would have been Captains, and much older than myself. Anyway, we shall never know – and to conclude my brief comments regarding the Wright family, they also had another daughter and a son, whom I never met.

So back to Wednesday 1 October 1952, during the afternoon of my first day in Cyprus, our initial visitors, Colonel and Mrs Walter Muller, arrived at Government House to stay with us for a few days. He was the Inspector-

General of the Colonial Police and he was in the middle of one of his tours of inspection round the Colonies. Like most distinguished persons I met whilst at Government House, Colonel Muller always treated me with great friendliness and civility. In fact, during the whole of my two months' stay in Cyprus, hardly any of the visitors ever treated me with anything less than warmth and courtesy. On the very rare occasions when I sensed that anyone was tending to be imperious towards me, I concluded that it was either because they were always aloof towards others; or otherwise, because they were ill at ease in their high positions and felt they needed to assert themselves.

I was however, always careful to show due respect towards these high-ranking persons and I was quite certain that most of them preferred being treated in a natural and unaffected way (as Rudyard Kipling would say: 'with the common touch'), rather than with the least degree of sycophancy! But the more I witnessed these important people behind the scenes, the more I realised that without all their trappings and uniforms, they were all just ordinary people like you and me!

On that second evening, we had another cocktail party, this time at the house of the Commissioner of Police in Cyprus – to entertain his boss! Here again we all went from Government House in the big black Daimler, with flags flying and a Police escort. I was just following the others into the throng at the party, when the host intercepted me anxiously and whispered in my ear: 'When will he be leaving?' I assured him that I would tell him as soon as I knew. In due course, I discreetly passed on the word to him as promised!

There was a medium-sized swimming pool at the end of the large croquet lawn in the back garden at Government House, and from the beginning of my stay, I made sure that I had an invigorating swim before breakfast whenever possible. On that second morning Colonel Muller must have heard me splashing in the pool since he joined me straightaway – and was obviously pleased to have some company for his dip. Later that morning, in my best uniform and sitting in the front of the Daimler with flags flying again, I accompanied HE and Colonel Muller on their tour of inspection at the Police Training School at Strovolos, not far from Nicosia.

I learned from the conversation in the back of the Daimler, that the Greek-speaking people in Cyprus (who were not really 'Greeks' in the true sense of the word) out-numbered the Turkish-speaking Cypriots by a ratio of approximately 7 : 2. Therefore, with the Greek-Cypriots' inveterate yearning for Enosis ('Union with Greece'), and the Turkish-Cypriots' total antipathy towards that concept, the British rulers had the difficult task of holding the balance of power, and maintaining the current peace and happiness between the inhabitants of the Island. My two 'passengers' however, went on to speak about the rebellion which had taken place in Cyprus about twenty years before, when some Greek-speaking fanatics had burned down the original Government House in Nicosia. After this rebellion, two steps were taken by the British rulers:– firstly, the Greek-speakers on the island had to pay for the cost of rebuilding the new Government House; and secondly, from then onwards, more Turkish-speaking recruits were enlisted into the Police Force than Greek-Cypriots.

In the afternoon after this morning visit, I found the head gardener at Government House, a man named Hannas, and asked him to show me

Government House

Government House, Cyprus, Main Entrance

round all the gardens. At the same time, I took a number of photographs with my trusty Leica IIIc camera, which my father had generously given me about three years before. The display of fruit and vegetables in the gardens was most impressive and Hannas was clearly delighted to have someone who was interested enough to admire all his successes. There were

128

oranges, grapefruit, lemons, tangerines, dates, pomegranates, grapes, olives, figs, melons, marrow, gourds and every conceivable type of vegetable. It was a most impressive show.

I suppose that the whole of the grounds surrounding Government House must have covered some sixty acres. In addition to the croquet lawn, the swimming pool, the tennis courts and those fruit and vegetable gardens to the south, in the front of the building facing the Kyrenia mountain range in the north of the island, there was a long driveway, with trees on both sides, running from the Guard House down to the Main Entrance joining the road towards Nicosia.

On Saturday 4 October 1952, the Mullers were joined by another visitor at Government House called Sir Patrick Coghill. It was the ADC's job to contact the Airport beforehand to ensure that Sir Patrick was given the full priority treatment on arrival, and at 5 o'clock I went out in the Daimler to meet him. Sir Patrick had been at Haileybury with Sir Andrew so they knew each other very well and I soon found that he was a most interesting and congenial person. He was currently the Intelligence Colonel attached to the Arab Legion in Jordan, and he was clearly a great authority and expert on all Middle Eastern affairs.

On that first Saturday evening with the Mullers and Sir Patrick Coghill present, we had the first of our many fascinating dinner parties which included plenty of interesting (and sometimes indiscrete) discussions round the table – and I only wish now that I had recorded far more notes about the contents of the remarks being made by these well-informed persons. At the end of these meals it was customary for the ladies to retire, so the Governor and his principal male guests (including me) could drink their Cypriot 'port' and smoke their tobacco (which I didn't), whilst continuing to discuss some other more serious topics!

After we rejoined the ladies in the drawing-room after that first dinner party, four of them played a few hands of bridge together, whilst Jill taught me how to play Canasta – the 'in-game' at the time. In the following weeks, after two of Jill's friends came to stay at Government House, we often played Canasta together after dinner.

The Mullers stayed at Government House for four days, whilst Colonel Muller made his many inspections round the Island; and after he left, he went on to do the same in Malta and Gibraltar. By the end of their stay, I noted in my diary that: 'Irene Muller never stopped talking!' I also recorded: 'Sir Andrew Wright seemed completely bored by listening to her prattling on.' Anyway, that snippet from my diary may not be totally irrelevant, because when Irene's 'thank-you letter' arrived later to Lady Wright, she found that her letter from Irene Muller was the one she had intended to be sent to the *Governor of Malta* and his wife – she had inadvertently switched her letters and envelopes! Presumably, Irene Muller had been so busy talking about trivialities that she had put her 'standard thank-you letters' into the wrong envelopes!

It seems very strange to me now but during Sir Patrick's stay, I was often present when he and the Governor were talking, really quite privately together. They never seemed to mind me listening into their conversations and in fact, they acted as if I wasn't even present – similar to the livery-servants of yore! For instance, on one occasion, Sir Andrew made the comment that he had heard that some Arabs habitually put urine on their hair to kill off the bugs and Sir Patrick immediately concurred with this important piece of knowledge! Another isolated snippet I noted was a conversation they made about Sir Patrick's younger brother Nevill, who was currently a Professor of English Literature at Oxford University. Sir Patrick was saying that his brother had recently published a most controversial translation of *The Canterbury Tales* into modern English, which many critics considered to be much too frank and forthright (for 1952)! I thought at the time that this seemed to be an interesting book to buy – but I have to admit that I never got round to buying it!

Sir Patrick stayed with us for ten (most interesting) days and during that time the Governor made sure that he arranged a number of suitable dinner parties with senior people on the island for Sir Patrick to meet.

On one occasion whilst talking about the 'Enosis problem' in Cyprus, Sir Patrick said that in his opinion he thought it was the Greek Orthodox Church that was primarily to blame for any unrest there was on the Island; it was the parish priests in particular who were stirring up the trouble. He illustrated this opinion by quoting a well-known Greek saying, which (translated freely) goes as follows:– 'If the priest farts; the congregation sh-ts!' Sir Andrew had a good laugh at that one and thoroughly agreed with its rationale!

I spoke to George, the Greek Cypriot driver of the Daimler about the racial situation on the Island and when I repeated Sir Patrick's local saying, he thoroughly agreed with it and went on to say that many people in Cyprus were very much in favour of British rule and wished them to remain here. It was the minority of extremists and Priests who encouraged the people to support Enosis – although there were also a number of Communists who make trouble. When I was in Cyprus later in 1953, Enosis had reached the graffiti stage. By 1955 there were terrorist attacks and murders – and from then onwards, the once peaceful, happy, prosperous island was split apart, with the British, Greeks and Turkish all being suspicious of each other.

In the late summer when I arrived at Government House, it was still deemed to be 'summertime' in Cyprus so there was little or no office work to be done in the afternoons, but on 20 October winter-time schedules began and from then onwards all the offices were open again from 2.15 pm onwards. To give some idea of the ADC's duties, I have included the following brief résumé of his commitments on a typical working day in the office:

- The 'Red-Boxes' from the Colonial Office, and the mail-bags from the Cypriot Secretariat and from other Countries had to be opened or left unopened as instructed and then taken straight through to HE's Office.
- Every morning with the post, there would also be the Reuter Report of World News, which the ADC had to read through carefully and pick out all news items relevant to Cyprus or the Middle East which the Governor should know about. Before taking the Report through to HE's Office, the ADC had to write a short précis on all the local items, and I always took great care in preparing these.
- Then all the telephone calls of visitors and the written invitations had to be dealt with and arrangements made and times confirmed and answered; and details of invitations checked carefully: for times of arrival – dress required – official car to be used? – Police escort need-

ed? – Speech by HE required? Etc., etc. All these details had to be confirmed and checked with Sir Andrew.

- Then, regarding the housekeeping at Government House:– the wine, drinks and cigarettes required for entertaining had to be checked and replenished from the cellar – the petty cash had to be checked – the wages and tips from the guests for the servants needed to be checked – the cash required for the market food and other supplies for the catering at Government House had to be checked and drawn – and there may have been some other miscellaneous details which also required the supervision of the ADC from time to time.

- The visitors' book in the Entrance Hall had to be inspected most days, to make sure that all the important visitors on the island were known to the Governor.

- In addition to all this, there were also a number of daily visitors to be received in the ADC's office. Some of these were quite regular, but on a typical morning there might be:– John Fletcher-Cook (the Colonial Secretary); Brigadier Garratt, (General Officer Commanding the Cyprus garrison); Mr Tornaritis (Attorney General for Cyprus); Mr Hochenhull (Cyprus's Publicity and Information Officer); Mufti Zadero (Assistant Commissioner of Farmagusta); Mr Clemens (Commissioner for Nicosia); Mr Davidson (Commissioner for Larnaca); or Mr Ross-Clune (Commissioner for Paphos). All of these had to be received by the ADC and then checked with HE before being shown through to his office.

The above list of commitments and responsibilities may or may not seem onerous at first sight, but like any job after a few weeks in the seat, all these tasks fell easily into place and the back-up from the Government House staff was excellent. Nonetheless, the biggest problem with the job was the possibility of unwittingly making some horrible mistake – and with the ADC's diverse job this possibility was ever present.

There were periods when the Governor was engaged elsewhere, particularly when the Executive Council was in session and on these occasions there was nothing much happening in the office so I was allowed to take a few hours off and maybe walk into Nicosia. I was later allowed the use of a small Austin car, which was a great boost to me, and this gave me much more freedom when I was off duty.

The swimming pool at Government
House

The terrace used for pre-dinner
drinks

The committee room where the
Executive Council met

Lady Wright arranging
housekeeping matters with Costas
and designing a cushion

Breakfasts in the mornings were a 'help-yourself' affair from a good selection on the hot-plate:–fried and scrambled eggs, grilled bacon and tomatoes and such like and there was always a selection of cereals available, and an abundance of fruit such as, bananas, oranges, figs, melons and grapes – the like of which were seldom seen in the Britain I had left behind in 1952.

I always made sure that I was already in my office well before HE came through to his office suite in the morning and if possible I made sure that I had prepared the Government Red Boxes and all the mail before he arrived. I soon realised that the Governor of a Colony such as Cyprus had a considerable workload of administrative duties to handle during the course of a week and I saw that this soon built up when he was out of the office for a period. With Minutes, speeches, letters, reports, questions and answers to prepare on a wide range of subjects, the Governor's Secretary was always busy typing. Then in addition to this there was a steady stream of officials coming in to interrupt him for discussions, decisions and interviews.

One morning during my early days at Government House, the Governor came through to go to his office with the usual 'Good Mornings', and almost immediately the buzzer on my desk sounded. When I responded eagerly to ask what was required he just said to me rather brusquely: 'Yes Brian; your hair is very untidy this morning – go off and give it a brush!'

On another occasion after the death of Sir Harold Briggs (a former Governor of Cyprus), HE declared that all flags in the Colony should be flown at half-mast on the following day. Next morning I had forgotten all about this instruction so until about 9 o'clock Government House was about the only Government Building in Cyprus disregarding his order! Sitting at my desk I suddenly remembered – and dashed out to the Guard House, and hastily ran down the flag to half-mast; and then ran back to my desk. I had just sat down again exclaiming a 'phew!' of relief, when the telephone rang. It was the Colonial Secretary, John Fletcher-Cooke who had just noticed the error from his window!

An unwitting faux-pas I also made during those weeks happened when I was showing one of the visitors through the building to meet Sir Andrew Wright. I had always been intrigued myself by the way in which the main sitting room could be divided into two halves, by simply lowering a dividing wall (complete with pictures and a communicating door). This particular visitor was obviously interested to see more of Government House, so I innocently demonstrated how this dividing wall worked. Sir Andrew heard about my indiscretion and he was not at all amused. He called me into his office and told me firmly to be much more on my guard when speaking to unknown visitors. There were many ill-wishing journalists always looking for trouble and eager to write critical articles about the Establishment. 'Don't do that again Brian!' That was another lesson learned!

A few words about the Executive Council of Cyprus, which was the equivalent of Parliament in the Colony:–

The Colony was divided into six Districts and each of these had its own Commissioner and a Cypriot Assistant Commissioner and its own small secretariat. At least once a week, normally on a Tuesday, there was a full Meeting of the Executive Council, and this was chaired by the Governor and attended by the Colonial Secretary and all the District Commissioners, as well as the Attorney General, and sometimes other luminaries, such as the Police Commissioner and the Army GOC and maybe other specialists as required.

The ADC had to check beforehand that everything was correctly prepared for the Meeting; but after that, since no other visitors were allowed to Government House on Tuesdays the ADC's presence was not required. This was a day therefore, when it was possible to take the morning off and perhaps visit Nicosia to draw out some money or to do some shopping. Sometimes the Meetings of the Executive Council would finish at 12.30, but at other times they might go on into the afternoon. In any case I see that I always made sure that I was back in my office from 12.30 onwards, so that I was available if required.

As a young, uninformed (but interested) observer at the time, it seemed to me that this simple style of Colonial Government in Cyprus clearly had its merits: The Governor and the Executive Council seemed to control the affairs of the Island with an even-hand and with some efficiency. For instance, there was clear evidence of good Law and Order standards in the country and a well organised Civil Service; and there was never any evidence of bribery and corruption within the system – an observation that could seldom be made concerning many other countries in the region. Also, in spite of the uneven split between Greek-speaking Christians and Turkish-speaking Moslems, the population generally speaking continued to live in apparent harmony with each other.

Furthermore, improvements were constantly being made – which I personally witnessed – in the infrastructure on the island, and it is fair to say that hospitals and medical facilities, schools, the Civil Service, Police Force, road systems and the power and water supplies to remote areas, were probably in advance of most of the other Mediterranean countries in 1952 – including the Levant, Spain (under General Franco), Greece and southern Italy, as well as the islands of Crete, Corsica, Sicily, Mallorca and Sardinia.

For instance, during my brief visit to the Lebanon, Jordan and Syria in 1953, it would have been quite obvious to a short-sighted man on a galloping horse that the organisation of the Civil Service and the infrastructure was considerably more disorderly than that in Cyprus under British rule. The chaotic Passport and Border controls in the Levant were simple examples of this.

Also, I heard Sir Andrew Wright relate a factual story over the dinner table regarding malaria. Soon after World War II, Cyprus and Sicily had a friendly competition to find out which of the two islands could eradicate malaria first. In the event Cyprus won the test by many years and in due course, Cyprus received a token bunch of grapes from Sicily in recognition of their success! As a corollary to this, when I had visited Corsica during 1951, we were strongly warned not to go camping anywhere along the eastern coastal plain of the Island due to the presence of malaria!

Sir Andrew Wright's policy as Governor of Cyprus was to be seen and to travel widely on the island and this was much to my liking because it meant that I was able to visit most of the country during my short two months. At various times we drove out towards all the main towns of Paphos, Limassol, Larnaca, Famagusta, Kyrenia as well as up into the mountains of Troodos and these trips were normally made by the Governor to mark the official opening of some local project such as an extension to a

Sir Andrew Wright at Kambos, presenting the Mukhtar with a Silver Badge

hospital, a Home for aged people, a new school, an improved water supply, inspecting a Scout Camp and Jamboree, or just to open a new branch of the Ottoman Bank. On two other occasions, we also visited the lovely remote hill towns of Pendacomo and Kambos where HE presented the Turkish Mukhtars (similar to the mayor of a town) with Silver Badges. I noted in my diary what really friendly events these last two visits were and it really was quite clear that the Governor's presence was much appreciated and revered.

On all these occasions, the ADC accompanied the Governor (and also Lady Wright at times) with me sitting in the front seat of the black Daimler and with the flags flying. As we drove along the roads and through the towns many of the bystanders would stop and salute the Governor as he passed and there is no doubt that these acknowledgements were spontaneous, benevolent, and certainly not in any way derisive! Once after one of these long journeys, the Governor complimented me because I always stayed wide awake and attentive during these interesting trips. He told me that most of his ADCs normally spent their time dozing in the front seat during these journeys!

An extract of my diary on Sunday 19 October, mentions one of the busy days we had:– 'I overslept until 8.30 this morning, so I missed my bathe. I had to open the mail for HE after breakfast. We left for St Paul's Church at 9.50 so that we arrived at four minutes to 10 precisely. The Bishop – who speaks in the same way as Margaret Rutherford – took the Service of Dedication. The Service was recorded and was broadcast at 6 this evening. HE read the second Lesson. Lady Wright left her scarf in the church, so I had to go back to retrieve it for her. We had several guests for lunch, including Gillian Wiseman-Clark, Brigadier Austin, Mr Tornarites (Attorney General for Cyprus) and a friend of Lady Wright from the TB Charity. After lunch we went off to Nicosia Race Course in the Daimler and the Brigadier's Jaguar. Our party occupied a box. I placed most of the bets for the people. I lost 4 shillings in all. Everyone in our party was betting 2 shillings. The horses were mostly quite young and were terribly excited, so the starter had a most difficult task lining them all up. I played against HE at croquet after we returned, and very nearly won! An early supper and off to bed at 9.30.'

More should be said about the formal Dinner Parties which took place at least once a week, and also about some of the other entertaining and parties we arranged at Government House during my time as ADC:

As mentioned it was one of the traditions in 1952, that Government House in all the British Colonies had a Visitors' Book in the Entrance Hall so that visitors could sign in if they wished, to inform the Governor that they were staying in the Colony. It was the ADC's duty to inspect this Book regularly and to inform the Governor if there was anyone outstanding who should be *considered* for inviting to one of his Dinner Parties. It used to amuse me to hear HE's comments about this. The signatories had to be very high-powered indeed, even to be considered for an invitation!

It was on Thursday 9 October that we had one of these many formal Dinner Parties, so I shall go into more detail about the format of these events:– The guests on this occasion consisted of, Air Marshal Sir Charles Guest (Inspector General of the RAF), Air Vice-Marshal Victor Bowling (Air Officer Commanding Cyprus) and his wife, Brigadier P.K. Powell (a Gunner, but I made no note of his title) and his wife, Sir Albert Gladstone (a Director of the Ottoman Bank in Cyprus), and Colonel Sir Patrick Coghill, who was still staying at Government House.

Ledra Street in Nicosia - four years
later, Eoka made this a killing ground

Forests in the Troodos Mountains

The Salt Lake near Larnaca

Beforehand, the ADC had to write-out a suggested seating plan which HE would then vet and make alterations to as he felt necessary; then, before dinner, the ADC had to ensure that the place names were put out correctly and that all was ready for the pre-dinner drinks. All the visitors had to be met and welcomed by the ADC as they arrived in the Entrance Hall, and they were then led through to join the others for drinks on the terrace, and introduced to the Governor and Lady Wright as well as to the other guests. He then had to be attentive, and to make sure that all the guests were being looked after with drinks and cigarettes.

At the appropriate time, after Lady Wright had given the 'OK', the ADC would ring the servants' bell and Kyriacos would come in and announce that dinner was ready to be served. The ADC made sure that everyone knew where they were seated and dinner would commence. Then, after the sweet course, the ladies would normally retire from the scene – to allow the gentlemen to have their port and tobacco by themselves and to speak about more serious matters! In due course HE would suggest that we rejoined the ladies, and then perhaps some might play a few hands of bridge, or just continue talking amongst themselves. Sometimes, when there were a number of important guests who had not met each other before, interesting discussions might continue for an hour or more. At the appropriate time however, the guests were escorted to the Entrance Hall and their cars called for, and finally it was the ADC's task to appropriately bid them all good-bye. On occasions after everyone had left, there might be a 'free and frank discussion' about some of the guests!

Although this was the procedure with the many formal evening affairs, there were also a number of less formal supper and luncheon parties. During my time, the Governor was quite judicious about ensuring that a wide variety of people came to Government House and had the opportunity of being entertained there; and these included many Cypriots as well as young friends, or those from service personnel stationed on the Island. I made a note about many of the persons who came to join in the fun, although unfortunately, I omitted to record in my diary some of their job titles, which might have been interesting to know some fifty years later. I have also excluded some of those who have already been mentioned.

Sir Andrew Wright concentrating on his croquet

The Commissionaire, Aghabios - An
old retainer, who had served loyally at
Government House for 50 years

Kyriacos. the Head Steward

However, here is an incomplete list to give some idea of the activity:

Sir William Battershill (a former Governor of Cyprus) and wife.
Prince and Princess Birabongse of Thailand.
Bishop Stuart of Jerusalem,
Major-General Thomas Brodie (GOC 1st Infantry Division, MELF)
Sir Panayioti Cacoyiannis ('an important person in Cyprus')
Mr Clemens (Commissioner for Nicosia) and wife.
Lady Mary Davidson (Lady-in-Waiting to Princess Marina).
Dr and Mrs Dill-Russell (Medical Officer on Cyprus).
Brigadier Garratt, (GOC Cyprus)
Commander John Grierson (Chief Test Pilot for de Havilland)
Mr Eric Hallinan (Chief Justice for Cyprus) and wife..
Mr Philip Hay (Private Secretary and Comptroller to the Duke and Duchess of Kent)
Brigadier Reginald Hobbs (Commander of 2nd Infantry Brigade)
Major-General George Humphreys (Admin GHQ MELF),
Colonel Irons (Black Watch)
General Sir Clive Liddell
Mr and Mrs Clive Mace (a Commissioner in Cyprus, and Jill Wright's future parents-in-law)
Sir Courtney and Lady Manifold
Princess Marina, Duchess of Kent
Duke of Kent
Brigadier Phillips (BRA)
Rev and Mrs Edmund Probyn (Chaplin to the Forces in Cyprus)
Mr Arthur Reddaway (Commissioner of Kyrenia)
General Sir Ouvry Roberts (Quarter-Master-General to the Forces)
Air Marshal Sir Alfred Sanderson (C-in-C Far East Air Forces)
Air Vice-Marshal Sharp
Brigadier Stevens
Mr Tornarites (Attorney General for Cyprus).

And there were others, including the wives of some senior officers serving in the Canal Zone and a selection of young servicemen, but the above list should suffice!

Government House, and Croquet Lawn

On one occasion at one of the less formal Dinner Parties towards the end of my time, one of the wives present, when she was told that I was the ADC to the Governor at Government House, didn't believe it. She must have thought that she was 'having her leg pulled' because she

thought that I was much too young to be the ADC. Also perhaps, my relationship with Lady Wright might have appeared fairly relaxed at times,
because Lady Wright sometimes referred to me using her jocular nickname
for me, 'Bold Sir B', even on those occasions. Anyway, the guest obviously
assumed that I must be their son or some other relation – and in the end,
she was really quite embarrassed about her faux-pas when it was confirmed beyond doubt that she had been entirely mistaken!

Another isolated snippet which I recorded in my diary, was when we were
entertaining Air Marshal Sir Alfred Sanderson – a most likeable and
friendly person – at one of these dinner parties. When I was speaking to
him and escorting him to the door at Government House, I inadvertently
referred to the Royal Air Force as the 'Raff'. He picked me up on my jargon
immediately with a mild rebuke:– 'No, No Brian! Even Gunners have to call
us the Royal Air Force – not the Raff!'

Nothing much has been mentioned hitherto about the frequent croquet contests we had after office hours and before we changed for dinner. There was
a fine croquet lawn surrounded by the covered terrace at the back of
Government House and this court was in constant use.

Croquet was an ideal recreation to have available at Government House, and
the game was always much enjoyed by the Wrights as well as by the many
guests staying there. Croquet is a remarkable game:– it is thoughtful and
absorbing in the same way as chess or snooker; and all the good players work
out their moves way ahead. Then it also requires considerable 'ball skill'; and
lastly the game is not physical nor too energetic, so it can be played by both
sexes, young and old – and also by those with certain disabilities, such as
Lady Wright with her hands deformed by rheumatoid arthritis.

We often played this game with great pleasure during my time in Cyprus,
and although the pairs playing together were frequently altered, it was
noticeable that the team which included Sir Andrew was normally the winner in these contests. He was a very 'focused' player – ruthless and uncompromising – although all the games were played with the greatest sense of
fun and enjoyment. Towards the end of my stay I really became quite skilful
at the game, although I never felt that I was quite the equal of Sir Andrew!

Government House, and Croquet Lawn

Remembrance Day on Sunday 9 November 1952 was an important event for all the British forces stationed in Cyprus and on the Friday before, there was a full rehearsal in preparation which included a military band and all the troops.

Unfortunately, Sir Andrew Wright was running a temperature of 102° on that day, so he was quite unable to attend. He therefore called me into his bedroom and gave me his instructions about what to do: 'Brian' he said, 'I should like you to take my place at the Rehearsal Parade today! This means that you will be acting as the Queen's representative on the Parade. Therefore, when the National Anthem is played, make sure that you don't salute with all the other officers. Are you quite clear about that?' (I *was* quite clear about that!)

So off I went to the rehearsal, all by myself in the back of the black Daimler limousine, as the 'Queen's own representative', escorted by a Land Rover and some Police motor cycles! In due course, the arrival of 'my' limousine was the signal for the rehearsal to start, and I practiced my part in all the ceremonies with the other many hundreds of troops on the Parade Ground. During the Service and March Past I had to stand on the dais in place of the Governor and then afterwards, to drive off again in the Daimler to terminate proceedings.

A senior Adjutant, Major Cole, took the Parade rehearsal and when it came to playing the National Anthem and he saw me standing rigidly to attention (being the only officer on parade not saluting) he sprang towards me straightaway to reprimand me. I soon put him right – in the nicest possible way – and all credit to him, he apologised immediately for *his* mistake! Driving back to Government House in the back of the Daimler with flags flying and escort of Land Rover and motorcycles, I couldn't resist a little chuckle to myself (2nd Lieutenant me!) sitting there alone in the back of that cavernous black limousine!

When I reported back to Sir Andrew Wright in his bedroom about the outcome of the Parade and told him about the saluting incident, he thought that was really funny and laughed out loud.

Sir Andrew Wright was still unwell for the Remembrance Day Parade itself two days later, so I accompanied Lady Wright in the Daimler without HE again. Crucially, I made sure that we arrived on the scene at the precise time of 10.50 a.m. and then went through all the procedures, as rehearsed. Since Sir Andrew was not present, there were some changes made in the procedures for the Parade, but unfortunately I was foolish enough not to make any precise notes about these in my diary. I did however record that the weather was unusually hot for the Parade and that I noticed at least one soldier fainting during the proceedings.

Sir Andrew's illness also prevented him from attending the Cypriot Regimental Association Dinner on the Saturday before the Remembrance Sunday Parade, which consisted of Cypriots who had joined the forces during the last war. HE was generous enough to say that I could go on my own and in his place, if I wished to do so – and I certainly *did* wish to do so! The Governor was to have been the Guest of Honour for the Dinner, so I sat in his position at the top table – though luckily, not called upon to make the main speech!

I mention this Dinner in particular, because I heard some extremely sad news during the course of the meal. In my exalted position on top table, I was sitting next to a Colonel Irons of the Black Watch Regiment and speaking about the Korean War, which was in full spate during that November 1952. He was telling me about the Battalion of the Black Watch which was currently serving with the Commonwealth Division in Korea and in the latest Issue of the Regiment's Magazine, it reported that a National Service officer called Nicoll, had recently been killed in action. I was really shocked to hear this name because a friend of mine at school called Nicoll was about the right age to be completing his National Service about this time. In those days at Charterhouse, all new boys were looked after for the first fortnight by an older boy called in school slang, a 'father', and David Nicoll, who was a Scot, had been appointed *my* father when I started at the school.

I was hoping against hope that the information was incorrect, but short-ly afterwards, Colonel Irons called at Government House with the arti-cle in his hand and I sadly confirmed that the unfortunate David Nicoll was the person who had been tragically killed in action in Korea. *The Black Watch Magazine* reported that he had opted to stay on for an extra month after he was due for demobilization since his Battalion was then being withdrawn from the line. On 8 August 1952, during those last few weeks, poor David had been killed by mortar-fire. He was just over 20 years old.

Two days after that Remembrance Day Parade, I also had a most important 'lesson for life' confirmed to me:– namely, 'that nothing is *certain*, until it is *absolutely certain*'. This beneficial lesson came to me as a result of the unscheduled visit of Princess Marina of Kent to Government House.

The Princess and her retinue were returning from a tour of the Far East, which had ended in the Remembrance Day Parade in Singapore. It was decided that their Elizabethan aeroplane instead of stopping in Cyprus on its way back to the UK, would land in Athens instead for refueling. Nonetheless, HE sensibly told me to make absolutely certain that I was kept informed regularly about their progress in case there were any changes in its flight path.

Accordingly, I spoke to my contact at Cyprus Airways on Monday afternoon and confirmed with him that although the flight was an hour behind schedule from Singapore, it was still intended to fly on to Athens as arranged. I had this confirmed again before I went to bed that night, although he did go on to say that they were flying in a new Elizabethan aircraft, which was notoriously troublesome. Therefore, in spite of these assurances, I made sure that I put out my uniform in preparation and told George, the Daimler driver, to be prepared for a call in the small hours. At 5.15 next morning, I was woken up by my contact at Cyprus Airways to give me the up-to-date news that the Elizabethan was currently passing over Cyprus and was continuing on its way to Athens as arranged.

I was then suddenly roused again at 7 am by yet another call to say that the aircraft had developed engine trouble and that the pilot had decided to turn back to Cyprus and would now be landing here shortly!

Action! I telephoned George – and got dressed and shaved in about two minutes flat – left a message for HE – and off we went to the Airport as fast as that sluggish old Daimler could go (which was probably less than 70 m.p.h.!) I arrived at the Airport about 10 minutes after the Elizabethan aircraft had landed.

I went up and spoke to Philip Hay the organizer of this trip who seemed quite a pleasant person, though at that point he was somewhat harassed because he was attempting to find out how bad the problem was. I then met and spoke to Princess Marina, Lady Davidson (her Lady-in-Waiting) and also to the Duke of Kent, who had all now descended from the Elizabethan, and were standing around waiting.

Admittedly, their journey had been very trying due to the unreliability of their Elizabethan aircraft, but I soon formed an unfavourable impression of them all! None of them seemed particularly friendly towards me (considering me a 'servant' perhaps?) and I thought that Marina appeared distinctly supercilious and aloof. I also noted in my diary that she spoke with quite a strong foreign accent and that, although her face was pretty, she had a rather sad look.

Her son, the Duke of Kent, was also standing on the tarmac by the aeroplane, so I went over to have a brief chat with him as well. He was carrying a super-duper Leica camera round his neck, so I used this as my opening gambit. I told him that I also had a Leica IIIc camera, and asked him to show me all the gadgets he had on his. I soon realised that he wasn't in the least interested in showing me his Leica nor in promoting a conversation with me, so our meeting proved to be short-lived! I could see straightaway that he was a very shy individual – after all, he was only seventeen years old at the time. But nonetheless, I formed the opinion that he was distinctly 'wet' and considered that he would clearly benefit from a week or two under RSM Brittain at Mons OCTU!

We found out that the engine-trouble was rather worse than anticipated, but that an alternative aircraft, an Argonaut, would be available at mid-day to fly them on to England instead. I told Princess Marina that I should be pleased to take them back to Government House until the other aeroplane was ready for take off and also that they could have some breakfast with us if they wished. I noted in my diary that she and Lady Davidson accepted this thoughtful invitation with the minimum of gratitude or grace! Before we left, I made sure that those at Government House were warned about our arrival and we then drove off in the Daimler. As soon as we started the first thing Marina did in the Daimler, was to close the inter-communicating window, so that I was cut off from them sitting in the back! I felt rather cheated by this, because I was really looking forward to hearing what they had to say to each other during their journey back to Government House!

Poor Sir Andrew Wright was still not fully fit, but nonetheless he was out of his sick-bed to welcome them when they arrived at Government House. Our visitors just had time to freshen up and have some breakfast before I escorted them back to the airport in the Daimler (again incommunicado!). After that meeting I have to say that I was not favourably impressed in the least by the way Princess Marina and her retinue had conducted themselves. I formed the impression straightaway, which was also confirmed in later years that the *closer* to Royalty you find yourself, the *less* of a royalist you become!

I couldn't help contrasting Marina's disagreeable aloofness towards me, with the friendliness (for instance) of General Sir Ouvry Roberts and Major-General George Humphreys during their short stay at Government House a few days later. When I took them to the Airport, they both shook me warmly by the hand and General Roberts said to me (verbatim): 'Well Brian, thank you very much for looking after us both so well during our short visit here!' I thought to myself, 'now that didn't cost him a bean to say that to me, did it?'

A few days following Princess Marina's unscheduled visit to Cyprus, Sir Andrew Wright told us an amusing story he had been told about their departure from Singapore on the previous day. After their official send-off, all the local dignitaries had thankfully returned to their homes in the humid heat and changed back into something more comfortable, when it was suddenly reported that her Elizabethan aircraft had developed engine trouble and was forced to return to Singapore. All the officials therefore had to quickly change back into their full uniforms, and then reassemble to give her another official welcome!

Probably due to the presence of his daughter Jill, and her girl friends Jean Birnie and Gillian Wiseman-Clark, towards the end of my time in Government House, HE decided to arrange a large Cocktail Party for about 60 young persons and this was a great success, especially as a public relations exercise. Amongst others, we invited some young officers from the RAF and the RNZAF (who had a squadron of Vampires based in Cyprus at that time) and also from the Army units stationed in Cyprus, as well as many other friends known to Jill and Lady Wright from the British, Greek and Turkish communities in Nicosia.

I also scored a few points here myself, because I had prepared the list of those attending fairly carefully beforehand, so I was able to introduce all those unknown to the Governor and Lady Wright by explaining where they came from, which helped them in opening the conversation with their visitors. They made a point of complimenting me on this when we were discussing the party afterwards.

As a result of some of those we met at this party, Jill Wright and her two girl friends decided to make up a party, which including two of the New

Zealand pilots; and the six of us went to a Dance at the Nicosia Club, which proved to be most successful and enjoyable. The Governor agreed to let us all go, so long as I was responsible for the girls and made sure that we didn't stay out too late. This kind of ruling is much easier said than done and in the event we eventually returned to Government House at about 2.30 am. When HE queried me next morning about the previous night, I told him that everything had gone really well and that we were all safely in bed again by about 1 o'clock. He may not have believed me totally but nonetheless, he accepted my remarks without question and continued to walk through to his office suite with a satisfied expression on his face!

Another little snippet that I duly recorded in my diary about social events in Cyprus, was an incident concerning the tying of black bow-ties when wearing dinner dress uniform. Nowadays, virtually anything is accepted without comment, but in the 1950s it was considered decidedly infra dig for anyone to wear a 'ready-made-up' bow-tie which could be just clipped on or fastened at the back. Also, most of these made-up bow-ties looked so 'perfect' that they could be easily spotted from right across the room!

It just so happened, that when I was in my late teens, I possessed one of the most excellent versions of these 'made-up bow-ties' that you could ever find. In addition whenever I wore it, I purposely screwed it around a little to make sure that it looked even more convincing that I had tied it up myself! On one occasion at Government House, the conversation turned to this subject and I was complimented on being able to tie my own bow-tie so well – a compliment that I lyingly accepted without comment. Having acknowledged their praises, I hoped desperately the no one would jestingly try to untie my permanently fixed knot!

On the next day I went swiftly to my friendly tailor in Nicosia and bought an *un-made up* black bow-tie for myself – and then stood patiently in front of the mirror in my room until I had eventually discovered how the knot was tied; an attainment that remains with me to this day!

It was now the middle of November 1952 and my time as ADC was fast running out. On 14 November I heard that my replacement, Captain Peter Bowring, would be arriving in two days time and that I would be leaving Cyprus on Saturday 22 November.

During those last few days, I arranged to have dinner in the Officers' Mess of 49 Field and then afterwards, some of the subalterns took me round Nicosia to sample some of the night-life in the capital.

We must have kept on the move during that evening, because according to my diary, we started with a drink in 'Chanteclair' Night Club – where I recorded there was an appalling girly floor show – then onto 'Femina', then 'Ambassador' and finally ended up at 'Cosmopolitan', where there was a pianist who played some pops and Tchaikovsky – not very well I thought – whilst some of the unattractive hostesses continued to ask us: 'you buy me a drink mister?' No! On consideration, I was not particularly impressed by all these Night Clubs' antics which we saw that night! After all this interesting socialising and drinking, I see that I managed to drive back in my little Austin car without any incident – and then to climb through a window in Government House which I had left open for the purpose; and then finally into my bed at 3.30 am!

The only other incident that I need to mention briefly before I end this chapter on my extraordinary experiences at Government House, Cyprus, is the flight that I arranged during my last week, in a new twin-engined Meteor jet aircraft.

My pilot on this occasion was a Polish RAF pilot and our Meteor I had the task of towing a target-banner for Vampire fighters to fire at over the sea along the north coast of Cyprus. This was a memorable experience for me, and the surge of power that the Meteor had as it was taking off was rather like sitting in a rocket. I also remember that the rate of climb was quite amazing; and within a few minutes, we were up to a level of 20,000 feet – and from that height, it was quite easy to see the whole Island of Cyprus. The other thing that I remember most vividly, was wearing that horrible, dirty, disease-ridden oxygen mask, which was evil-smelling beyond belief! It must have been doing the rounds at the Airport for many years without ever having been cleaned or sterilized. I remember that experience very well indeed:– it was rather like having to chew on a filthy, smelly, disease-ridden, sweaty bit of old rag all the time during the flight!

I thoroughly enjoyed my last few days in Government House in November. I was by then very familiar with most of my duties as ADC, and in any case, as soon as I had collected Captain Peter Bowring from the Airport on 16 November, I started handing over all the duties to him.

Remembering the minimum of helpful and meaningful instructions I myself had received from my predecessor, I made sure that I passed on to Peter as much help and advice that I possibly could. I also gave him plenty of tuition on the croquet lawn, so that he was fully prepared for the fray!

Thoughtful as ever during those last few days, Sir Andrew Wright made sure that I had enough free time to drive about in my little car. This was

Homeward bound in 1952

the period when I had enough time to have a really good look at places like Peristerona, Kyrenia, St Hilarion Castle, Bellapais Abbey, Morphou and the lovely north coast of the Island, which I had only seen briefly during my previous weeks.

So my extraordinary stay in Government House was now coming to an end and on the evening of Friday 21 November I said my farewells to the family and to all the servants, who I now knew so well. On the next morning, I boarded a Corvette at Famagusta, called *HMS Empire Lifeguard*, and set off on a calm sea towards Port Said, once again.

After that extraordinary, fascinating, demanding, exciting, rewarding, unforgettable, enlightening and privileged interlude at Government House in Cyprus I would shortly be returning once again to reality – and to 29 Field Regiment RA – and to resuming my allotted part in the 'Army Game'!

ADC's Austin by some village building bricks

Roadside café between Nicosia and Larnaca

Looking south over the Central Plain from Kyrenia Mountains

Winnowing grain in Kyrenia Mountains

CHAPTER 9

Back to Reality
in 29 Field

The voyage on *HMS Empire Lifeguard* from Famagusta to Port Said was both pleasant and uneventful, and this was followed by the 80 mile road journey southwards again to Gineifa, which was just as fascinating and interesting as it had been two months before.

When I reached Ava Camp on Sunday 23 November, I found that I had arrived at a most opportune time, because I had just missed the main Inspection of the year – that of the CRA (Commander Royal Artillery) who made a yearly Inspection for all the Gunner Regiments in MELF, and it had been the turn of 29 Field Regiment the previous Thursday!

Much to my liking therefore, this big Inspection was now 'all over' – although there were still signs 'all over' that this Inspection had just taken place. I saw Sergeant Caddick of Baker Troop when I went into Battery Lines and he remarked to me: 'If you had stood still for 2 minutes last week Sir, you would have found yourself painted!'

Whilst I fully understood the reasons for keeping the men busy and occupied, and for making sure that all the Regiments were keen and efficient, I was never enthusiastic about excessive and unnecessary 'bulling' which always happened when preparing for these 'extra special' inspections. Superficial appearances (i.e. the Army slang word, 'bullshit') were of paramount importance on these occasions, so everything that could possibly be polished and painted, was polished and painted again whether it needed it or not.

For instance, consider the situation with painted curb stones in the MELF camps. Whilst these curb stones make the driveways in desert camps look neat and tidy, in the Army, this can be taken beyond the extremes of time-wasting and extravagance. In some Camps in the Suez Canal Zone (but not in 29 Field) I saw that some had used dozens of painted 'jerry-cans' as 'curb stones' to make the driveways look uniform and smart. Admittedly, there was an order from HQ that forbad the use of 'serviceable' jerry-cans for this purpose, but this ruling could easily be evaded, because it was quite simple to make a 'good' jerry-can into a 'damaged' one at the stroke of a hammer! And I know that this certainly happened on occasions!

To make this stupidity and waste even more stupid and wasteful; not only were jerry-cans a most vital piece of equipment for transporting water and petrol in the desert, there was also a small factory in the Suez Canal Zone for the sole purpose of producing more jerry-cans for all the MELF Units!

The day after I arrived back at 29 Field (24 November), I wrote in my diary: 'I have spent most of the past 24 hours telling all the others about my experiences in Cyprus, and I am getting quite fed up with it all!' But then everyone in the Officers' Mess was extremely (and genuinely) interested to hear how I had got on in the job, so I had to be extremely patient in answering all their repeated questions (again and again) – whilst also bending over backwards not to appear pleased with myself! The situation was neither pleasant nor simple.

Furthermore, I fully understood how envious all those Regular Subalterns and younger Captains were, when they saw me (a very junior National Serviceman) receiving all this attention and kudos, especially when every one of them could have done the job just as well as I did – and more important, would have furthered their Army careers into the bargain. So I was in a most delicate situation for a period and I made certain that I never opened a discussion about my stay in Cyprus, and I was very careful to show not the least cockiness nor cleverness about the whole episode.

In spite of all my efforts, I noted in my diary a week later (1 December):– 'I can sense a slight jealousy in certain members of the Mess, particularly Nigel Hacking and John Flinn (who were both excellent Regular

Lieutenants), because it was *I* who had been sent to Cyprus as ADC. I suppose it is only natural, but I do find this really irksome, especially since I have made every effort to speak on the subject as little as possible.'

It was just two days after I had returned from Cyprus that the Adjutant, Captain Peter Roberts, called me to the Regimental Office to show me (and also to compliment me upon) a batch of extremely flattering telegrams which had arrived from all the BTE Generals.

There were no photocopiers in Regimental Offices in those far off days, so when I was next ROO (Regimental Orderly Officer), I surreptitiously opened that file again and copied out all the telegrams by hand to make sure that they were not lost forever!

- Brigadier Garratt, (GOC in Cyprus), to Sir Brian Robertson, (Commander in Chief of MELF):

  'Capt. Bowring now arrived and in process of taking over from 2/Lt Goodliffe as ADC to Governor. Governor wishes me to express his great appreciation for the services rendered by Goodliffe which have been of a high order and would like this brought to the notice of the appropriate authorities.'

- General Sir Brian Robertson (Commander in Chief of MELF) to CO of 29 Field Regiment RA:

  'HE the Governor of Cyprus and the GOC BTE express their appreciation of the good work done by 2/Lt Goodliffe during his time as ADC. His services have evidently been of a high order.'

- General Sir Francis Festing, (GOC of British Forces in Egypt) to CO of 29 Field Regiment RA:

  'GOC, BTE wishes to add his appreciation and thanks to those of the Governor of Cyprus for the good work done by 2/Lt Goodliffe whilst performing the duties of ADC.'

- Major General Thomas Brodie, (GOC 1st Infantry Division) to CO of 29 Field Regiment RA.:

  'The Divisional Commander wishes to add his thanks for the services of 2/Lt BWGoodliffe and considers his performance most creditable particularly in view of his very short experience."

Well, well, well – now back to reality!

Surprisingly, after my diversion in Cyprus, I soon settled back into Regimental and Battery life in the Suez Canal Zone. I had been under no illusions about its temporary nature nor the extraordinary circumstances surrounding the appointment. Furthermore, I was really keen to find out more about life in MELF.

The officers and men in all Regiments are constantly changing, and this was particularly the case during the years of National Service. Each month there was a steady drain of soldiers being demobilized; and conversely, a constant flow of incoming, semi-trained servicemen. Naturally, this was the aspect of National Service which the Regular soldiers disliked so much. Inevitably, at any one time, there were always a number of National Servicemen who were nearing the end of their two years, and were therefore becoming 'de-mob-happy'.

The Battery Commander of 8 Battery, Major 'Barney' Brook-Fox, had been on leave in Cyprus last September, so when I rejoined the Regiment, I met him for the first time. He was a wiry, tough individual with a stiff leg, which he presumably received whilst fighting with 8 Army in the desert. He was a person I never liked very much, although he was probably considered a dedicated and efficient soldier to his seniors. He was certainly a stickler for keeping high standards, and there is no doubt about it – no one ever took liberties with him! As I got to know him more, I always felt that his fellow officers under him in the Battery worked *for* him rather than *with* him. This was the kind of leadership that I least admired.

I thought that Barney was much more concerned with cleaning and polishing up the guns and all the other equipment for the sake of appearances (i.e. 'bullshit'), rather than using this time more sensibly for training the gunners! As a young conscript, I never fully agreed with the polishing and painting aspect of the 'Army Game' – especially when pursued with too much enthusiasm.

From the start, I was very favourably impressed by the officers and men of 29 Field. There is a well known Army saying which goes:– 'There are no bad Regiments, only bad officers', and it's a saying that I firmly agree with. Perhaps 29 Field was fortunate in having more than its fair share of high calibre and likeable officers, but I always felt quite sure that if we had needed to be involved in any conflict or war, our Regiment would surely have given a very good account of itself – and in 1952 and 1953, this eventuality never seemed far from reality.

I wrote in my diary on 18 December 1952:– 'The Mau Mau problem in Kenya is still far from settled. Sir Evelyn Baring has just gone to England to discuss the matter with Mr Oliver Lyttleton. The Lancashire Fusiliers (who had been stationed not far from us at Geneifa) were sent out to Kenya a week or so ago, and we have heard that they don't like the situation there at all – but then it should improve within a month or two. It is quite surprising how much antagonism there is for the British throughout the world...'

During my first week back in the Canal Zone, it was the MELF Athletics Championships at the so-called Olympia Stadium at Fayid, and even though I was really well out of training at this point, I was immediately involved in our 440 yard and 880 yard relay teams. Ted Burgess, who had now been promoted to Captain, was organizing our Regimental effort, and he was very pleased to have me back with them again; and as a team, 29 Field performed better than most other units in the Championships.

Ted Burgess was one of the Regulars I thought most highly of in 8 Battery, and surprisingly enough, I was quite friendly with him at the time, even though he was much senior to me. I was not surprised to learn in later years, that he had risen to the rank of Major General in the British Army in NATO.

The Athletics Meeting at the end of November 1952 was one of the few occasions when we met those from other Regiments in MELF, and I noted that I spoke to at least eight people during that week who were known to me either from my schooldays (John Bayman was one), or from Oswestry, or from Mons. I also noted in my diary that the DRA (Director of Royal Artillery), General McKay-Lewis, looked out for me during the games, and congratulated me on the telegrams he had seen coming in from Cyprus. This may be a small point, but I gave him high marks for that.

Without the big practice schemes involving other units, or these gatherings like MELF Athletic Championships, life in the Suez Canal Zone revolved almost entirely around your own Camp and your own Regiment, and it

As GPO of Baker Troop, standing by 'George Baker' Truck

could be several weeks before meeting anyone else from another unit. Life was like being isolated together on a ship in the open sea, so the attitudes shown by the Commanding Officer and the senior officers were crucial. Luckily, I found that life at Ava Camp went along quite agreeably, and with the minimum of squabbles and contretemps.

I was pleased that Barney Brook-Fox had decided to appoint me GPO (Gun Position Officer) of Baker Troop, which was a position I had always thought would be to my liking – and so it turned out. My main problem at this stage though, was to re-learn the Gunnery knowledge I needed for the job!

The Gun Position Officer was the right hand man of the Troop Commander (a Captain), and he was the one responsible for looking after all the ORs in the Troop of 4 x 25 Pounder Guns and their vehicles; and when out of camp on schemes, the GPO was the one in charge of setting up and organising the Gun Positions, and controlling the Guns when moving and firing. It was never an easy job to do, and it was often quite demanding – but at most times it could be very satisfying.

My Troop Commander in Baker Troop was Captain (Mac) Mackenzie, and whilst he was in charge of all the Troop activities in camp, when we were

Mac and three of the Sergeants at the end of a Scheme

Quad, Limber and 25 Pounder Gun deploying

out on schemes, he was seldom seen at the Gun Position, because his job was to liaise with the Infantry Battalion we were supporting and it was his task to observe the fire from the forward O.P (Observation Post) and give corrections to the guns during shoots.

"Number One, Fire!" - on the Ranges

There must have been about 35 persons in Baker Troop under the Gun Position Officer. These were:– the Troop Leader (another Subaltern if there was one), the TSM (Troop Sergeant Major), the four Sergeants and five other Gunners manning each Gun, the Drivers of the four Tractors (or Quads) and the Command Vehicles. Then in the GPO's Command Post, there was the Troop Signaller, the Driver, and at least two Tec Accs (Technical Assistants) whose job it was to calculate the ranging details for the guns when firing.

The Regiments in MELF were seriously under-strength in 1952, so there were seldom any Troop Leaders during my time and we were never able to man all four Guns when out on schemes. Also the majority of our vehicles, with the exception of the Land Rovers, were in a poor condition. Few, if any, had been replaced since the war, so many were in a badly worn out and unreliable state, and needed frequent servicing by the REME mechanics attached to the Regiment.

The TSM (Troop Sergeant Major) of Baker Troop during my time was a likeable old campaigner called Fletcher. He was a typical Cockney, who I always thought must have been brought up near the Elephant & Castle. He was a loyal and dependable colleague to have, and true to his type, he was quick-witted and street-wise. He was also an outstanding scrounger, so

TSM Fletcher – the old campaigner

if we ever needed more red-oxide paint or tyre-blacking for an inspection, Fletcher would know straightaway where he could 'win' or borrow some for us.

I suppose he must have been about 35 years old when I knew him, and he frequently interested us with tales about his experiences during the War. As a young Regular, he went to France with the Highland Division of BEF and took part in the early débâcle in 1940. He was with the 8th Army afterwards and went right through the campaigns in north Africa, Sicily and Italy. He once told us how, during the evacuation of Dunkerque, the French population at Boulogne had stood by the quay spitting and jeering at the British soldiers, as they spiked their guns before departing hurriedly back to England.

On another occasion, he reminisced about that long drawn out and bloody battle outside Monte Cassino in Italy in 1944. He told us how he saw many American soldiers killed unnecessarily there, because they just stood up on the skyline, apparently thinking it was somewhat 'cowardly' to lie low and out of sight from German sniper-fire! He also told us how the GI's always expected a plentiful supply of creature comforts when they went to battle, such as coca cola and other goodies, and also made sure that there were plenty of earth-moving machines to prepare their positions.

The Sergeants on the Guns were also Regulars, and most of them were old enough to have seen service during the War. I suppose they were still in their twenties at the time, and most of them were hoping to progress to Warrant Officer in due course. But before they could be promoted, they had to pass some written exams, and many looked forward to these with some dread. I expect that Fletcher was one of these, unless he had progressed to WO2 before the tests had been introduced.

Of all the Other Ranks in Baker Troop, about 20% were Regulars, whilst the other 80% were National Servicemen about the same age as me. They were a real assortment, and it was during this period that I grew to know and to like all the fascinating regional accents from around the country which I continually heard spoken. For much of my time as GPO, the Troop

Gaskell from Wigan – the Baker Troop signaller

Command Post comprised of a Geordie called Brown, Stacey from Norfolk, Dodd from the West Country; Gaskell my signaller from Wigan, and drivers from Scotland and Birmingham; then, with Fletcher the Cockney added, this made a good mixture of accents to listen to!

There were many times when I felt quite sorry for the ORs having to put up with such frequent guard duties, night patrols, road block duties, inlying pickets, BC's inspections and camp fatigues – although in the main, they accepted these chores with remarkable cheerfulness and

Baker Troop Command Post Team (l to r)
TSM Fletcher, Gaskell, Snape, Langford , Brown, Stacey and Dodd

Brown (Geordie) and Stacey from Norfolk battling with Sandsgraph

good humour. However, it was quite noticeable how their spirits rose as soon as we had left Ava Camp and driven off into the .'miredahm' on one of our schemes.

I frequently played in the Baker Troop Soccer Team during those months, so I knew many of my OR colleagues really quite well, and I always found

Mad Dogs and Englishmen play in the midday sun!

them a most congenial and good natured bunch of people to be with – although I always had to remember that this was the Army, so I had to be very careful not to become *too familiar* with them all! Later in September 1953, when I was transferred to RHQ for my last three months, I was really sorry to move on, because by then I had seen most of them develop from the time they had first joined the Regiment as raw recruits from Oswestry.

Captain Mac Mackenzie, my Troop Commander in Baker Troop, was an efficient and dedicated soldier, and although I found him a supportive boss and companion to work with, I never became really friendly with him. He was tall and slim, and had a moustache and glasses – and I never saw him wear shorts! I always unkindly concluded that he had skinny, knobbly, white knees which he wanted to keep hidden! He came from the Liverpool area, and he must have been about twenty-six when I knew him. . To my mind, he was much too interested in the show and superficial appearances that went with the 'Army Game', rather than the more important need to produce thoroughly well-trained soldiers. This may have been due to the influence of Barney Brook-Fox, because Barney could be very disparaging during his Saturday Inspections if he considered slackness was creeping in, and poor Mac saw every criticism of Baker Troop as another demerit point on his Army Report. Barney seldom gave any praise or showed any satisfaction, and I always felt that he took little or no account of the shortages of men available to maintain the high level of polishing and bulling that he demanded so fervently.

With all the Units in MELF at least 20% under strength at that time, and with the many commitments for guarding in their camp and elsewhere in the Suez Canal Zone, as well as camp commitments, inspections and fatigues – this meant that everyone was frequently involved in one duty or another. I therefore always had very little sympathy with Barney's detached view.

I wrote in my diary on Monday, 13 April 1953:– 'We are duty Battery again this week, so Baker Troop only had Stacey (my Norfolk Tec Acc) and two drivers left for training this morning. I gave Langford's reconditioned Quad (or Gun Tractor) a 406 (the monthly vehicle check). The paintwork on it is bad, so we are having him excused fatigues so that he can paint it up. The

Winching a Quad from soft sand

engine and steering are now perfect, so it is excellent to drive. The rest of the morning I spent training up Stacey on the Artillery Board. He is now much faster and more accurate than he used to be, so he should be very useful when we go out on the scheme next week. Evidently, Mac had a row with Barney last Saturday when he was told off after the 'working inspection'. Mac told him about the large number of fatigues and other duties which the blokes are having to do, and how this inevitably affects the amount of preparation possible for these inspections – Barney just doesn't want to listen to any 'excuses' like this.'

I, of course, agreed wholeheartedly with Mac's opinions and comments, but this sort of plain speaking to seniors is normally not greatly appreciated – especially by the likes of Barney Brook-Fox! I never liked Barney's style, and always thought that he was badly lacking in the best leadership qualities.

But returning again to Mac:– before he had joined 29 Field, he had trained as a Staff Officer in an Ack Ack Gunner Unit (neither of which were much admired by many officers in Field Regiments), and I always thought that these inclinations showed through to some extent in Mac's approach to activities in 8 Field Battery. I also never really felt that he had much depth of knowledge in the intricacies of Field Gunnery. Later however, when the time came for him to leave for another Staff job in 3 Brigade, I realised that he had taught me a great deal during the time we worked together, and I was really sorry to see him leave the Regiment. After writing my regrets in my diary on 21 October 1953, I also commented: 'Mac thinks that Barney didn't like him because he was Ack-Ack, and so he gave Mac a mediocre Army Report accordingly.' Ah well, I thought to myself, that's all part of the 'Army Game'!

Having written about those in Baker Troop, I should briefly mention a few of my other colleagues in 8 Field Battery:– Captain Ted Burgess, who soon left the Regiment in the new year and returned to England, was in charge of the Battery Command Post, whilst Captain Peter Brereton was the other Troop Commander in Able Troop. Peter was an Old Wellingtonian, and a most amusing and pleasant individual, and his presence always made life enjoyable in the Regiment. He was also a good practical soldier and with a wide knowledge of Gunnery. He was senior to Mac, and I noted in my diary that they had a number of cross words together because he sometimes thought that Mac was trying to 'dodge the column'. I often thought myself that Mac was quite happy to 'skive off' on a trip to Fayid, rather than look after some training session in the Battery!

Peter Brereton was very good with words, and he once told us that he some-times wrote under a pseudonym to the correspondence columns of *The Times*, with a purposely contentious and perverse letter in order to provoke some indignant and scathing replies. Peter knew exactly how to antagonise the ex-Colonels reading his unreasonable anti-Army nonsense, and was quite delighted when the newspaper published outraged replies, calling him, 'totally unaware of the facts', or 'an ingenuous correspondent', or 'a complete ignoramus'! When I read about this incident again in my diary (which I had quite forgotten) I had another good laugh about it, as we had all done over fifty years ago.

I was very fortunate in having such a pleasant and convivial bunch of com-panions in 8 Battery with me. The other three Subalterns about my age during those early months were, John Gilmour and Mike Martin, both very competent and most likeable young Regulars who ran the Battery Command Post (which controlled the two Gun Positions), whilst the Able Troop Gun Position Officer was the National Serviceman, John Stansfield.

John Stansfield, GPO of Able Troop

The four of us controlled the eight Battery guns when we were in training or on the ranges, and we always worked well and most amicably together. Both John Gilmour and Mike Martin were Sandhurst-trained, and they remained with 29 Field during all the time that I was in the Suez Canal Zone, although they both also went off for additional training on specialist courses during that time. I always thought that John Gilmour would do very well in the Army, but I never heard any news about his subsequent progress. Mike Martin on the other hand, I did hear about:– sadly, he died of some ailment very early in his life (this is mentioned more fully in Chapter 16).

John Stansfield, David Secher-Walker, John Gilmour and Dick Brimelow returning from swimming at 10 BOD

For my first few weeks with 8 Battery, Mike Martin had been my GPO in Baker Troop, so luckily, working with him and Mac had been my introduction to Regimental life as an officer. After I returned from Cyprus, and the Regiment received the complimentary telegrams from BTE Headquarters, Mike was genuinely pleased for me, and he strongly advised me to sign on as a Regular with that on my Army Record!

The other Gun Position Officer, John Stansfield was an Old Wellingtonian who was much the same age as me. We saw a lot of each other during those months, and we were very close friends at the time. We had hoped to go on holiday together, but in the event, this was rightly refused by Barney, because we were the two main GPOs in 8 Battery, and our absence at the same time would have left the Battery unnecessarily exposed. John was a most convivial and friendly companion to be working with, and I see that we frequently moaned together about Barney's overbearing attitude in 8 Battery, which we both considered needless, and indeed, counter-productive.

On 12 March I wrote in my diary:– 'Last night over dinner, John and I had a long chat about the Army, and we are both of the same opinion:– there is far too much unnecessary bulling going on in 8 Battery! At the moment we are very short of men, and yet we spend so much of the available time concentrating on cleaning, scraping and painting, instead of training, which is far more useful and needed. Mac and Barney are the main causes for this, because they are both much too keen on bulling – such as polishing the brass radiator caps, the petrol tops and the tops of the fire extinguishers. Also, one of the petty rules which we both think is so unnecessary is that all the personal photographs by the beds in the men's' tents have to be put away during Barney's Saturday inspections!'

On one occasion, John Stansfield and I were told to make sure that all the ORs in Able and Baker Troops were consuming enough salt and drinking enough water. This was always a potential hazard in the intense dry heat of the Suez Canal Zone, and the Regiment had recently sent a soldier to hospital due to 'heat exhaustion'.

So off we went together into Battery Lines with a bag of salt and some water – and also with a firm resolve to ensure that everyone had his fair dose of both! After our little pep talk, we found that a few of the ORs were still reluctant to do as they were told, so John just took a chunk of salt out of the bag, and said irritably: 'Come along now, stop wasting time! Just look how easy it is!' And with that, he quickly swallowed the lump down whole, and took a large gulp of the water. A short time afterwards, he had to make a hasty exit and – out of sight – was violently sick! It was not long after this incident, that special salt tablets were issued to all the troops in the Zone, so this whole problem was overcome in a much more sensible and palatable way!

A Khamseen wind at mid afternoon

By November, December and January, the temperature at night in the Suez Canal Zone was much lower, and happily, the numbers of worrying flies also gradually decreased; but it was also during these 'winter' months that the 'khamseen' could be expected. This was the unpleasant, hot, sandstorm wind which came from the south, and it could continue to blow for several days on end. The wind could reach speeds of up to 85 mph and the temperature could rise by 17° in two hours.

On Sunday 7 December, I noted in my diary: 'It is an ominous sign out here if the wind changes to the south and there is a smell of oil from the oil wells near Port Suez. The smell was in the air this morning, and sure enough, at about 10.30 a sandstorm had started. The old stagers may not consider this to be a bad khamseen, but it was quite sufficient for me. Everything in our tent is now covered with a fine layer of sandy dust.'

A few weeks later we had another dose of khamseen, and this time it was much fiercer and lasted several days – and by the time it had blown itself out, the tent which I shared with Mike Logan (another National Service Subaltern in 79 Battery), ended up badly torn and battered.

But the 'winter' was not long. On 21 February I wrote: 'It is noticeably warmer now during the day, and I am sorry to say that the flies are also returning after a welcome relapse.'

The sun shines most days throughout the year in Egypt, but sudden rain storms can also happen at any time, although I remember it raining just three or four times during the whole of my stay in the Zone. There was a particularly heavy thunderstorm however on 4 March, and this caught some of our troops by surprise who were out on a scheme in the desert. We were always warned never to sleep in a wadi because this could be very

Mike Logan inspecting our tent after the Khamseen

Officers' Mess at Ava Camp

dangerous if a heavy rainstorm occurred further up country during the night. On this occasion, the rain came during the daytime, and some of their baggage and equipment had been inadvertently left in one of these dried-up water-courses. Suddenly, due to one of these localised rainstorms, a big tide of sandy water came rushing down the wadi and carried off everything in its path! After the weight of water had subsided, some of their possessions had to be retrieved hundreds of yards down the wadi. At the time, this happening was used as a graphic warning to all.

The Christmas period was a rather special time in any Regiment, especially when abroad. This was my second Christmas in the Army, so I felt that I was now passing the halfway mark. In 29 Field, we organised a number of events and parties in the messes to keep us all occupied, and many of these included plenty of beer drinking! We had a concert when talented and untalented people gave various turns on the stage – most of which were on the coarse side! The officers gave a rousing chorus of *Standing on the bridge at midnight* and a few other songs like *They're shiftin' father's grave to build a Sewer*, and *I belong to Glasgow* and *Rollin' up the Clyde*. Then most of the young Subalterns were called up to tell a joke – much to the enjoyment of all!

There were three other particular turns in the concert which I noted in my diary. The first was given by one of the Sergeants who performed a very funny (but most irreligious) skit on a vicar's sermon about life in the Suez Canal Zone, which started with the incantation: 'Ace, King, Queen, Knave!' as he crossed himself – another Sergeant gave a rendering of Stanley Holloway's *Battle of Hastings* – and the other was a very clever and up-market skit about a Troop Command Post, as seen by William Shakespeare!

But in addition to this sort of entertainment and conviviality, the Regiment also organised cross-country runs and hockey and soccer matches between the Regimental units. I thoroughly approved of all this activity, but I was totally against continuing all the early Morning Parades as well as Barney's regular Saturday Morning Inspections during these Christmas weeks, instead of allowing a few concessions for the troops. Barney however, probably saw any relaxation as a sign of weakness or slackness, rather than as a possible means of boosting morale for his troops who have to endure a surfeit of camp fatigues, inspections and guard duties. Being closer to the ORs than he was, I heard all their grumblings as a result of his decisions, and I considered his man-management techniques decidedly foolish and counter-productive.

Officers' Mess at Ava Camp

I noted in my diary on Saturday, 20 December: 'The BC had his weekly inspection this morning, and as usual, he found much to criticise about the 'bulling-up' of the guns and vehicles. The main reasons for the low standards are because so many of our ORs have been away on guard duties and fatigues – and also because the Sergeants themselves have been so occupied with other commitments. In addition to this, during the whole of the past week our guns have been used for the cadre course'.

As a result of this 'bad' inspection, Mac, gave all Baker Troop a bollocking on the following Sunday morning, and also a pep talk about improving standards, and went on to tell them they would continue to have early morning parades during the Christmas week. I personally thought all this was quite absurd, but then this was Mac's way of demonstrating to Barney that he was 'tough' rather than 'slack'. To me, it was all just an unnecessary part of the 'Army Game' – and in essence, the reason why I never seriously considered signing on as a Regular.

It is interesting to compare the attitudes shown towards this bulling in the British Army of 1952/3 – of which I was so critical – with those of the part-time Territorial Army I joined after demobilisation. When I trained with 298 (Surrey Yeomanry) Field Regiment RA (TA) between the years 1954 and 1963, we spent the minimum of time 'bulling' up our equipment, but then, when we went out firing on the Ranges, we were just as efficient and sharp as 29 Field Regiment had been in the Suez Canal Zone. I understand that attitudes have changed in the modern British Army, where there is now far less concentration on 'window-dressing', and far more emphasis on training the troops well.

But concluding on our Christmas Day of 1952:– the officers took round the traditional 'Gun Fire' (tea and rum) to all the OR's tents first thing in the morning – then there was a short Church Service with Christmas carols in mid-morning – and this was followed by a booze-up for the officers, WOs and Sergeants in the Sergeants' Mess! For lunch, the officers then served the turkey lunch and a bottle of beer to all the ORs. I noted in my diary that, 'everyone seemed jolly and satisfied.'

The main meal for the officers was in the evening, and I recorded on the day:– 'It was an excellent dinner. John Stansfield, Mike Logan, Dick Brimelow (all National Servicemen) and I celebrated together with two bottles of champagne! Burning paper hats in the Mess was a popular sport with some of the other more senior officers tonight!' – that sounds very puerile and dangerous! 'As arranged, I drank a toast to Mum and Dad at 12 o'clock.'

It will be appreciated that the general situation for us in BTE was fairly tense during the beginning of 1953, and it was on 17 January that I wrote in my diary:– 'There is a big flap on now because 'Black Sunday' is fast approaching. It has been re-emphasized that all soldiers must carry loaded weapons, and in addition, various rules have been issued, such as guarding vehicles when out of camp. Barney is talking to us tomorrow about the situation. Evidently Cairo is in ferment; General Naguib has jailed several Army Officers and has dissolved all Political Parties. It looks as if there could be some problems for us quite soon.'

On 22 January I noted:– 'Barney gave us another short talk about the Egyptian situation. He mentioned again about the perilous position of Naguib at present and also that many people seem to be converging on Port Said, Port Suez and Ismailia, so it is most likely that there will be some show-down with us on 'Black Sunday' (25 January).'

In the event however, nothing out of the ordinary happened on that 'Black Sunday' – but in the following year Nasser did depose Naguib, and then made himself President of Egypt.

The local Egyptian population was always a possible source of hostility and there were a number of important points in the Suez Canal Zone which needed to be specially guarded for 24 hours a day. There were, for instance, the Married Quarters and the Water Filtration Plants; and also the large Ammunition Dump by Lake Timsah near the central town of Ismailia. There were others.

It was 29 Field's responsibility to guard this last important installation for three weeks during February 1953, so preparations were duly made by the three Batteries to take a week in turn. Our Battery was to be the first, so on 1 February, the 8 Battery convoy of six vehicles, with 65 OR's, 6

Sergeants and 4 Officers, plus all their bedding and personal kit, set off to take over from 80 Light Ack Ack Regiment RA.

When we arrived to look round the site, we soon realized why so many guards were required. The storage depot was spread out over a large area of uneven ground, and one side of it was open to Lake Timsah. There were two Guard Rooms, one at each end of the site, and telephones were located at strategic points. During the night, the prowler guards used mortar flares and searchlights to make sure that no one was trying to come in from the lake. 10 prowler guards were on duty all night, and 6 similar prowlers were used during daytime.

I mention all these details merely to illustrate just how much effort and organization (and cost) is always involved, when guarding an important site like this against terrorists, for 24 hours every day.

As so often happens when on Guard Duty – *nothing* at all happened! As the week progressed, everyone inevitably became more and more tired from lack of sleep. On Friday, 6 February I wrote in my diary:– 'I took over from TSM Fletcher at 1 a.m., and didn't finish in the morning until 6 a.m. The

Lake Timsah Aummunition Dump

Long Lagoon at Timsah Ammunition Depot

blokes are definitely getting quite tired now after all this continual night guarding. Three sentries in No.1 guard were reported asleep or dozing on duty, and Barney saw them this morning. Unfortunately, Bombardier Lister was one of them. He's a Regular who has just been made up to Bombardier, and so he was immediately stripped. That will now put him back for a few months as far as promotion is concerned. Some of us went into Ismailia today, which is the first time most of us have had a chance to see the town and the shops there – and there are plenty of cheap watches, cameras, lighters, socks and shoes on offer from the shops and the street traders, who were all very persistent!'

8 Battery was finishing on Saturday, and I wrote that day:– 'We have seen no action whatsoever this whole week, as expected. But last night we did have a laugh: Sergeant Prentice saw a fishing boat approaching quite near to shore, so he fired a mortar flare towards it to have a better look at them. The flare was a dud and therefore failed to go off, although he saw the cartridge land with a big splash right close to the boat. When he fired a second flare (which did ignite this time), he saw the fishermen rowing away as fast as they could go, with their oars all over the place! They obviously thought that they were being bombarded! We all complimented Prentice on the accuracy of his shooting!'

On the last Sunday, when we were clearing up the site in preparation for handing over to 79 Battery, Barney was in one of his well known 'flaps' and was stomping around finding fault with everything and criticizing everyone in general! I wrote at the time how unhelpful I thought this sort of peevish behaviour was to those working with him, but that was Barney's way and although we all disliked his attitude intensely, perhaps this was the only way he knew of keeping us all on our toes – and I have to admit that it certainly did that!

The officers in 8 Battery took the week's duties in turn, and as a result, John Gilmour, Mike Martin and John Stansfield all travelled back a day before the rest of us. When they came out to greet us dressed in their civvies, Barney was absolutely furious with them. He thought that this was very slack even though it was a Sunday. I wrote that 'Barney gave them all a real bollocking for not wearing their uniforms!' That was our Barney!

Soon after our spell at Lake Timsah, I was again writing frequently in my diary about the tense situation existing in the Canal Zone. On 7 May I noted:– 'All this week, we have been digging defence pits round the Camp so that we can defend ourselves more easily if we are attacked. Everyone seems to be flapping again about the situation and are taking extra precautions and checks with the guards. We read on the *MELF News Sheet* that an armed Egyptian had shot and wounded a Brigadier's wife near Fayid yesterday.'

On 10 May I wrote further:– 'Everyone thinks that there will be a flare up out here soon. All the camps nearby are frantically digging slit trenches. At Ava Camp we have now extended our barbed-wire out beyond the 'Dhobi compound' so that the Egyptians can't infiltrate through here unnoticed. Our local Egyptian – Busty – had always been allowed to live in a tent in the Dhobi Compound by the entrance to Ava Camp and there he earned his living selling sweets and other goods and also providing a laundry (dhobi) service.

'We have now dug slit trenches all round our camp. General Neguib has declared that he will not discuss the Canal Zone matter any further, and so the Cairo Talks are ending forthwith. He said that he would consider nothing other than unconditional evacuation of the Suez Canal Zone. Therefore, back to square one!'

Then three days later I wrote:– 'BTE is now on full alert. Everyone goes around armed to the teeth. Unfortunately, for the whole of this month, 29 Field has to provide the wretched Road Patrols from Gineifa down to Port Suez. We heard yesterday that a road patrol up north had captured three 'westernised oriental gentlemen' (I used different phraseology in my diary) and killed 4 others cutting the wire!'

These Road Patrols consisted of two vehicles, manned by a Subaltern and six soldiers, which patrolled all through the night. Their objective was to prevent the Egyptians from digging up and stealing the expensive copper telephone cable, which ran alongside the 25 mile stretch of road down to Port Suez. If ever the wire was tampered with, this would be immediately detected by HQ, and the road patrols would be alerted by wireless communication to go to the place where the wire had been cut.

Like all patrols and guard duties that I ever did, these stints were extremely boring because nothing significant ever happened! The whole night was spent either parked, or driving up and down the road, all the time listening to the radio tuned into HQ. We all had our share of running these night patrols, and I must have taken them out at least six times. To keep my patrol usefully employed, I often gave driving instruction to some of the ORs, and organised competitions for firing the sten guns at tin cans and other targets. We seldom practiced firing sten guns on other occasions, so this was quite a novelty for us all. These guns were really cheap and horrible weapons to use. For one thing, they had no rifling in the barrels so this made their firing direction most inaccurate; and for another thing, they spat out the empty cartridge cases at the side of the barrel, so it was essential to hold the gun in the correct way, otherwise it was quite possible to lose a finger or two!

The Commanding Officer of a Regiment can make a very big difference to morale, both for good or for ill, and it was during February and April that we had a change of Command in 29 Field. As a very inexperienced Subaltern, I was really in no position to judge the capabilities of either of the COs I served under in the Canal Zone, but I personally I approved of both.

When I joined the Regiment at the end of August 1952, the CO was Lt Col Chris Hutt OBE, and he must have been the person who decided to make the bold and contentious decision to put my name forward for that position of ADC in Cyprus, rather than select some other far more obvious choice from amongst his Regular Officers. With the benefit of hindsight, I should imagine that this decision must have caused some resentment in the Regiment, although no one ever expressed this view to me. It is a fact however that Col Hutt was not a very popular CO with many of the other Regular Officers in the Regiment.

Many said for instance, that he could have done more to improve conditions in Ava Camp by spending more money on outside labour, but I have no idea whether or not this was a fair criticism. In any case, it was in February that Chris Hutt left the Regiment and returned to a Staff Job, whilst he was replaced as CO by a Lt Col 'Tiny' Shoreland in the following April. Now Shoreland was a person I knew much better, because for my last few months with 29 Field, I was transferred to Regimental Head Quarters (RHQ), and appointed as his Intelligence Officer on schemes, a position which was rather like being his Personal Assistant.

Shoreland was a friendly and avuncular man, and he had some good ideas for reorganising the Regiment. We soon saw that he meant business, and that he was efficient, fair-minded and decisive. I wrote in my diary on 9 April.– 'This CO is going to make quite a difference to this Regiment in a short time. He seems a likeable person, and one great point in his favour is that he mixes with the Subalterns, and listens to what we have to say. He talked with a crowd of us for some time during the Dinner Night last night.' I have introduced Colonel Shoreland into these recollections at this stage, because we shall be hearing more about him before too long.

During 1952 and 1953, there were various Colonial Pioneer Corps Units as well as Colonial Guards Units stationed in the Suez Canal Zone, and although I never noted in my diary exactly what their functions were, I expect that they provided some essential services to the BTE troops, as well as covered some of the guard duties needed.

On one Sunday, when I attended a Church Service at 10 BOD with John Stansfield, Mike Logan and Mike Martin, we had a most interesting meet-

The 10 BOD Swimming Pool

ing with one of the British Majors who was stationed with an East
African Pioneer Corps Unit near Fayid. He drove us back to Ava
Camp in his car, and I made a few notes about his remarks. He told
us, for instance, that the Kenyans always ate exactly the same food
every day – for the whole year. They used to have a bean stew for
lunch, and then a meat stew for dinner, and if any of these stews were
not *exactly* to their liking, or slightly below standard, there was a
near riot! He also went on to say that most of the Kenyans had more
than one wife, and that each wife would cost about 12 cows, so if
a father had many daughters, he was quite a wealthy man!

However, I thought that his most interesting comments were about the
tribal dances they performed at their festivities. He said that they just
loved performing these dances whenever possible, but although they had
dozens and dozens of different routines in their repertoire, most of these
dances were so explicitly sexual that only one or two could ever be demonstrated to the general public. He said that this was always a great disappointment to Kenyans, because it was the highly sexual dances that they
enjoyed performing the most!

We used to see one of these East African camps from the Treaty Road whenever we drove north to Fayid, and not far away, there were other camps occupied by the Mauritian and Seychellois Guards Companies. These Colonial Units always intrigued me, but I had no idea at the time that in due course, I should be seeing one of these Companies much more closely.

To supplement the Regular Officers in charge of these Colonial units, a few National Service Subalterns after their training at Mons Officer Cadet School, were drafted in to swell their numbers. This was probably considered an unfortunate posting for many who had completed their Gunnery training, but to ensure that they received some more conventional Regimental training, they were swapped for a month with another Subaltern in a more typical Regiment.

I was pleased to be told at the beginning of May that I had been selected for one of these exchanges, and that I was to be seconded for the whole of June to 84 Mauritian Guards Company in Fayid. This was excellent news since it would mean a complete change of scenery for a month, as well as a totally different experience for me. I was therefore looking forward to 30 May – although subsequent events were to make me look even more eagerly towards that particular date....

It was also during May 1953, that due to rumbles of possible trouble in Egypt and the Suez Canal Zone, some of the British Newspapers sent over reporters to find out 'first-hand' what was happening in BTE. None of us ever saw any of these reporters, but in due course, when we read their reports in the newspapers, we all had a really good laugh in the Mess. Their articles were not only extremely alarmist in their content, but the comments they made had little or no relevance to the situation we saw around us. It was from this little incident that I learned another important lesson for life:– always to be distrustful about any 'factual' information I read in the tabloid newspapers!

We later heard that the reporters writing these articles had made their 'thorough investigation' by spending half a day drinking and dining in the Officers' Mess in Fayid – one of the most insulated of all places in the Suez Canal Zone – and then flying back again! On 19 May I wrote in my diary:–

'After reading all these frighten-ing reports in the papers today, I shall have to write home straight-away to reassure them that the war has definitely not started out here yet!'

Life in the Suez Canal Zone con-tinued to include many periods of boredom and inactivity in camp, interspersed by several days of intense action when we were out on training schemes. This was always the way of Army life, but during the 'State of Emergency' in 1953, one particularly irksome task for the junior officers, was to ensure that the Regimental tele-phone was manned at all times. As a result, this tiresome job had to be covered normally by the Regimental Orderly Officer (ROO) out of office hours. However, every

Mounting the Guard at Ava Camp as Regimental Orderly Officer

situation in life has its plusses and minuses, and although these periods of inactivity could be a real pain at times, the definite plus side was that we had long periods available for reading.

I see from my diary that during these months I first read *Alice in Wonderland* (with great enjoyment), as well as many of the classics, such as *Wuthering Heights, Vanity Fair, A Tale of Two Cities*; and some excel-lent novels by Robert Louis Stevenson and Thomas Hardy. I also read most of the Neville Shute books (very popular at the time), and also the well known novel by Daphne du Meurier, *My Cousin Rachel*, which impressed me very much. I mention all this in some detail, because my reading of this last novel, *My Cousin Rachel*, was about to cause me to make the most almighty blunder. But wait! Let me first explain another important matter in this episode.

A short distance from Ava Camp was a Water Filtration Plant which supplied the water to all the camps in the southern part of the Suez Canal Zone, and this was naturally an important installation that 29 Field had to guard and protect. This particular Guard Duty was one of the least popular commitments amongst us, because of the thousands and thousands of tenacious mosquitoes which infested many parts of this site! When guarding there, the only way we could prevent ourselves from being bitten to blazes, was to button up our shirts tightly both at the neck and the sleeves, and then to souse ourselves with a repugnant concoction provided by the Army, which repelled both insects and human beings in equal measure!

As always, there were a few of the ORs who thought that all this palaver was quite unnecessary (or maybe sissy), and therefore only partially applied the remedy – but they only made this stupid mistake once! I have never seen such swollen forearms as the ones I saw on a few of those returning from a session at this Water Filtration Plant. Unfortunately, I made no notes in my diary about how long it took for these people to fully recover after this terrible onslaught, but it must have taken them several weeks of extreme discomfort.

Luckily, we seldom provided this particular Guard Duty, but 29 Field did have to supply a so-called 'Inlying Picket' (consisting of eight ORs and a Subaltern), which had to remain in camp when on duty, and had to be on call to rush out to the Filtration Plant's assistance if ever it sent up a red flare, showing that it was being attacked. In practice however, this alarm had never ever been given, so being detailed for this particular 'Inlying Picket' was not an onerous duty in the least.

Anyway, I learned that the film of *My Cousin Rachel* was being shown on the Saturday night at our local open-air cinema just across the road in 10 BOD, and since I had enjoyed the book so much, this was a film that I just *had* to see. The trouble was that I was in charge of the 'Inlying Picket' on that particular night. But then, I thought to myself, that Inlying Picket had never, ever been called out. So I thought to myself, without telling anybody, that I would just take a chance, and quietly slip out of camp, and go across the road – for only for a couple of hours after all – just to *make sure* that the Producers of the film had done justice to that excellent book!

Well, on *one* point I was *absolutely correct*. The Inlying Picket had *never, ever been called out, up to 23 May*. However, whilst I was sitting there critically watching *My Cousin Rachel* – a red flare was reported by the Guard Room as having gone up over the Water Filtration Plant – *for the first time ever!*

Anyway, my colleague, John Kenny, (without the least ill-feeling shown towards me I must report) soon stepped into the breach, and rushed out to defend the beleaguered Water Filtration Plant, only to find that the whole emergency had been a false alarm! But the fact that it had been a 'false' alarm, of course, made no difference whatsoever to my predicament. I knew that I would now have hell to pay for my irresponsibility. If something *can* possibly happen *however unlikely* – then it *will damned well happen, some-times*! How many times do we need to have this fact proved to us? I should, of course, have learned this important lesson from the unscheduled stop of the Duchess of Kent's Elizabethan aircraft in Cyprus last November – but no.

But back to *My Cousin Rachel*:– although Dame Fortune must have had a really good laugh at my expense over this whole episode, she also decided to do me a good turn as well. Since I was due to leave on my temporary post-ing to 84 Mauritian Group on the following Saturday, my time was fast run-ning out!

In fact, it was not until the following Wednesday that I was eventually summoned in to see the Commanding Officer, Lt Col Shoreland – and I often wondered if he had purposely allowed this delay of four days to pass. In any case, by the time I went to see him, he really had very little room for manoeuvre, so he just gave me a good telling off, and then sentenced me to three extra days of Orderly Officer before I departed on the following Saturday! In the normal way, I feel sure that my punishment would have been for a much longer period.

It was quite interesting (and revealing) to observe how some people react-ed to my aberration: When I apologised to John Kenny about the incident, and thanked him for taking out the In-Lying Picket in my place, he was most gracious in taking my apology, and did so without any apparent hard feelings whatsoever. Also, I was surprised to find how understanding and mild Barney Brook-Fox was in his rebuke to me. Major George Bridge on the other hand demonstrated his unforgiving nature. I noted in my diary: 'George ignored me today and barely acknowledged me with a 'good morning', although when I had come back from Cyprus, he was all smiles and 'hello Brians'. I'd really like to kick him up the arse' – this was a verbatim remark from my diary!

Subsequently, whilst I was completing my three days ROO on the trot, the Orderly Sergeants began to look rather quizzically at me and asked me why, but I remained non-committal all the while and eventually Saturday morning arrived. !

On my last day as ROO, Friday 29 May, I was reading my book in the Regimental Office after lunch, when the Fire Alarm suddenly went off. I dashed outside, and saw that one of the tents was 'up in flames'. I telephoned for the Zone Fire Engines and then went to the fire – but luckily there was no wind on that day, and by the time I reached the tent in question, the problem was under control. Nonetheless, it was very frightening. The blaze probably lasted no more than a minute! With the extremely dry atmosphere we had in Egypt, fires like this were always a potential hazard, although I can't recall this trouble ever happening again during my time at Ava Camp.

Louis Schneider, the Subaltern from 84 Mauritian Guards with whom I was exchanging, arrived at 29 Field on the Saturday, and I duly showed him round the camp and introduced him to those in the Mess. The next day, Louis accompanied me up north to the Mauritian Camp, Pope Hennessy, near Fayid in MELF 15, and he too, showed me round my new surroundings there. I saw straightaway that all the facilities at Pope Hennessy were infinitely better than those at Ava Camp, so I felt sure that I should be well looked after during that next month!

Another Chapter of these recollections is now told. This one started with an almost overwhelming accolade after my time in Cyprus – and concluded with a most gigantic raspberry! – Such is life!

CHAPTER 10

Mauritian Guards
and All That

In the Suez Canal Zone in 1953, most of the camps of the Regiments of 1 Infantry Division – like Ava Camp – had been established and occupied for less than two years, so they were still of a temporary nature. Some improvements, like extra buildings, were being added from time to time, but during my sixteen months with 29 Field, all the sleeping accommodation and the officers' and sergeants' and OR's messes consisted of tents with concrete bases, whilst the only permanent buildings were the Regimental Office, the Guard Room and armoury, the troops' Canteen and kitchens, the vehicle maintenance building, and the water tower and showers.

It was not similar throughout the Zone. Whenever we drove northwards to Fayid – a distance of some fifteen miles – it was quite noticeable that some of the other BTE camps seen from the Treaty Road were much better laid out and established than ours in Gineifa. Many camps had been

The 'superior' Canal Cottages at Pope Hennessy Camp

Officers' Mess at Pope Hennessy Camp 84 Mauritian Guards Group

set up in the Suez Canal Zone many years before, and some of the better RAF camps by 1953 looked like permanent barracks. Pope Hennessy Camp, which 84 Mauritian Guards occupied, was one of these well established, superior camps.

I was well pleased when I saw my sleeping accommodation for the next month, which consisted of a well-furnished semi-permanent 'Canal Cottage', which I would be sharing with Peter Gordon, another National Serviceman. I was equally happy when I saw the Officers' Mess, which was really excellent compared to the tented one we had at Ava Camp. It was a solid stone building surrounded by an attractive little garden and shaded terrace, and all the furnishings were similar to the standard of a decent hotel. I was certainly quite happy with my first impressions of the place and I wondered briefly how Louis Schneider was reacting to his inferior quarters at Ava Camp!

Peter Gordon seemed to be a pleasant enough companion and I saw that he was obviously quite a clever individual – although I noted in my diary that 'I don't think Peter will ever hit the high spots.' He told me that he had received his Commission just a few months before and he went on to say in his soft Scottish accent that 'contrary to Mons, that big monster 'Sense of Urgency' is seldom, if ever, seen here at 84 Mauritian Corps!' I was really looking forward to this interlude at Pope Hennessy Camp, but I certainly didn't sense from our conversation that I was about to experience a taste of the real Army! I also thanked my lucky stars that I had not ended up with a posting like this after my training at Mons OCTU!

When I later met the other officers in the Mess that evening, I soon discovered that they were a very mixed bag. Apart from Peter Gordon, there were two other National Service Subalterns, neither of whom I took to very much – which is the reason why I hardly mention them again in my diary. Then there were three Mauritian Captains who seemed pleasant enough, and the Adjutant, Douglas Urquart, who I immediately thought was a cut above the rest. Apart from Douglas, I thought

that the other British Regular Officers were a strange and unappealing bunch. They were also not particularly welcoming towards me as a newcomer and I soon found that they were decidedly cliquey. When I first met the Quarter Master Captain, his derogatory opening gambit was: 'these Mauritians will kill you!' I noted at the time that he must be a foolish and unpleasant person – and sure enough, that is exactly how he turned out!

The acting Commanding Officer, Major Austin, was not present on that opening Sunday evening, so I didn't meet him until next day.

Officers' Mess at Pope Hennessy Camp 84 Mauritian Guards Group

However listening to the others talking about him round the table, I noticed that not one of them had a good word to say for him! His nick-name was 'the ogre', and by the end of that first meal, I really started to feel quite sorry for the man. Nonetheless, when I met him next morning and he 'greeted' me in a blunt and ungracious manner, I soon realised why he had managed to build up such a bad reputation for himself! With the advantage of hindsight however, I can now see that the poor fellow was suffering from a severe dose of inferiority complex, although at the time I was unable to appreciate this fully.

On the first Monday, since Peter Gordon was Orderly Officer and had to dismount the Guard, we were woken up at 5.30. Breakfast in the Officers' Mess was at 6.30 and I had been told to report to Douglas Urquhart in the Adjutant's Office at 7 o'clock. Since it was June, the office hours included mornings only up to lunchtime and for the next month, I was to be his assis-tant. I soon found that Douglas was very competent at his job and also a pleasant person to work with. I could soon see that he was the linchpin of the whole Unit – although I doubt if many in 84 Group really appreciated the contribution he was making behind the scenes.

Between his many swear words (I noted in my diary!) he told me a few things about the units I had just joined:– He said that 84 RPC Group of Mauritian Guards consisted of 9 Companies and these were located in dif-ferent camps throughout the Suez Canal Zone. All the soldiers in each Company came from the islands of either Mauritius or Rodrigues or Seychelles, but the different nationals were never mixed up together in the same Company, because there could be so much animosity and rivalry between them! He said that this problem always had to be remembered whenever we arranged overnight accommodation for soldiers from the var-ious Companies. That last year, a ferocious fight had broken out after an inter-Company Soccer match and as a result of this, one person had been killed and many others badly injured!

Nonetheless, he said that the Mauritians and the Seychellois in 84 Group were mostly intelligent, happy and obliging individuals and they were far better educated than the Kenyans and the Tanzanians in the East African Royal Pioneer Corp Contingents. Most of the soldiers 84 Group came from the island of Mauritius, because its population, including the sister island of Rodrigues (about 370 miles to the East), was close on a million people, whereas the Seychelles (which is a widely spread group of islands about 600 miles to the North) had a population of only about 50,000, most of whom lived in the main island of Mahé.

Mauritius was of course the home of the extinct Dodo and like Rodigues and the Seychelles archipelago, all these islands were uninhabited until the French discovered them and then started colonising them in the 18th century. It was not until after 1810 that the British eventually took them over. The natives of the islands are now a real mixture, made up of Indians, Negroes and Europeans, and they variously speak Creole, English, Hindi and French!

During my month at Pope Hennessy Camp, I always found the Mauritians a likeable bunch, although, sad to say, I also noted that some of our worst mannered British Officers in the Mess were often unnecessarily rude towards them – like to the Quarter Master Captain already mentioned. On that first day in the office with Douglas Urquhart, he touched upon this matter and told me how critical he was about the conduct of some of his fellow Officers within the Group towards the Mauritians. He went on to say however, that he had met the newly appointed Commanding Officer of 84 Group and he thought that this new man should soon influence the situation for the better.

The second day after my arrival at 84 Mauritian Group was the Coronation Day of Queen Elizabeth II – Tuesday 2 June 1953 – and since I was Orderly Officer, I had to remain in Camp all day long whilst there were many parades being held elsewhere in the Zone. I was quite happy about this, because it enabled me to listen to all the broadcasts coming in from Britain throughout the day and I found this most interesting.

Two days later, as part of our celebrations in MELF, a grand Coronation Ball was arranged at the Officers' Mess in Fayid, and since the opportunity of attending a mixed party like this was so rare, some of us from 29 Field made sure that we joined in all the fun. This was, in fact, the only occasion that I ever went out with any girls during the whole of my time in Egypt!

With Mike Martin, Ronnie Hambleton, Ray Kelly and the girls at the Coronation Ball in Fayid, 4 June 1953

As might be surmised, there were very few young girls living in the Suez Canal Zone during 1953. I suppose the only ones would have been those working in the Military Hospital or in HQ Offices or on the telephone exchanges in places like Fayid and Moascar. Maybe life was different for soldiers working in the main centres, but for those stationed in any of the camps scattered throughout the Suez Canal Zone, there was very little opportunity for any of us to socialise with girls, except perhaps during infrequent visits to the Officers' Club in Fayid.

Mike Martin, my friend in 8 Battery, had asked me to join his party for this Coronation Ball, which he was organising with two other Regular Subalterns in 29 Field, Ray Kelly and Ronny Hambleton. Ray was our key man in arranging our partners for the evening, because he had a girl friend working in HQ and she had agreed to invite three of her friends to join us. On the night therefore, we laid on two of our Land Rovers and we all met up in the Officers' Club at Fayid.

It was a really splendid event and included, a good dinner followed by a 'London' cabaret; bagpipers from the Inniskillings and dancing all through the night. The girls, who were daughters of senior Officers, were very good company and after the event, Mike Martin eventually dropped me off at Pope Hennessy Camp again at 5.30 next morning. We all agreed that the party had been a great success – and at the same time, we had done our duty to our new Queen!

The temperature on most days at this time of the year was well over 100°, and during the day this felt like a hot blast whenever you went outside from the cooler air in the office. The Office Building of 84 Mauritian Group was built with thick stone walls, and Douglas Urquhart's method of keeping these rooms bearable was to make sure that all the doors and windows were kept open during the early morning cool and then, from 9 o'clock onwards, closed so that the warm air was kept out for the rest of the day. We then had a fan to keep the air circulating inside. To prove his point, on one day we tried keeping the doors, shutters and windows open for much longer during the morning, and it was noticeable how the ambient temperature soon felt several degrees higher.

Ronnie Hambleton and Mike Martin

Officers' Club at Fayid on the Great Bitter Lake

Since this was high Summer, we only worked in the Office from 7 o'clock until lunchtime, so being much closer to Fayid, I had plenty of opportunity for looking round the shops in the afternoon and also for visiting the Officers' Club for a drink with John Gordon. We also went for many swims in the Great Bitter Lake, even though the water was unpleasantly salty. This sort of relaxation was seldom, if ever, on agenda when I was at Ava Camp, because transport was far too restricted and difficult to arrange. My month with Mauritians was therefore the period when I visited Fayid most.

In the Mauritian Group office, I soon discovered that the biggest time-waster was the telephone system in the Canal Zone – at times it was really quite appalling. The Telephone Exchanges in those days were all manually operated, so sometimes the Exchange was slow to answer or the telephone line was out of order or maybe the telephone lines were completely full. Then sometimes when you eventually got through to your required number, the extension line was engaged or there was no one to answer the telephone or the person you were calling was unavailable! It was all extremely irritating and frustrating – and time-wasting.

On 19 June, I wrote in my diary:– 'At times in the office, I can hear Major Austin getting very irate with the poor young girl on the HQ switchboard – either because she doesn't understand the number he is asking for, or perhaps because she keeps him waiting for too long. In any case, he is disgracefully rude to them. Although Major Austin may be good at organising the duties for the Mauritian Guards which he needs to do, his manners are appalling and he is absolutely hopeless at managing his fellow officers, especially those junior to him.'

On another occasion in the office, I noted in my diary that Douglas Urquhart was on the telephone within earshot of Austin, when he remarked to the caller in a jocular way: 'Oh, that doesn't matter; everyone is mad up here anyway!' I heard the 'ogre' grunt his disagreement with *that* remark. A little later in the conversation, when Douglas went on to say: 'Ah well then, perhaps it's only you and me who are mad!' To which I heard the ogre grunt (quite seriously): 'Huh! That's more like it!' Later that day – when Douglas and I were alone – we had a really good laugh about that trivial incident.

One of my principal tasks in the Adjutant's office during that month, seemed to be making and confirming the travel arrangements for batches

Near Fayid on Great Bitter Lake

of some 80 of our soldiers who were taking leave in Cyprus; and with the chaotic telephone system in the Suez Canal Zone, this could easily take many hours of my office time to complete! I know that Douglas much appreciated my efforts.

Apart from the enormous waste of time in making all these arrangements as mentioned above, the worst problems caused by these holidays in Cyprus were the frightful increase in VD cases which occurred after each batch of 'holiday makers' had returned to duty! I noted that this problem was getting out of hand by June, so when the new CO arrived, he decided to call upon a 'higher being' – in the form of the Roman Catholic Priest – to improve the critical situation. Just before I left 84 Group, some palliative measures were already being implemented. The Priest and one of the Mauritian Captains had held sessions with all those about to depart for Cyprus, telling them about the dangers of entering that 'den of iniquity'. Whether or not all this cautionary advice had any effect, I never learned. However, at least *some* positive attempt was made to help save those 'holiday-makers' from their hazardous impulses!

The new CO of 84 Group, Lt Col D.P.Roissier OBE., proved to be a good choice for the job and he was also a man of substance. He had previously been in the Indian Army and after he had taken over, he raised the overall standard of the Mess at a stroke. Just one last telling comment about our poor, unfortunate 'ogre', I noted in my diary:– 'it is comical (but also sad of course) to see how obsequious our Major Austin is towards the new CO.' I really can't help feeling sorry for him now, can you?

Douglas Urquhart had been a pleasant, helpful and amusing person to work with and during those weeks, he taught me a great deal about running a Regimental Office (or indeed, any other office). I learned about Douglas, that after World War II, he had tried to run a pub at Farnborough for a period, but after this had proved unsuccessful, he decided to return to the Army to find his feet again. In those days, this problem of readjustment after the unsettling period of World War II was quite common for ex-servicemen. I noted in my diary that there was another Major in the Pope Hennessy Mess at that time, who had become bankrupt after failing in a market gardening venture. As a result of his debts, the unfortunate person was attempting to re-establish himself in the Services so that he was in a position to repay his borrowings.

As you know, there were only four Subalterns in Pope Hennessy Camp, so during my secondment to 84 Group, I must have been Orderly Officer for at least seven times; and although Orderly Officers at 84 Group were virtually unsupervised, the ordained duties were much the same as those at 29 Field:– Namely, dismounting the Guard, making a tour of the Camp and inspecting the perimeter wire, inspecting the Ablutions and Cookhouse, asking if there were any complaints in the Canteen, counting the weapons and ammunition in the Armoury, and then, after mounting the new Guard at 5.30, writing the Report.

During the night, the Orderly Officer often checked the prowler guards in the camp, to make sure that they were being attentive. This could be quite blood-curdling at times, because the Mauritians were particularly trained to really shout out their challenges whilst on Guard Duty. The procedure here (and elsewhere) was that, if the guard heard something suspicious outside or inside the wire compound, he should shout out: 'Halt! Who goes there?' – and if the answer was 'Friend', then he would say:– 'Advance and be recognized!' If there was no answer at all; then there was no messing in those days – he was ordered to fire.

We frequently heard reports in our *News letter* about Egyptians wandering outside the camps at night and then running off when challenged and in the Zone in 1953, this was really serious. If the challenge was unsatisfactory, the guards were ordered to shoot. The large Base Ordnance Depot (10 BOD) opposite Ava Camp – which had so many desirable goods piled up high – acted as a magnet for all Egyptian thieves in the locality and during the course of the year, there were quite a number of shooting incidents there which 'drew blood'.

It was about this time, that we heard about a tragic accident, in which an over zealous Orderly Officer putting his guards to the test, wandered outside the perimeter wire and when challenged, ran off into the darkness. The guard involved, fired his rifle at a venture – and shot the officer dead!

On another matter completely:– I had been selected during the previous month (with Harry Cotter another National Serviceman, and a Regular Sergeant named Cole) to represent 29 Field in an inter-Regimental Modern Pentathlon Competition which was being arranged to start on 7 July. During May, June and the beginning of July therefore, the three of us practiced and trained in the five events involved whenever possible.

Modern Pentathlon comprises of horse riding, fencing, pistol shooting, swimming, and cross-country running (in that order). However, since there were only camels to ride in the Suez Canal Zone, an event for motorcycle scrambling (or trialling) was fortunately substituted for the horse riding!

The running (2½ miles) and the swimming (300 metres) didn't present problems for most competitors, but many needed extra practice and tuition in the other three events:– motorcycle trialling, fencing and pistol shooting.

In 29 Field, we had Matchless motorcycles as well as BSA motorcycles to practice with, but since the BSA bike was the more sluggish of the two, we always rode the Matchless ones. The rules for the motorcycle scrambling event were as follows:– There would be 10 hazards marked out on the course with white tape, and at each hazard, the rider would be penalized for dismounting, touching the ground with his feet, crossing the boundary tape, or getting stuck in the sand and needing some help to keep moving.

This was Sergeant Cole's best event, so he was able to help Harry and myself when we went off to practice together in the desert. By 7 July, although Harry and I were still very inexperienced and a little apprehensive about the hazards in store, we were a little more confident about controlling 'our steeds' than we had been just a few weeks before!

For the fencing instruction with the epées, we had to go to the Army Gymnasium in Fayid, so whilst I was stationed with 84 Group at Pope Hennessy Camp, Harry used to pick me up in a Land Rover on the way to our training sessions together. We were told that we would be fencing against all the other competitors during the day and that each bout would last 3 minutes, unless there was a touch of one of the epées first. If there were no touches, or if both touched at the same time, this would count as a double defeat. Whilst we were training at the gymnasium in the 'novices area', we noticed that one or two of the other competitors were real experts at this sport!

The pistol shooting we were able to practice on our own. The competition consisted of firing 20 shots at a silhouette target at a distance of 25 yards. When firing a revolver (which has quite a 'kick' in it after pressing the trigger) the prime rule was to keep the firing arm absolutely straight and rigid when you fired. All this quick firing from the hip, and picking off tiny targets at forty yards as seen in the Western films, is total rubbish!

At the end of June therefore, I said all my goodbyes to all at 84 Mauritian Guards Group and returned to Ava Camp. Thinking about my stay afterwards, I wish that I had seen much more of the Mauritian troops at work and at play. Foolishly, I never asked to spend part of my time out of the office, so I remained as Assistant Adjutant for the whole of that month and the only time I ever became involved with the Mauritians' activities was when I was Orderly Officer. Nonetheless, I still found my stay at Pope Hennessy Camp different and interesting, even though the miscellaneous bunch of officers in the Officers' Mess were really not at all to my liking. By the time I left, I never revised my view that they were the most unfriendly bunch of colleagues that I ever met in the Army. But in addition to this, another disadvantage to my remaining as Assistant Adjutant for the whole of that month was that, by sitting in the office for most of the time, I had lost most of my sun tan by the time I returned to Ava Camp again!

After I was back at 29 Field, I wrote in my diary on that Saturday 27 June 1953:– 'I am really pleased to be returning to this friendly Mess again. It was almost like coming home, with all the, 'glad to see you back again' from all the blokes I saw again. John Stansfield and Dick Brimelow are still away on leave, and I am waiting to finalise my holiday arrangements with Ian (Sinclair) and Harry (Cotter). Harry now thinks that he will only be able to take two weeks leave, because he will be returning to the UK in August.

Big fire at 10 Base Ordnance Depot

'This afternoon, there is a big fire in one of the sheds in 10 BOD and a great cloud of black smoke is billowing from it, and the fire engines are there tackling the blaze.'

The Pentathlon Competition started with the motorcycle trialling on Tuesday, 7 July. The day before, we had been taken round the course for us to look closely at the ten hazards and to make sure that we knew exactly what was in store for us all! We heard that there would be 60 competitors in all, which meant that 20 Units had sent in teams.

When the motorcycle event started, each member of the team went off in turn, and the next rider started as soon as the previous one had completed the course. Sergeant Cole went off first for us and when he came back, he said that he had lost 12 points out of the possible 100, which sounded quite good to Harry and me.

I went off next, and I wrote in my diary:– 'The first 500 yards at the start of the course was over loose, stony and bumpy sand, which was easily covered by standing up on the bike. Then came the first hazard:– this was up a stony, bumpy wadi – I came off! The second was over bumpy stones, and then up a bank – again, no go! After that however, things improved for me. I somehow got through the next three hazards without any faults at all, but then I stumbled again. Some of the hazards were really quite frightening and I have no idea how I managed to do them. One hazard in particular was going down a very steep bank for about 50 feet and then ending with a sharp turn to the right through loose sand at the bottom! I got through this hazard all right! By the end of the course I believe that I managed to manoeuvre 5 out of the 10 without any faults! I failed most when the hazard was going up bumpy sides. The ones coming down a bank I found less difficult. It was all quite a new experience for me and I also thought it was quite good fun – but only after I had finished! Fortunately, Harry Cotter finished as well, so all three of us completed the course. Harry seemed to have done a little better than me. We didn't do so badly, because we noticed that a number of the other teams failed to finish at all.'

After this first event, we learned that we were lying 11th (out of 20) – Sgt Cole came 4th out of 60, whilst Harry was 40th, and I came 44th!

The next day was fencing and for this event we had 57 bouts to complete, which took most of the day. I noted in my diary:– 'With this kind of fencing for the pentathlon, the first jab/hit with the epée wins, but if both competitors stick each other at the same time, it is recorded as a double defeat.

All set for the Motor Cycle Trials for the Modern Pentathlon

Sergeant Cole had many of these double defeats and we saw that he often finished his contests needing to straighten up his badly bent epée! I finished the day by beating a rather good Major in 14/20 (?) who had been doing rather well, which I thought quite gratifying! When we returned to camp, we went out and practiced with the pistol shooting again, and blazed away with about 70 shots a piece.'

On Thursday 9 July, I wrote:– 'Sergeant Cole scored 13 hits out of 20, and I got 14 on the target. In the afternoon I played Basket Ball for the Regiment. We swiped up an RASC team 45-7. I am rather stiff today in my thighs, due to all that standing up during the motor cycling on Tuesday. I hope that I can shake this off before the running on Saturday.'

In the swimming, I recorded that I came 38th with a time of 7 minutes and 9 seconds, but unfortunately, I failed to write down any more details about that day's competition.

On the last day, Saturday, I wrote:– 'Harry wasn't feeling too well. He had been sick during the night, which wasn't a very good start for the cross-country run! Sergeant Cole went off first for us, and came in looking ghastly – he is too old for this running really! I went off soon after he came in. The course was fairly hard going over soft sand, but it was only 2½ miles, so I kept going all right. I found it rather difficult to judge how fast I was running, since the result is judged only on a time basis. I finished quite freshly and did a 21 minute 50 second round. In the afternoon I played cricket for Baker Troop against Charlie Troop, and saw *Prisoner of Zenda* in the evening.'

I later noted that in the Pentathlon Competition, our trio team had come 12th out of the 20 units competing, so we felt that we hadn't completely disgraced ourselves after all our efforts!

In conclusion, although the deserts to the west and south of Ava Camp – where our firing ranges were situated – were well known to most of us by the end of our time in MELF, the next Chapter takes a look at our expeditions into the Sinai Peninsular to the east of the Suez Canal, an area of desert, which we investigated just twice during the whole of our time in Egypt, and a region where Moses wandered for 40 years with the Israelites in about 1450 BC.

CHAPTER 11

Into the Wilderness
of Sinai

Towards the East of the Suez Canal is the wedge-shaped Sinai Peninsula. It is about the size of Sicily and stretches 100 miles across to Israel and Jordan and some 250 miles southwards from the Mediterranean down to the Red Sea. It is wilderness for the most part, consisting of loose sand, wadis, bare mountains and barren rocky ground. Little lives there.

It was during March and April of 1953, that we made two lengthy journeys deep into Sinai. The first was during a large Military Exercise called *Longbow*, which involved most of the Middle East Land Forces; and the second, was an expedition we made to the mountainous southern part of the Peninsula, when we visited the ancient Monastery of Saint Catherine.

The objective of Exercise *Longbow* was to test our ability to wage a moving offensive far into the wilderness of Sinai, and as soon as we heard this intention, we knew that our main problem would be the dreadful state of our vehicles, which were always liable to break down at any time! Most of these vehicles had been in heavy use for some ten years, and no doubt, if there had been more money in the national coffers, many would have been replaced long ago. The only new vehicles I ever remember seeing in the Army were the Land Rovers, which had come in to replace most of the wartime American Jeeps.

In preparation for Exercise *Longbow*, we went out on a number of one day training schemes from Ava Camp, and after one of these on 11 March, I wrote:– 'Up at 6.30 this morning, since Baker Troop is out on a one day scheme. We prepared four gun positions and practiced some 'crash actions' (that's setting up the guns quickly, after receiving orders when on the move), and we were quite pleased with ourselves, because our fastest time from receiving the order to 'shot one', was $3\frac{1}{2}$ minutes. We also practiced some anti-tank actions. This morning we started on the Geneifa Range just south of Egg Hill and moved westwards towards the 'enemy'. At this point, Mac's carrier conked out and left him stranded for a few hours in the morning and then two other trucks also broke down during the day and had to be towed back – oh dear, this modern Army! George Baker (my GPO's truck) behaved itself fortunately.

'Our last position was near the bombing range, just south of the Police Post. It was quite late (5.15 pm) when we saw an RAF jeep drive up to look at some targets nearby. Luckily, TSM Fletcher went over to have a chat with them and they told him that the RAF was about to start bombing here in thirty minutes' time! We therefore decided to get the hell out of the place! As we were driving back to camp, we saw some Lancaster bombers flying overhead! Dinner Night tonight. Afterwards, some of us went up to the Sergeants' Mess to say goodbye to Sgt Barnes, who is leaving tomorrow.'

Exercise *Longbow* started on Monday 16 March 1953, so on that day the 29 Field convoy (including some spare vehicles to cover for breakdowns!) moved off northwards at 10 o'clock towards the swing-bridge at El Firdan, just north of Ismailia. This was the best route for taking so many vehicles across the Canal (elsewhere there are only ferries). The one big snag with using El Firdan bridge however, was that it was very costly to keep the Canal closed for longer than is absolutely necessary (£1E per minute I noted!), so the time taken to cross the bridge was crucial. As a result, there were Military Police everywhere along the road to make sure that the convoys kept moving quickly!. Having crossed at El Firdan without mishap, we drove southwards down the eastern bank to El Shatt, where we sat in our collection area and waited for *Longbow* to start on the following evening. We had travelled 110 miles, and already two of our vehicles had broken down and were being repaired by the REME mobile workshop!

It is well known, that on schemes like this, life is either frantically busy or dreadfully boring and inactive. During the boring periods, hours and

Across El Firdan Bridge and driving down the East side of the Canal

hours are spent just waiting around for orders to come through on the wireless for the next move. Having reached El Shatt on that afternoon, we were given some briefing meetings about the forthcoming Exercise, and then we spent the rest of Monday and the whole of the following day, just waiting for all the fun to begin.

We were told that during *Longbow*, we should be driving more than 60 miles eastwards – much of it by night – across the 2,500 foot high Mitla Pass, and then on towards Nakhl, a small, isolated, mud-hut town which lay in the dusty plain beyond the mountains, midway between the Suez Canal and Aqaba in Jordan.

I noted in my diary some of the instructions we were given about *Longbow*, which I had to pass onto the others:
- Smokers had to be very careful about smoking under the camouflage nets (and there were many smokers in those days.)
- There must be no collection of people around the mobile kitchen at mealtimes – thus making an easy target for enemy aircraft strafing.
- Drivers must keep a good distance between vehicles when on the move during daytime.
- Weapons must be carried at all times.
- Vehicles must never be left unattended.
- All camouflage had to be taken down at night.

- Always sleep alongside your vehicle at nights for protection – with vehicles on the move in the darkness, sleepers out in the open can so easily be run over!
- Never sleep under vehicles, because these tend to 'settle down' in loose sand!
- Be very careful to prevent road accidents.
- Never camp in a wadi, in case of a flash storm occurring higher up the wadi.

All these precautions were discussed and circulated in all Units, but nonetheless, after *Longbow* had ended, we learned that as many as six soldiers (none in 29 Field) had been killed during that week's activity! Since the Exercise involved plenty of night driving, most of these accidents were due to road accidents.

It was during another large scheme like this, that I witnessed the worst accident I have ever seen. In those days, the field kitchens normally cooked their meals, by using a horizontal, petrol burner (rather like a flame thrower). On one occasion, I was close to one of these field kitchens when a burner exploded (or otherwise got out of control) and in a trice, the poor young cook using it had been horrifically burned. They tried to cover him up quickly, but I feel sure that he subsequently died from his burns. When I spoke to our doctor Bill Cattell about the accident afterwards, he said that when a large part of the skin is burnt off like that, the body dehydrates very quickly. This horrible incident has been a strong warning to me ever since; never, ever, to underestimate the dangers of handling petrol anywhere near a naked flame; the extreme heat that petrol can so quickly generate is quite terrifying.

It was during *Longbow* that our old campaigner, TSM Fletcher, introduced us to the wonders (and the dangers) of what he called, an 'open-Benghazi', for preparing a really 'quick brew' of tea: He filled the kettle with water and prepared the ground with some stones as a good base to support the kettle, then soused the sand underneath with plenty of petrol, put the kettle on, stood well back, and carefully threw a lighted match under the kettle. There was a mild explosion and a sudden conflagration, and almost immediately the water in the kettle was boiling! Although we

Making height towards the Mitlah Pass

Look westward in the Mitlah Pass

did sometimes use this method for brewing up quickly, most of us preferred instead, to continue using the much slower primus stove for brew-up time!

At dusk on the Tuesday, all the vehicles and guns were formed up in close order at midnight, in readiness for the start of *Longbow*, and then at 2 o'clock in the morning, the convoy began its arduous night drive up to the Mitla Pass – each vehicle following the tiny night-tail-light of the vehicle in front. For much of the time there was soft sand on either side of the road, and as we drove along in the semi-darkness, we could see that quite a number of our vehicles had already driven off the hard surface and were bogged down in loose sand, waiting to be winched out.

Most of the Army vehicles had windscreens which elevated, so this made visibility at night much easier for the driver, but even so, night driving was always very tiring and stressful, and we were all very pleased when we saw John Gilmour from our Battery Head Quarters to meet us at first light, and

Preparing to move again

to show us a suitable spot for our vehicles to pull off the road. He told John Stansfield and myself (the two GPOs) as much as possible about the general situation (which was not very much!) and when I went back to check on the Baker Troop vehicles after the move, I found that one of the quads (or gun-tractors), together with its limber and gun, had been damaged in a road accident during the night and had been told to return to camp. This was not particularly bad news for me, because it meant that I should now only have two guns to look after for the rest of the week, which will make my life much easier!

The next four days were frenetic for everyone involved. The most frustrating part of a big Exercise like *Longbow*, is that only the minimal amount of information ever reaches the troops on the ground. For long periods, nobody seems to know what is happening, or why we are doing what we are doing! Orders came down telling us to move on to the next map reference, but explanations seldom accompanied the order, and for days on end, the whole picture is totally confused. As a result of this, assumptions are made and rumours abound. It is rather like playing football in a thick fog:– no one knows what the score is; or who is winning; or even where the rest of your team is! On the other hand, I expect that real warfare is equally confusing at times, so it could be said that schemes like this are excellent practice!

During Wednesday, we drove along the road through barren, rocky mountains, frequently taking up gun positions on the way to support our infantry who were advancing ahead. As soon as our targets were out of range, we had to move forward again. From our fourth position, with evening approaching, John Stansfield and I received orders for us to drive forward about 8 miles with our Taras and prepare new gun positions for Able and Baker Troops to occupy after darkness.

Just in range on the way to the Nakhl Plain

Night occupations are never simple at the best of times, but when the ground is as rocky and uneven as it is in these mountains, positions are particularly difficult to prepare and to occupy. But before the darkness had completely closed in, John and I had each completed our preparations, so all we had to do now was to wait for the guns to arrive. We therefore gathered together for a convivial 'supper party', and ate up our 'iron rations', washed down by the distinctive taste of sweet, hot tea and condensed milk.

On Thursday 19 March, I wrote about this night occupation and the action on the following day:– 'We had a long wait for the guns, but eventually, they arrived at about midnight after a difficult night drive. By this time it was bitterly cold. Thankfully, all the vehicles arrived safely, so we directed the guns in with the help of hand-torches to indicate the white marker tapes, and then sent all the vehicles back to the wagon lines in the rear. The guns were set up in line by means of lights, and then most of us got some sleep. When we checked the 'zero lines' of the guns in the

George Baker ready to move off again

morning, we found that they were within 3 minutes of perfect! We felt quite pleased with ourselves!

'We didn't stay in this position for long, but moved out at about 10 o'clock, and then got entangled with all the other traffic on the road for several hours, and were constantly held up and delayed. Eventually we saw the flat plain stretching out before us and when we later reached this, we found that there was much less traffic on the road. We were ordered to make many 'crash actions' and everyone's tempers began to fray a little under the strain.

'We received hardly any information today (Thursday) about what was happening in the engagement;– although whilst on the road, we were variously told off by the umpires, for not being staggered enough – or otherwise, for having our vehicles too far apart! We occupied many different gun positions during the day and were often ordered to move on again before we had time to even set up the guns. We were on the move so much that we had no time for any food or even for brewing up! We travelled about 35 miles and took up our final position in the middle of the Nakhl plain at dusk. Eventually, we all had something to eat at 8.30!'

Shaving during a break in the action

And on the Friday morning I wrote:– 'The

reconnaissance party (including me) had to move forward at 0445! We laid out positions by the front line and the guns came in at 0830. I had a shave after the position had been organised. No breakfast was possible for the recce party because we were receiving targets throughout the morning – and lunch was also missed because, as usual, we were ordered to move on again at midday. We occupied two more positions nearer Nakhl, and although an Auster (light aircraft) dropped a note at one stage to say that armoured cars were seen in the north, nothing came of it.

'Our last gun position (on Friday) was on very broken ground in sight of Nakhl, which consisted of a mosque and a small fort surrounded by a small group of mud buildings – in the middle of nowhere! The town lies in a vast plain with numerous wadis, and in the far distance, a range of mountains was just visible. The only vegetation was the usual tufted grass and prickly bushes. We have still been given no definite information, but the rumour is that we shall most likely be moving again this evening, because we know that the scheme ends on Saturday! Tonight we had our combined breakfast, lunch and supper at 8.30 pm!'

'Char up' time for the George Baker Team: TSM Fletcher, Gaskell (Signaller), Langford (driver), and Tec Accs, Stacey, Brown and Dodd (behind)

On Saturday, 21 March, I wrote in my diary:– 'We travelled back to the Mitla Pass during the whole of the night from 11 o'clock onwards. To add to the chaos armoured cars pounced upon the convoy of vehicles and disorganised us. Our guns came into action but no one knew what was happening in the dark. I took over the driving of GB whilst Snape (my driver and batman) drove the carrier. The column was going along very slowly, and sometimes all the vehicles stopped completely – caused by drivers falling asleep at the wheel whilst they were temporarily delayed! (When you are driving in a large convoy at night, it is extremely difficult to know for certain what is causing any stoppage up front, unless someone gets out, walks up the column and investigates – but the front vehicle of the column may be a mile or more ahead!). It has been quite a hectic exercise, and everyone is now very tired – and tempers are short. The shouting which came down the convoy when we were stopped due to some drivers ahead falling asleep was loud enough to wake the dead!

Baker Troop taking up another Gun Position

'At first light (Saturday morning) we were again attacked by tanks, but this time, we were able to get into action, and we really pasted them – we were adjudged to have knocked out about 5!! We moved on towards the Pass, and collected in a Dispersal Point about a mile from Colonel Parker's Memorial (the person who originally constructed the Mitla Pass). We took up a position as a Battery, and while the others recced, I took charge and fired on a number of targets – the enemy were attacking all round. The Exercise was declared finished at 12 noon.'

It seems from this account, which is taken almost verbatim from my diary, that I was saved by the bell, although I might well have won a medal for that action, if it had been during wartime! (Only kidding!) I finished that page, Saturday 21 March:– 'We started back at midday (no lunch again!) and reached the other side of the Pass just before dark, where we formed a closed *laager* (in the shape of Δ) for the night. Once again we gratefully received our food for the whole day at 8 pm – all in one go!"

We left early next morning (Sunday), because 29 Field had to be ready to cross the bridge at El Firdan at 11 o'clock on the dot! As we drove along, I normally stood up in my George Baker truck with my head through the roof opening, so that I could look back and keep an eye on the Baker Troop guns following behind. I noted a little incident in my diary about the drive back, which shows that, even in March 1953, I still found much of this 'Army Game' a bit of a joke:– 'After crossing the bridge, we went by the road through Ismailia, so I managed to get a few snaps of the place. The

Homeward Bound at the end of Longbow

guard was being mounted on one of the Army buildings as we passed, so the guns (and me!) were given an almighty salute. A Sergeant stood over the other side of the road, and called the guard up as I passed. I had a chuckle as I returned a salute.'

When we reached Ava Camp later that afternoon, we were all quite weary, and our faces were nicely tanned after all that exposure to the elements. We also returned with many lessons and experiences learned – most of which could never have been gleaned from any Training Manuals!

An occurrence I witnessed during *Longbow* saddened me greatly:– In the middle of one of our night drives, the whole column was held up for some time because one of the vehicles had broken down and just refused to start again. After a few minutes, the REME mechanic found the trouble. Some water had been mixed in with the petrol, so the whole system needed to be drained off. Some evil villain must have siphoned off petrol in some of the jerry cans – to be sold off no doubt – and then topped them up again with water! Such is the selfishness and wickedness of man!

During *Longbow* however, I once again discovered just how supportive and likeable the vast majority of the ORs are to work with, in spite of all the pressures, lack of sleep and the other trials that come with these Exercises. I was always greatly heartened to see how they responded with such continued good humour, helpfulness and cheerfulness – and this is not a retrospective observation viewed through rose-coloured glasses. I see that I made similar comments elsewhere in my diary. Generally speaking, I found the ORs in 8 Battery a fine mixture of people. Having said that, during the stresses of *Longbow*, I did discover one rotten apple in the Baker Troop Command Post barrel, and I was determined to remove that person as soon as possible.

The day after our return to Ava Camp on Monday 23 March, I wrote:– 'All the vehicles and equipment are being overhauled today. I spent most of the day testing Stacey and revising all the TARA-work. I have to make sure that he passes this Class III TARA Exam which is being taken next month. I can then make him my Tec Acc 1, and Brown my Tec Acc 2 straightaway. I have to get rid of that wretched man Dodd from Baker

Troop as soon as possible! On *Longbow*, he showed that he was unhelpful when the pressure was on, and he is a definite weakness in the Troop Command Post. He is so different from Stacey and Brown who are both calm and dependable in a crisis. Although Stacey lacks knowledge at present, he is eager to learn. Brown has recently arrived in the Canal Zone but has picked up TARA-work very quickly. They also work well together, and are pleasant to be with, and show initiative. I must get Stacey through that test next month.'

Three days later on Thursday, I wrote:– 'I took Chambers' quad on a 406 (a monthly vehicle check) this morning. Up to the break I was teaching Stacey about 'C of M' (all about weather, wind and temperature, and how these affect the range and line of the shells). I am making him set up the graph continually so that he is well practiced in this. It is with this 'Stephen's Graph' that most of the candidates fail the test. Dodd has at long last left Baker Troop. We have given him to BHQ!! What a present!'

Before I leave these two weeks following the end of *Longbow*, I am including just a few more random notes which give a little more insight into life at Ava Camp, as well as into the 'Army Game'. On Saturday 28 March I wrote:– 'It was the BC's inspection today as usual, starting with the guns at 9.30. Preparations beforehand had gone quite well until one of the limbers was found to have some rust on it. For a time, Mac got really excited about this and 'threw a wobbly', but the 'crisis' quickly passed after Barney had inspected the guns and vehicles and given them a most favourable report! I can now always depend upon my quad drivers, Chambers, Drayton and Langford to do their best for these inspections – I play Soccer regularly with them – and I always tell them to really 'pull the stops out'. Also, by now, they are all experienced, and know exactly where Barney habitually looks to find the faults!'

Most of the Gunners really loved their Football, and I found it both useful and enjoyable that I often played in our Baker Troop Soccer team (but never as captain). Strangely enough, very few of my fellow officers in 29 Field ever took much interest in the game, mainly because most had been to rugby-playing schools, and didn't really understand the rules of Soccer. Speaking generally, this was one of the big 'divides' in the

Army in those days. The officers were mostly interested in Rugby, whilst the men played and understood Soccer. I thoroughly enjoyed these Soccer games we played together and I always found that my interest in the game was a great help in my working relationships with my Gunner colleagues in the Battery. I was a knowledgeable supporter of Fulham Football Club at that time, and I used to know many of the Teams that other ORs supported all round the country and I made a point of reading the Soccer pages in the newspapers. When all else failed, there was always that dependable common bond which I had with them.

We used to play our Soccer matches on hard, rough, bumpy pitches, so although sliding tackles were definitely out, it was still quite easy to finish a game with grazed knees and arms. Some of our players were really quite skilful, but on the whole I just about managed to hold my own, although one unfortunate incident sticks in my mind. In one of these matches, I gave away a crucial penalty to lose the match, when the ball bounced up unkindly in the penalty area and hit my hand! Life can be so unfair at times!

I was always surprised how little interest Barney used to take in the success of Baker Troop Soccer Team, even though we very nearly won the inter-Troop competition. On 4 April I wrote:– 'we had a football match against Charlie Troop (79 Battery) this morning, and luckily my toe and knee are both OK now. We had a good game and won quite convincingly 3-0. Unfortunately, Staff Hill (PTI) was a poor referee, and this rather spoilt the game. Chambers plays very well at centre half, and our forwards: Crawford, Langford, Brown (Geordie), Evans (Scouser), and L/Bdr Rouse are quite a good bunch of footballers and really play well together. I played at back with Drayton as usual, and our goalkeeper was L/Bdr Mills. Mills is fairly safe, but he is rather unsure with some of the high crosses and during this game he nearly gave away a goal because of this. Barney acted typically when he came into lunch and sat right opposite me in the Mess. He didn't so much as mention the match we had just played. I thought that he could have just said 'that was a good game Brian'. I gave him very low marks for that – but then, that is his way. He hardly ever congratulates anyone for anything.'

***

Every year, the Batteries in 29 Field organized one or two expeditions to St. Catherine's Monastery in the southern mountains of the Sinai Peninsular, and I was pleased to be included in the 8 Battery trip organised by Barney at the end of April. About twelve of us went in this party, and it also included Colonel 'Tiny' Shoreland (who had just joined the Regiment), as well as Mac and Lionel Savin.

St. Catherine's is one of the oldest Monasteries in the world:– it was founded in about A.D.530 by the Byzantine Emperor Justinian for the purpose of accommodating the Christian pilgrims who went to worship at Mount Sinai – also named, Mount Moses or Gebel Musa – which stands 7,497 feet high, and is the place where Moses – according to the Scriptures – received the Ten Commandments from God. The Monastery is built at the foot of the Mountain.

From Gineifa, St. Catherine's Monastery is a round trip of some 400 miles, and in 1953, this was no simple journey, because there were few good roads in the Sinai Peninsular and much of the country further south along the western coastline consisted of loose sand and all the tracks leading into the mountains were very rough and unreliable.

Waiting for the Ferry at El Kubri near Port Suez, at the South end of the Canal

222

At 10 o'clock on Saturday 25 April, our convoy of four Land Rovers with trailers, crossed the Canal on the ferry at El Kubri, just north of Port Suez, and started the drive down the eastern coast of the Gulf of Suez. For the first 50 miles the road was good, but just past the Shell Oil Wells at Ras el Sudr, the proper tarmac road ended and the track became dusty and bumpy. Eventually this track also petered out, and we had to cross a stretch of soft sand which the wind had blown over the track. This meant that plenty of pushing was needed to keep the Land Rovers on the move and it took us 2 hours to cover about 6 miles. Luckily, we struck the track again, and after that difficult stretch, we agreed that it was time to stop for lunch!

The route continued along the coast, until we passed the old copper and turquoise mines at Abu Zenima – well known to the Pharaohs – and just beyond this small settlement, we stopped for the night. By this time we were all begrimed and dusty, so a swim in the sea was most welcome. We had brought a good supply of 'iron-rations' with us, so we finished our first day, whilst watching the sun go down over the Gulf of Suez, by devouring an excellent beef stew and potatoes, prepared by our commendable ACC member, Corporal Tucker.

Early morning by the Gulf of Suez

On Sunday 26 April I wrote:– 'it is nearly 100 miles from here to St Catherine's Monastery, and since it stands at 4,925 feet above sea level, we know that most of the day the track will be climbing. In the morning, we waited for the sun to rise before we had another bathe, and after an excellent breakfast of fried bread, sausage and bacon, we continued on our way down the bumpy route along the coast. After 20 miles we turned inland up the Wadi Sidri, towards the Oasis of

The wilderness near Wadi Sidri

Feiran, and from now on we were in the mountains and our rough track had impressive high peaks on both sides. Occasionally we passed a Bedouin on a camel, and sometimes we even saw Bedouins just walking by themselves in the middle of nowhere! When we reached Feiran, we drove right through the oasis and then stopped for lunch beyond it. The oasis was much larger than I had imagined. It was about 2 miles wide,

Hobbled camels in the Wadi el Sheikh

Nomads we passed in Wadi el Sheikh

and had many palm trees and cultivated fields, and also quite a number of small, square huts made of stone, which had thatched palm roofs and small holes in the walls for windows.

'After lunch, we had about 40 miles further to drive, and we followed the bumpy track along various wadis, first towards the east, and then towards

The Oasis of Feiran

'The Garden of Moses' at Feiran

the south, climbing through some magnificent mountain scenery, until we eventually reached St Catherine's at about 3.30 pm. We parked our Land Rovers on some flat ground nearby, and went over to the Monastery straight-away, to ask for a look round. Father Claud, one of the Greek Orthodox monks, gave us a tour of the place – for a small consideration, and why not? – and I was very sur-prised to see how small the place seemed from the inside. There had been many more monks living here in the past, but now there are only 16 residents, although the Monastery has plenty of other accommodation for visitors if needed. The monks seem well provided for:– they now have a generator for electricity on the site, and the gardens outside seem bountiful, and there is an abundance of water from the well.

First sight of St Catherine's Monastery

Parked outside the fortress-like Monastery walls

From the outside, the Monastery looks rather like a fortress, and in the past it had been very necessary to be well protected from the marauding Arabs who would otherwise have attacked the monks for their treasures. Its walls are between 39 and 49 feet high and they are almost square in shape – measuring 93 yards and 83 yards in length. Until recently, the only way into the Monastery had been by means of a basket and a rope and pulley, but there is now a small gate constructed in the southern wall. The walls date from the original foundation, but God in his wisdom, allowed much of the East and North sides of the ramparts to be shattered by a severe earthquake in 1312, so these had to be reconstructed soon after that date. Outside the Monastery, there is an impressive walled garden which is well watered and shaded by tall cypress trees. The garden is tended carefully by the monks and it provides the Monastery with a wide range of fruit and vegetable throughout the year.

Within the walls of the Monastery, the focal point for the monks is the ornate Greek Orthodox Church of the Transfiguration and in addition, there are many other buildings for the small community and their visitors, including dormitories and a small Mosque and Minaret. The Library is also an outstanding feature since it contains one of the largest collections of Arabic and

The Bell Tower of the Church of the Transfiguration

Father Claud and the 'Burning Bush'

Early morning at the top of Gebel Musa
(Mt Sinai)

Turkish writings in existence. However, the monks consider that the most prized possession of St Catherine's Monastery is the unimpressive shrub just inside the walls, which believers imagine to be *the* actual 'Burning Bush' described by Moses in Exodus, Chapter III, verse 2.

The place where our Land Rovers were parked was at the foot of the Mount Sinai, just a short distance from the start of the stone steps leading right up to the summit, built by the monks years before. On Monday 27 April I wrote:– 'Lionel Savin, Fowler and I decided to climb up to the top of Mount Sinai before breakfast this morning, so we were up early, and set off on the slog at 7 o'clock – and it really was quite a climb. If we had known how hard it was going to be before we started, we might not have been quite so enthusiastic about climbing it! Anyway, we eventually reached the very top, where there is a small stone chapel and a tremendous view – but then it really needed to be, because it is a climb of 2,572 feet! We were scheduled to leave at 10 o'clock, so we couldn't dawdle at the top, but returned down the steps as quickly as possible, to make sure that we missed none of that excellent breakfast waiting for us at the bottom!'

Before leaving St Catherine's Monastery, we filled up all our empty jerry cans with cold water from their well, and started retracing our steps northwards through Watia Pass and then westward

Looking down at St Catherine's

The Chapel on the top of Gebel Musa

down Wadi el-Sheikh until we reached the Oasis of Feiran again, and there we stopped to have some lunch. Before long, we were surrounded by many local kids, persistently asking for 'bakshish' and 'ceegarettes'. On this second visit we saw a little more of the place, and we could readily understand why it has been called the 'pearl of Sinai'. I noted in my diary that I saw grapes, dates, peas, maize, barley and many other cereals all growing there abundantly. I also learned that there are many tamarisk trees in the oasis, and this is the tree that scholars believe provided all the manna so much referred to in the Scriptures (Exodus, Chapter XVI, verse 15)

After leaving the Oasis of Feiran, we followed the bumpy track westward down the Wadi Feiran until we reached the Gulf of Suez, and there we stopped for the night. Next day, Tuesday, we retraced our steps up the coast and arrived back to Ava Camp in the mid afternoon. It had been a most memorable trip.

I was soon back 'in the swim' again:– the following night I was in charge of the Road Patrol, so I spent the night on the road driving up and down to make sure that the expensive copper telephone wire remained where it should be!

On 6 July, I passed the marker in my diary: "only 5 months more!!!" All of my National Service friends, who had been in the Regiment when I arrived last September, were now approaching the end of their two years' Service, so I was pleased in July when I finalised my holiday arrangements with two friends of mine, Harry Cotter and Ian Sinclair. We agreed plans to travel through the Levant and Cyprus together.

Both Harry and Ian were being demobilised in September, so they had been rather late in arranging to take this leave, and for this reason, their Battery Commanders in 79 and 145 only allowed each of them to stay away for 14 days. Barney on the other hand, agreed to let me have 21 days. Our leave would be starting soon after 1 August.

During the whole of July, we were making our plans. We spoke to many others in the Mess who had made various journeys abroad recently, and

An evening swim in the Gulf of Suez

decided to start at Aqaba in Southern Jordan – then make our way north to Amman via Petra – then onto Jerusalem, stopping at Amman, the Dead Sea and Jerash – then to Damascus and Beirut – and then across to Cyprus, and back to Port Said. We thought that all this promised to be quite an interesting trip! In 1953, Jerusalem was a divided city, and it was forbidden to enter Israel after your Passport had been stamped in Jordan.

We had our TAB injections and vaccinations, wrote some letters for hotel bookings, went to the British Consulate near Port Suez for our Passports, and also arranged our visas from the Civilian Repatriation Bureau at Moascar. On 19 July we heard that our flights to Aqaba were agreed, but that the actual date in August would be confirmed nearer the time. For money, I arranged to take £E20 in cash and £40 in Travellers' Cheques.

We were now all set to find out what the Levant had in store for us.....

GPO's George Baker Truck

Vicky Saumarez

CHAPTER 12

Travels in
the Levant

We were unable to start our holiday until we received a confirmed reservation on one of the regular supply 'planes that flew from Fayid to the British troops stationed in Aqaba. Eventually, we heard the welcome news that we could join the next 'meat run' flight which was leaving at 6 o'clock on the morning of Friday 7 August 1953. We therefore informed the Adjutant, and made our final preparations accordingly.

I was up before 3 o'clock on that morning, but when I went along to collect Ian and Harry from their tent at about 3.30, I found that they had both dropped off to sleep again! We therefore had a last minute rush round to get ready to leave, followed by a mad dash in the duty truck to Fayid Airport so that we could complete all the necessary health and baggage formalities before the Hermes flight took off.

Aqaba was a dusty little Jordanian port of little consequence in those days, and as we flew in, I saw that there was just one cargo ship anchored in the calm, crystal clear sea in the Gulf. There was an Officers' Mess and a NAAFI established for the 'O' Force stationed in Aqaba and I was surprised to find that the British contingent was really quite large. It must have consisted of over 800 troops, including personnel from the RAF to look after the Airport, a contingent of the Royal Corps of Signals, the REME and the RASC, as well as a Company of Guards, and a Battery from the 80 LAA Regiment, Royal Artillery. I never learned why Britain needed to have so many troops stationed in this remote part of Jordan, but in those days, we seemed to have troops located in so many different places round the world. For instance, I know that we also had a detachment of troops in Libya at that time.

We were making for Ma'an – a small town about 80 miles to the north of Aqaba, and not far from Petra – and when we made enquiries in the

The REME convoy south of Ma'an

Officers' Mess about travelling there, we learned that a REME convoy would be leaving in a few hours' time; so we quickly ensured that we were included amongst the freight! Although it may seem lucky that we found this transport so easily, we had been told that British Army vehicles were regularly driving northwards into Jordan from Aqaba, so we were quite confident that we should have little difficulty in hitching a lift.

I noted in my diary that the road out of Aqaba was quite a newly improved one, but that recent heavy rains had washed away parts of it, so we therefore had to make a few detours. After driving about 10 miles north however, the road for the rest of the 65 miles to Ma'an was in excellent condition. The country to start with was sandy and rocky with the usual dry, prickly vegetation, but we then climbed up to over 3,000 feet and drove through a mountain range, and here we started to see more signs of life and vegetation and there were also a few herds of sheep and goats to be seen.

Ma'an itself was a nondescript, dusty, mud brick town, which stood at about 4,000 feet above sea level and had grown up due to the coming of the railway line in the 1890s. When our convoy passed through the little town-

Harry chatting up friendly locals in Ma'an

ship in 1953 to drive on to the Arab Legion Fort beyond, many of the inhabitants suddenly appeared from their houses to gawp at this big event! The Arab Legionaries at the Fort made us very welcome when we arrived, and gave us some coffee and some flat bread. We could see straightaway, that they had great respect and affection for the British Army. We also noticed at Ma'an how smart and soldierly the Legionaries were when they were on duty and also how much they were respected by the local inhabitants.

We slept in the back of one of the trailers for that night and since we had no sleeping bags or blankets with us and were well above sea level, we were absolutely frozen by the morning. I wrote in my diary: – 'our hands remained numb until the sun came up in the morning and started to make the blood circulate once again!'

For breakfast we feasted on a tin of pears and some biscuits, and after the convoy had departed northwards at 6.30, we started to chat with a friendly Corporal in the Arab Legion who came over to meet us outside the Fort. He knew Petra and the area very well and since he had the day off, he agreed immediately to act as our guide, which was to prove a great help to us.

The town of Wadi Musa and Petra lay about 25 miles to the west of Ma'an and our Arab friend soon arranged a taxi for the day for us costing £5 and then took us into the town to reserve rooms at the local Station Hotel for the following night. After that he took us to a local shop to buy some food for our lunch. This consisted of grapes, some biscuits and some tinned cheese – we decided against buying any flat bread because we thought it looked rather 'suspect'. When we selected the grapes, we had a really good laugh together. There must have been 30,000 grapes on display outside the shop, but there were also clouds of flies all over them! As we were buying them, Harry made the droll remark, 'I would guess that we have a ratio here of about ten flies to every grape!'

On the way to Wadi Musa, we stopped at the well-known Ain Musa (Moses' Spring), which still provides all the water needed for the town. According

to the Bible, this is the place where Moses (in about 1490 B.C.) struck the rock twice, 'and water came forth abundantly' (Numbers Chapter XX).

The water was cool and crystal clear and so we had a good long drink, filled up our water bottles – and made sure that we washed all our fly-ridden grapes really thoroughly!

Although the country round here is semi-arid, the mud hut town of Wadi Musa itself looked well provided for, because I noted a wide variety of crops being grown nearby, including marrows,

Moses' Spring near Petra

238

Approaching the Siq at Petra

courgettes, tomatoes, figs, dates, olives, oranges and vines; and in addition to this, we also saw a number of herds of sheep and goats.

We again saw the respect with which British Army Officers were held in 1953, when we were received most cordially at the spotlessly clean Police Station there. Our Arab friend and guide soon arranged for some ponies (at a good price of 70c each) to take us on, and by 9 o'clock we were riding our docile mounts towards the 'rose-red city', some 2 miles away.

This ride was a most memorable journey: – for the first mile or so we made our way down the wadi, called the 'Gate of the Siq'. We then saw some old tombs carved in the rock-facings on either side of the valley. Soon the valley started closing in, and we found ourselves riding down a narrow gorge for more than half a mile, with cliffs on either side rising to some 300 feet – 'the Siq'. Without warning, this gorge suddenly opened out to reveal a most spectacular Temple called 'the Treasury', carved right out of the red sandstone rock face.

This is the impressive entrance into the historic site of Petra, and the remainder of the old city is to the right of the Treasury, where the whole

Through the Siq to the Treasury at Petra

The Treasury at Petra – the broken column has since been repaired

Tiers of rock cut tombs at Petra

The theatre cut out of the rock at Petra

area opens out into a wide valley. There are no remains of any dwelling houses for the people here, but there is an impressive Roman amphitheatre on the left, with a capacity of some 7,000 people – which amazingly, has been completely carved out of the hillside rock.

Otherwise, most of the site consists of numerous tombs carved out of the rock faces all around the valley – some quite simple, others much more elaborate. The 'Urn Tomb' for instance, is really outstanding. However, the most spectacular struc- ture on the whole site is

The Amphitheatre at Petra

the so-called 'Monastery' building, which is located on a plateau overlooking the rest of Petra, so to see it requires a strenuous climb. Again, this construction is carved out of the rock face in a similar way to the 'Treasury', but this structure is even more impressive and far better preserved.

On the site in general, we were all surprised to find so little excavation work in progress, even though it was clear that many areas would greatly benefit from some additional expert delving. Perhaps much of this has been accomplished and revealed during the intervening years up to 2000.

Petra remained forgotten and neglected until the 19th century, when it was rediscovered by the Swiss traveller Jean-Louis Burckhardt in 1812. The poet John Burgon (1813-1888) immortalised the spectacular 'lost city' when

243

Our Arab Legion Guide at Petra

he wrote in his famous poem:

'But from the rock as if by magic grown,
Eternal, silent, beautiful, alone!
Match me such marvel save in Eastern clime,
A rose-red city – half as old as time!'

Petra was founded by the Edomites in about 1000 B.C., but soon after 300 BC, they were driven out by the Nabateans who made this the capital of their extensive empire.

In ancient times, Petra owed its outstanding prosperity and success to its location in the Esh Sherah mountains, with its well-placed pass through the high range, as well as with its plentiful supplies of freshwater. The city is situated at a point where trading caravans could easily pass through the mountains in both an easterly and westerly direction, and thereby reach the ports on the south-eastern Mediterranean coastline as well as the markets in the Orient and China.

The Nabateans were therefore in control of this key route, and were able to prosper from all the trade passing through. Petra's golden era lasted for some 200 years between 100 B.C. and 100 A.D., and it was during this period that the 'Treasury', the 'Monastery' and most of the other outstanding monuments were constructed. The Romans eventually took over in 106 A.D. and subsequently the Byzantines. However, it was as a result of a bad earthquake in A.D.551, as well as the decline of Byzantium and the resulting increase in Arab raiders, that the city was eventually deserted.

Back at Ma'an on the evening after our visit, we confirmed that our train would be leaving at 7.40 am in the morning, and so we bought 2nd class tickets to Amman costing £1 each, and then went back to the hotel where we gratefully received our first cooked meal since leaving Fayid on the previous morning. I wrote in my diary briefly about the Station Hotel in Ma'an: – 'The room is really quite comfortable, but there is no electricity and although the lavatory does actually flush, it is a pretty low grade one! The cost of the room, including dinner, bed and breakfast, was £1 each, which seemed quite good value to us. Breakfast next morning consisted of a double fried egg and flat bread, butter, jam and cheese. This flat bread seems to be produced in most of the Middle East. It is quite palatable but at times, we found that it is not particularly hygienic for some British digestive systems!' Regarding the train tickets, I wrote, 'it is not worth paying more for the 1st class seats because they are virtually the same as 2nd class. There are bus-like wooden seats in the 3rd class section.'

It was a distance of about 130 miles from Ma'an to Amman and we soon understood why the journey was going to take as long as 9 hours. Not only

A stop at El Qatrani, 45 miles south of Amman

did the ancient German locomotive seldom reach as much as 30 miles per hour, but there were also many long 'social' stops at all the intervening stations! The train's arrival in each town was a big event! I wrote in my diary: – 'On the way, we passed about 6 trainloads of Muslims going on their pilgrimage to Mecca. They were very colourful types and seemed as interested to stare at us, as we were to gawp at them! As we approached Amman, the country became a little more prosperous and from Deba northwards there were more ploughed fields and different types of agriculture from those we had seen before. I also saw a few herds of sheep and goats on the slopes. We eventually arrived in Amman at 5 pm and since we have spent now £15 from our communal purse and have little Jordanian money left, we telephoned our hotel in Amman and arranged to cash a cheque there.'

Amman is the Capital of Jordan and although it is built on the ruins of ancient Biblical and Roman towns, the buildings in the new city have been built during the decades since the railway track was completed at the end of the nineteenth century. We had reserved rooms for one night

Amman Capital of Jordan in 1953

Amman Capital of Jordan in 1953

at the Hotel Continental in the centre of Amman and before we had our evening meal, we had a quick look round the city. We knew that Amman was a modern city and that the only site of any interest was the Roman amphitheatre near the city centre, so we had a good look at this and little else.

The Biblical town of Rabbat Ammon is famous in particular for one compelling story in the 2nd Book of Samuel, Chapter XI, when (in about 1035 B.C.) King David shamefully ensured that Uriah the Hittite was killed in the battle besieging the ramparts of the town – so that our 'dear little David' could marry Uriah's most beautiful wife! This was yet another example of 'sex transcending all!'

Our hotel in Amman was a modern one, but nonetheless, we had our sleep suddenly cut short in the early morning when the muezzins started their loud chanting from their nearby minarets. It was the first time that we had ever heard these piercing, clamorous wails (which last for about 30 minutes!) and it made a lasting impression upon us all.

Winnowing the corn near Jerash

We liked the taxi driver who had brought us from the railway station on Sunday, so we decided to book him again for our trip to Jerusalem on the following day. We negotiated a fare of 5 Dinars (£5) with him – and as arranged, he was outside our hotel at 8 o'clock on the following morning.

Our first stop on that day (10 August) was at Jerash, about 35 miles to the north of Amman, and this was well worth a visit. It is thought that the city was originally founded by Alexander the Great (356-323 B.C.), although most of the remains we saw were constructed during the Roman era, during and after the time of Christ.

Jerash must be one of the most beautiful and best-preserved provincial Roman cities in the Middle East. It is surrounded by hills, so it can be easily seen by climbing one of these hills and looking down on the whole city – with its Temples and Arches and its Forum surrounded by Ionic columns and with its main street (the Cardo) leading down some 800 yards of colonnade up to the North Gate.

When we visited Jerash in 1953, the site had remained virtually untouched

The Oval Precinct at Jerash

The Cardo, the main street leading from the Precinct to the North Gate, Jerash

Jerash, August 1953

by excavation in recent years, although there was clearly much more to be revealed. In the past few decades however, much restoration work has been carried out, so today this ancient city is an even more impressive sight. It was interesting for us to observe the imposing remains of ancient Jerash and then compare it with the primitive, disorder of the 'modern' Arab town nearby.

From here the road goes to the west, and then starts descending into the Dead Sea Depression far below. As we drove downwards, we passed a startling notice by the side of the road which simply stated: 'Sea Level'! At this point, the road could clearly be seen to continue its descent hundreds of feet further downwards. As we descended, the ambient temperature in the car rose until it became stifling!

We drove about 60 miles southwards down the valley of the River Jordan, which lies more than 1,250 feet below sea level, and we then stopped briefly to look at Jericho, an ancient oasis city near the west bank and about 14 miles north-east of Jerusalem 'as the crow flies'.. Although this is the site of one of the oldest cities in the world (thought to date back to about 7000

Near Jericho in the Dead Sea Valley

Harry and Ian – 'Look no hands' in the Dead Sea

B.C.), there was little of historical interest to be seen here. Our lasting memory of the region was the hundreds and hundreds of Palestinian refugees we saw encamped in their distinctive, flat, black tents. These refugees were the result of the recent war between the Arabs and the Jews. It was a shocking sight to behold, but it is quite possible that the people we saw at that time, were the forebears of those Palestinian refugees who are *still* encamped there in similar tents to this day. As Robert Burns might have remarked: 'Even today, they continue to nurse their wrath, to keep it warm.'

Our last stop before driving on to Jerusalem, was to have a bathe in the Dead Sea – the world's saltiest stretch of water. In Arabic its name is Bahret Lut – the Sea of Lot – and it has a salt content of over 25%. No fish are able to live in its waters and even humans find it quite hazardous! When we went in for our exploratory dip, we found swimming very difficult, because feet tend to float above the surface and this can be dangerous, because if any of the salty water gets into the eyes, the effect is excruciating. We were warned that if we ever put our heads under that water, life would just not be worth living! Fortunately, tourism in Jordan had pro-

253

The wilderness in the Judea Hills

gressed sufficiently by 1953, for a fresh water shower to be available after we had finished our experiment!

Jerusalem was now just 25 miles away by road, and after leaving the mostly fertile valley of the River Jordan where we had seen maize, tobacco, tomatoes and various fruit trees being cultivated, the road climbed up and went westward through the arid and inhospitable hills of the Judea wilderness – just the sort of country mentioned by Christ in his parable of *the Good Samaritan*: 'A certain man went down from Jerusalem to Jericho, and fell among thieves...'

We had booked in at the YMCA Hostel in Jerusalem and when we arrived, we were pleased to find that it was well situated close to Herod's Gate and just outside the old city walls. This location suited us admirably, but there was another plus – the food they served us was really excellent!

Jerusalem was a divided city in 1953, split between the Jewish part (which we were unable to visit) and the Jordanian part (which included most of the old city). It is worth briefly mentioning here, the complicated circumstances that led to this illogical situation.

Jerusalem, with the Mount of Olives in the far background

When the Ottoman Empire collapsed after World War I, the Province of Palestine was inhabited by Muslim and Christian Arabs, together with an increasing number of Jews who now wished to re-settle in their 'promised land'. It was agreed by the League of Nations that Britain would be given the unpleasant responsibility of administering the country, but this proved

Damascus Gate in Jerusalem

to be an increasingly difficult task. As the 1930s progressed, sporadic fighting broke out as the Arabs objected more and more to the way the Jewish population was gaining in numbers and gradually using their ascendancy to take over the whole country.

After World War II and the resulting upheaval in Europe, more Jewish people wished to move into Palestine, and since Britain was still responsible for maintaining law and order, their troops had the thankless and unworkable task of restricting the flood of Jews pouring into the country. This led to Jewish terrorist attacks on both the Arabs and the British, and the situation soon became quite untenable for the British. Eventually, in 1947 Britain took the crisis to the United Nations, and warned that it would be withdrawing its troops in the following year. The UN voted to divide Palestine into two states – one Jewish, and the other Arab, whilst Jerusalem would become an international city. The Jews accepted this arrangement, but the Arabs refused; and the unworkable situation continued and worsened.

Britain therefore, thankfully withdrew its troops on 14 May 1948, and soon after this happened, the Jews, led by David Ben-Gurion (1886-1973) proclaimed the State of Israel and a war broke out between the Jews and all the surrounding Arab countries!

Street Scene in Jerusalem

It was Israel who gained the upper hand in this conflict and by the time the UN had negotiated a cease-fire in 1949, Israel had increased its territory by nearly a quarter and almost a million Arabs had lost their homes and possessions and had fled as refugees to neighbouring Arab countries, mainly Jordan. Ever since then, the Arabs have hated the Jews with an inveterate hatred and have sought revenge. When we visited Jordan in 1953, just four years after this bitter conflict, we saw this hatred and resentment wherever we went.

As soon as we arrived in the divided Jerusalem, we soon saw how fascinating and vibrant the city was. We had travelled very little in the Middle East before this time and we were really amazed. We had never seen anything like it in all our lives! Before long however, we also appreciated the other side of the coin.

Apart from the inveterate hatred the Arabs had for the Jews, we soon saw that there was much poverty in the city, and the other most distasteful aspect of the city was the 'un-Christian' attitudes displayed by so many of the 'men of God' we saw at the sacred religious sites. In Jerusalem, all the different Christian Sects are strongly represented – the Roman Catholics, the Anglican, the Eastern Orthodox, the Coptic and the Armenian Churches (and there maybe others) – and by the time we departed from the city, we had

St Francis Street, the old market place, Jerusalem

Hookahs at work in a cafe, Jerusalem

developed a lasting disgust for all the hateful rivalry we saw being shown by the majority of these clerics between themselves. (See page 380).

But before we started our sightseeing of Jerusalem in earnest, we had two important admin tasks to complete: – firstly, to find out the dates of the next ships sailing from Beirut to Limassol, so that we could make our plans for the rest of our holiday; and secondly, to make sure that our Passports were correctly stamped to show that we had in fact entered Jordan by way of Aqaba, where we passed through no Passport Control.

We soon completed our first essential task: – the Travel Agency told us that the two most suitable sailings would be on the night of Sunday 16 August or Saturday 22 August, so we decided to book our passages on the earlier one. This was quickly done, but our second task presented much more of a problem, and it took us many hours to accomplish. It involved 'queuing up' – a term quite unknown in the Middle East – at the crowded, disorganised Immigration Office and after we had eventually reached the front of the throng, being told that our Passports couldn't be stamped until we had produced a letter of confirmation from the British Consulate! So off we went to the British Consulate and after this formality had been completed, back we went again to the pushing and shoving at the Immigration Office to get our

Passports stamped. Not for the last time did we find the systems of administration in the Levant countries absurdly disorganised and chaotic!

It was Tuesday 11 August by then, so we now realised that we should have to leave Jerusalem in three days' time. We decided to spend the rest of that first afternoon looking round the old city by ourselves, and then to arrange a guide for the whole of Wednesday and Thursday.

It is now hard to fully appreciate just how strange and extraordinary it was for us three youths, uninitiated as we were at the time, to be walking round this Old City of Jerusalem for the first time. Everything we saw was so completely new to us: – the crowded narrow streets with their ancient vaulted passageways and arches, the street sellers, the people sitting on their chairs smoking hookahs, the beggars, the maimed, the nuns and the monks, the Moslems and the other colourful churchmen, the persistent shopkeepers inviting us again and again into their shops and the other passers-by who kept offering their services as our guide; the fruit markets with masses of water melons and other exotic fruits, the sweet-smelling shops with colourful spices, beans and other food displayed in their open sacks, the metal merchants hammering out their bangles and broaches – there was something of interest to catch our attention at every turn.

The massive Mosque called the Dome of the Rock, which stands on the site of the Temple built by King Solomon in 10th century BC, dominates the city, and there are numerous other mosques and old churches wherever you look. However, it was not until our little guide Joseph – one of the many Christians living in Jerusalem – started telling us more about the well-known religious sites in the city,

A street scene with man smoking his hookah

259

Street water seller (avoiding the camera), Jerusalem

A refugee girl (avoiding the camera), Jerusalem

Church of Gethsemane, Jerusalem

that we began to realise just how much guesswork and speculation there is being used by the experts in attempting to locate these sites. For instance, no one really knows for certain where either Calvary or the Holy Sepulchre are actually located; and even the most impressive Via Dolorosa – the Sorrowful Way – which is supposed to follow the route taken by Christ with the Cross up to Calvary, is open to much doubt. The city has been destroyed and rebuilt so many times since 30 AD that the narrow street called 'Via Dolorosa' is now situated well *within* the present city walls – which were not built until the 16th century by Sultan Suleiman the Magnificent

This is the reason why we were all particularly impressed by the Mount of Olives and the Garden of Gethsemane, which still overlook the city as they did in the time of Christ. Most of the other important sights on the other hand have changed so much in the past two thousand years that it is easy for cynics to leave the city feeling decidedly sceptical about much of the information being given out so readily.

Our guide Joseph showed us the most impressive Via Dolorosa and the XIV Stages of the Cross in some detail: – starting from the place where Christ had been tried by Pontius Pilate (now covered by a Chapel); and the courtyard of the Procurator's Palace (also now built over); and the cellar where Christ is supposed to have been imprisoned, which included the two holes where His feet had been – this really sounded like a big chunk of kiddology to us – and then onto the very old Church of the Holy Sepulchre (built 335 A.D.); and the supposed site of Calgary, now also well *within* the city walls and covered by another Chapel.

Via Dolorosa in Jerusalem

At all these Churches and religious sites, the Priests from the various Religious Sects were standing by, constantly pestering us for money and then squabbling amongst themselves about the handouts we had given them. I wrote in my diary at the time: 'We do loathe the way all these clerics persistently ask for money. We have come to the conclusion that the Greek Orthodox Priests are the worst offenders – and they aren't even part of our team!' – that was another of Harry Cotter's wry comments!

We went to the Wailing Wall and then on to Bethlehem – now built over and unimpressive – and the Pool of Siloam (St John Chapter IX) – and to the Mount of Olives and the Garden of Gethsemane – and also (most impressive) an alternative possible site of the Garden Tomb, which I thought was far more feasible than the gaudy Church of the Holy Sepulchre.

We finished off the last day in Jerusalem by buying some presents and souvenirs from a local gift shop near Herod's Gate which we had often visited,

At the Wailing Wall

and we had a long chat there with a big crowd of very friendly Arabs about the general situation in their unhappy and divided city. I noted in my diary, that although they showed not the least bitterness towards the British, the Jews were quite a different matter. They really hated all Jews fervently. They told us how the Jews had seized so much of the Arabs' wealth after that ill-fated War of 1948, and afterwards, they had refused to pay them any compensation whatsoever. For instance, one of the Arabs told us that his family had owned a large orange

The 'Garden Tomb'

grove near Jaffa four years ago, but now this had been taken from them. When we finally departed from Jerusalem, we all had many mixed feelings.

Very early next day, Friday 14 August, we had reserved three seats in a car which made the early morning 'newspaper run' to Amman, 60 miles away, so this was sure to drop us off in good time to catch our morning train to Damascus.

The Chrysler car was duly waiting for us at 3 o'clock in the morning outside the YMCA Hostel and whilst we drove eastwards out of Jerusalem, the muezzin were just beginning to make their raucous calls from their minarets across the city. Two other passengers were squashed into the car, and as we went along, the driver stopped periodically to drop off batches of newspapers along the way. When we reached Amman, the driver dumped his remaining bundles in the main street – and then demanded an extra 200 Fils to take us to the station! We decided to 'live and let live', and paid up the extra money without too much fuss. Nonetheless, we did find it galling to be caught out like this so simply! Another 'lesson of life' was learned: – 'Always fix the price of the taxi fare *before* the trip!'

The train journey to Damascus was about 140 miles and after leaving Amman, the railway track took its route up a fertile river valley towards the garrison town of Zarqa, where a main contingent of the Arab Legion was permanently stationed. Our Captain Ronnie Hambleton from 29 Field, happened to be seconded to the Legion at Zarqa during that August, so we had telephoned him from Amman and told him when our train would be passing through. Sure enough, we soon saw Ronnie on the platform, all smiles, waiting to meet us for a chat. There was a great affinity between the Arab Legion and the British Army in 1953, so at any one time there were always a number of selected British officers attached to the Legion as advisors. Ronnie said that he found this temporary secondment very interesting and frequently spoke to the Legion's Intelligence Officer, Sir Patrick Coghill, whom I had met in Cyprus.

After this 'social' stop of some twenty minutes, our train proceeded northwards along the plateau about 3,000 feet high and then across the border into Syria. I noted in my diary: 'The country we passed through is sometimes extremely stony, but in other parts it appeared quite fertile. It looks as if cereals will be growing in much of this land during the next few months.

'We had as companions (in our 1st class compartment costing 800 Fils each) a prosperous and wise old man of about 57 and his son. He is the Pasha of a village south of Amman near Gebel Nebos. We talked with him most of the time, and he gave us a good insight into the Jewish and Arab problem. He says, without bitterness towards us personally, that the British Government let the Arabs down by giving away the land which was rightfully Arab, and by putting so many Arab refugees into Jordan. For this, the people will never trust the British Government again. He said that there is bound to be another war in the region before too long. He said that he loathed the Jews with an inveterate hatred'.

He was known as Thomas Pasha, and he was travelling to Damascus to see his other son, who had trained as a doctor at the Hammersmith Hospital, in London. As his name indicated, Thomas was a Christian, and he acted as our self-appointed guide during much of our stay in Damascus. He knew the city very well, and told us much about its history.

Modern Damascus as it was in 1953

Modern Damascus in 1953

The River Barada running through
modern Damascus in 1953

Modern Damascus as it was in 1953

The old Market in Damascus

The daily fumigation of the Old Market near our hotel

Damascus was first mentioned in Egyptian records as early as 2500 B.C., so even in Old Testament times it was considered an ancient city. In fact, many believe that it is the oldest 'continuously inhabited' city in the world – another possible claimant is Cairo. It lies at over 2,000 feet above sea level, and is about 60 miles eastwards across the Lebanese mountains from the Mediterranean Sea and Beirut. It was then the modern capital of Syria, and a strange blend of the very old and the new – with its Great Mosque and old Citadel surrounded by the ancient city; and connected to the new city, with its trams and modern buildings and its spa-

'A street called Straight'

267

cious gardens and the clear waters of the Barada river running through. We were certainly most impressed by what we saw.

Thomas showed us where it was best for shopping and took us to the old Market and to the Via Recta – 'the Street called Straight', mentioned in the Acts of the Apostles Chapter IX, verse 11. He also showed us what is meant by the term, 'the eye of a needle', as mentioned in Christ's saying: 'It is easier for a camel to go through the eye of a needle than for a rich man to enter into the Kingdom of God' (St Mark Chapter X, verse 25). This saying had always worried me as a child. No one had ever bothered to explain that the,

Thomas in discussion with Ian and Harry

St. John the Baptist's Tomb in the Great Mosque of Ummayyad

so called, 'eye of a needle', was the nickname given to the low, arched entrances through the city walls, which the loaded camel caravans found so very difficult to manoeuvre when entering Damascus.

The Great Mosque of Ummayyad is also quite a sight to behold. It is an immense building and we heard that it is the oldest mosque to have survived intact during all the turbulent times since it was originally built. It was first built as a Christian Church in 5th century, but with the spread of Islam, it was rebuilt and converted into a Mosque in A.D. 708. I noted that the mosaics we saw by the cloisters were extremely old, and we were also told that the tomb within the Mosque contained the body of St John the Baptist – although I have never since read confirmation of this in any reference book.

Neither Ian, Harry nor myself had ever been inside a Mosque before, so we thought the whole experience was very strange and memorable: – the slippers at the entrance, the floors all covered by fine Persian carpets, the high roof inside the building and the enormous dome; and then, the absence of any women inside the Mosque, and all the male worshippers, either walk-ing around gossiping with each other,

A street in the old city

or prostrate in prayer – or in sleep! It was a spectacle well worth seeing.

It was a very good hotel we had in Damascus, although once again, we seemed to be surrounded by nearby minarets, from which all the noisy muezzins did their best – and succeeded – in waking us up in the small

Roof sleepers in the early morning in Damascus

269

hours! The nights were very hot during our stay in the city, and when we looked out of our windows in the early morning, we could see that many of the locals kept cool by sleeping on their flat roofs under the stars.

During that Saturday we were taken to see a wood mosaic factory and the old city again and bought some more knick-knacks and some Damask brocade table cloths (costing £1 each). We also visited the home of Thomas's son. But our short time in Damascus was fast running out, and although we wished to stay longer and to see more, our passage to Cyprus was booked on Sunday night, so we were bound to leave next morning.

After having a final meal with Thomas Pasha and his family, we gave our grateful thanks for his help during our stay. We drank the appropriate toasts to the Royalties of our two countries and also to both our countries and their peoples, and finally said our goodbyes. When we returned to our hotel that night, we all felt that we had made a small contribution to the general *entente cordiale* between our two countries! Next day we left the city with many happy memories.

Delays at the Frontier

Lebanese landscape

Our Chrysler taxi, which we shared with two other passengers, left Damascus at about 7 o'clock in the morning, and our journey westward through the mountains was an interesting one: We started by driving up the fertile valley of the River Barada, and even though it was now high summer, there was plenty of water in the river available for irrigation. Then, after leaving the river valley, we entered more mountainous country which was rocky and infertile.

At the Frontier, we had the usual long delays whilst all the red tape and other formalities were completed – and eventually, we were able to continue into the Lebanon. We drove through the Baider Pass which cuts through the mountains rising to over 6,000 feet on either side, and then downwards towards the coastal plain, where the temperature soon became noticeably warmer. The country here was much more prosperous and fertile and along the side of the road there were melons and other fruits being sold in abundance. By the time we reached Beirut at about 11 o'clock, it was baking hot.

In 1953, Beirut was a very prosperous city. It was nicknamed 'the little Paris' and it was one of the most important banking, educational and trading centres in the whole of the Levant. Sadly, some twenty years later, civil war and bloody strife between the Moslems and the Maronite Christians (and others) had changed this happy situation for the worse. Most of the benefits which had been derived from all this success and wealth, were then thrown away – and maybe lost to the region for ever.

Our first task in Beirut was to collect our tickets from the Shipping Agents which we had booked whilst in Jerusalem. We next needed to have our Passports stamped before we could board our ship, *The Fouadieh*, which we saw docked in the harbour.

When we reached the Passport Office, we found the place extremely crowded and in utter chaos – in fact, much the same as it had been in Jerusalem! After eventually jostling our way through the small entrance door, we saw that the rules were quite simple: – 'it was every man for himself'. After our passports had been stamped, it was equally difficult for us to get outside the office again. It seemed quite clear that this ridiculous situation happened every time a passenger ship set sail from Beirut Harbour!

It took us almost two hours to complete these simple tasks, so there was little time remaining for us to see much of the city. We bought some necessary food and then went straight on board the ship to secure a suitable spot for the crossing. Luckily, the weather was calm. As the light was beginning to fade, *The Fouadieh* set off to Limassol.

Beirut Harbour

CHAPTER 13

Reprise In
Cyprus

The Fouadieh sailed at 7 pm in the early evening, and since the night was warm and the sea remained calm, we slept on deck as intended. We befriended a young Cypriot on board, whom we had previously 'met' in the scrum at the Beirut Passport Office, and we shared our supper and breakfast together, which consisted of an odd mixture of olive bread, peaches, bananas and biscuits! When we reached Limassol, our boat stood out to sea for a short while, waiting for the Custom's Officials to come on board to check our Passports – which they did quickly and efficiently. The contrast between this and our experiences in Beirut and Jerusalem was just laughable!

On the beach at Limassol with our Cypriot friend

With the help of our friendly young Cypriot, we caught the bus from Limassol to Nicosia, and booked our rooms straightaway at Greta's Garden Hotel, a small hotel in the centre of the city recommended to us by John Stansfield, Mike Martin, Dick Brimelow and others who had passed that way.

The rest of that day, we had a good look round the narrow streets of the old city of Nicosia, a city founded as long ago as the 7th century BC, and I was very happy to have another look at Matexas Square, Socrates Street and Ledra Street. We had a walk round much of the 3 miles of Venetian battlements which encircle the city, and since we had all decided to have a sports jacket made during our stay in Cyprus, I took Harry and Ian to the tailor called Nicolaon, who I had used during my previous visit. Nicolaon recognised me as soon as I walked in through the door, and according to the custom in many shops in Cyprus at that time, he immediately offered us a welcome drink of thick Turkish coffee and a glass of water or a cold orangeade. After choosing the material for our jackets and being measured up, we saw some more of the town, and then finished the day with an excellent evening meal at Greta's Garden Hotel.

Whilst we were discussing our holiday over dinner, we all agreed that although the past ten days in Jordan, Syria and the Lebanon had been really fascinating and most enjoyable, Cyprus appealed to us the most because we felt so much more 'at home' here. The whole country seemed to be far better organised:– most people spoke English; the traffic drove on the left; the road signs were the same as those at home; the pillar-boxes were painted red; and the policemen looked much more trustworthy! It was, in fact, rather like Britain in the sun! I wrote in my diary next day: 'This is the first time during our holiday that we have been given some really good bacon and eggs, some decent bread and butter and some *fresh* milk. Also, after hiring a car tomorrow, we are all quite happy about driving ourselves on the roads out here. I'm sure that I am going to enjoy these last few days in Cyprus.'

Although Barney had allowed me to have three weeks' holiday, Ian Sinclair and Harry Cotter would now have to leave the Island in three days' time. We therefore had to plan how best to use the limited time remaining. After settling all our finances to date, we went out to find a suitable car to hire.

We knew that this might be no simple matter, because the car rental industry in those days was in its infancy, and it was mainly run by petrol and repair garages as a sideline. Also, since there were so few new cars reaching Cyprus in 1953, the ones on offer were a very mixed bag. Most of the cars we saw were fairly old, whereas all the good ones were either too big for us or too expensive. We walked round Nicosia for some time searching without success, but eventually we came across the ideal choice:– a newish, open-top Morris Minor costing £1.50 per day, which would be available for us on the following morning.

Next day we collected the car with great delight, and drove it off towards Famagusta, where Ian and Harry had to arrange their passage back to Port Said in two day's time. Our delight was short-lived however, because after driving a few miles, we suddenly noticed that the petrol gauge was almost empty! The wretched garage must have drained the car down to the very last drop of petrol. Caught again! Anyway, we just managed to limp to the next filling station without mishap, and before long we were happily driving eastwards once again.

After arranging their passages for the following Friday, we looked around the Venetian battlements of Famagusta, and then drove a few miles northwards up the coast, to see the remains of the old Greek city of Salamis – which was visited by St Paul and St Barnabas in A.D. 45 (Acts Chapter XIII, Verse 5). The city had been founded in about 1180 BC, and it was on the sea off Salamis that the Greeks had won a great naval victory against Ptolemy I of Egypt in 306 B.C. Salamis became an important Graeco-Roman port, although a few hundred years after St Paul's visit there, the harbour gradually silted up which caused its importance to decline.

This was the first time that I had seen Salamis, and I was rather disappointed by what I saw. It had obviously been a very large city in its heyday, but much of the area in 1953 remained virtually untouched by the archaeologists and the amphitheatre and temples were mostly overgrown and barely discernable. I noted in my diary: 'the forum (or main square) with a number of columns standing is the most visible part of the site, but I am quite sure that a few years of excavation work on this site will uncover a tremendous amount which is of interest.'

View of the North Coast from the Kyrenia Mountains

We had a swim and a picnic in one of the coves on the east coast, and then returned north-westwards through the Kyrenia Mountains and the northern coastline, which is one of the most attractive parts of the island. We drove through Lefkoniko, and onto Buffavento Castle and then Bellapais Abbey before driving southwards to the central plain back to Nicosia – a journey of about 120 miles.

Next day, we had another most enjoyable trip. We drove north-wards again, and went to the spectacular old Crusader castle of St Hilarion, perched in the mountains at over 2,000 feet, and then down to the lovely ancient harbour of Kyrenia, with its solid 12th century

KYRENIA HARBOUR-CYPRUS.

Kyrenia Harbour in 1953

Kyrenia harbour and Roman lighthouse

St Hilarion – the Crusader castle

With Harry Cotter at the Queen's window at St Hilarion

castle and Roman lighthouse; and then later along the north coast for a swim and a picnic. Few people live in the beautiful north-eastern corner of the Island – the 'pan-handle' – where the country is wild and rugged, and where the roads are narrow and tortuous. It lends itself to ambushes and bandit hide-outs, as shown just two years later, when Grivas and the EOKA started their murderous campaign for Enosis which soon divided this peaceful Island.

Time was fast running out for Ian and Harry, and on Friday we drove again to Famagusta to say our goodbyes. The whole holiday had been a wonderful experience for us, and we all agreed that the £30 we had each spent on it had been well worth the cost! We had had so many laughs together, and during that jam-packed fortnight, a cross word had never passed between us.

I watched *HMS Empire Peacemaker* making its way down the coast from Farmagusta, and then I drove back alone to my hotel – perfectly contented. I wrote in my diary that night:– 'I am really looking forward to this next week by myself. I can do just whatever I please, and I can go to some of those parts in the west of the island that I have never seen before.'

On the week that Ian and Harry had departed from Famagusta, I also noted two events in my diary which were of great interest to all of us stationed in the Middle East. On Thursday 20 August 1953, I wrote:– 'There is currently some turmoil in Persia (Iran). A coup d'état is reported, and the Shah has at last overthrown Mossadegh, and regained power – what a chaotic country!' Of course, unrest of this nature might well cause repercussions elsewhere in the area.

On the following day, I also noted another quite different matter:– 'I have read today that there have been a number of bad earthquakes in the Ionian Islands off Greece, and at least a hundred people have been killed.' There were, in fact, more earthquakes towards the west of Cyprus during September 1953, when some 40 more people were killed.

On the Sunday, I booked out of Greta's Garden Hotel until the following Tuesday, and with the hood of my little Morris Minor firmly down, I set off on my trip round the western part of the island:– 'I drove south through some vineyard country and along the coast to Limassol; then further west, past the British sovereign base at Akrotiri, and stopped on the way to see the Crusader castle of Kolossi (nothing much) – and then on to Curium'.

I was very pleased to have had a really good look at Curium (or Kourion), because it turned out to be one of the most impressive sites I saw on the Island. It had been an old Graeco-Roman city, originally founded by the Mycenaeans in about 1400 BC, and it must have been quite a prosperous city in its day. There are many interesting remains of buildings covering a large area – including a well-preserved public baths and a basilica – but the most spectacular sight of all is the Greco-Roman amphitheatre, which is located high on the cliffs overlooking the coastal plain far below. Curium was still an important city in Byzantine times, but as the power of Byzantium declined, it was subjected to continual Arab raids. Then in A.D.365, it was struck by a terrible earthquake from which it never recovered.

Curium amphitheatre in 1953

When I revisited this site in later years, I found that much reconstruction and excavation work had been completed in the meantime. As seen by the photograph of the theatre taken in 1953, most of the stone slabs at that time had been removed or scattered. These have now been replaced or put into position again.

It was not until the late afternoon that I finally left Curium and continued to drive westward along the picturesque coastal road towards Paphos. On the way, I stopped briefly to look at the Rock of Romios, situated in its pebbly bay, the place where Aphrodite, – the goddess of love – is said to have emerged from the foam in all her glory! As light was beginning to fail, I parked the car by the deserted rocky shoreline just south of Paphos.

In 1953, there were no buildings whatsoever along this stretch of the coastline. Nowadays, the area has been transformed by the construction of a string of modern tourist hotels, each with its own new sandy beach and jetty, as well as by a network of service roads nearby skirted by holiday homes and villas. After parking that night, I slept in the car, and then in the morning, had an early morning swim, before eating an excellent breakfast at a nearby tavern for just 2 shillings (10 pence)!

Undeveloped Paphos in 1953

The Soli amphitheatre ravaged by time

That morning, I had a brief look at Paphos, which I noted was an unimpressive town, and then drove northwards to Polis, and afterwards eastwards along the coast towards Morphou. This northwest region is a most attractive part of Cyprus. The coastline is rocky but there are many sandy bays, and the country is both rugged but fertile. There are banana plantations in the area, and grapes are cultivated in every suitable space. On the way along the northern coast I stopped at Soli, which was on my list of places to visit. I found that there was nothing much to see of this old city, which was once such an important centre for exporting Cypriot copper. Even the Greek amphitheatre (which was shown on the postage stamps at the time) was in a much neglected state, and at the time had none of its original stones left in place.

Copper has been mined in Cyprus for more than 5,000 years and in the Greek language, 'kypros' is the word still used both for the metal and for the name of the Island. In 1953, copper was still being mined in the hills near to Soli, but the mines were then being owned and run by international companies. As a result of this, there were many expatriate families living in the area. I mention this last point because of a small incident that happened to me on that day.

Prickly pears, carobs and palm trees near Paphos

I knew that the beaches further east towards Morphou were not so good for bathing, so I was keen to find a suitable sandy beach for me to swim along this north-western stretch of the coastline. At last, I saw a deserted sandy beach to my liking, and although there was a large notice by the car park which stated that the beach was strictly reserved for employees of the near-by mining company, I was quite sure that this inhospitable notice had nothing to do with me. I therefore parked my little car and changed into my swimming trunks for a swim.

As I walked across the virtually deserted beach towards the sea, I said (most amiably) to a young wife sitting there with her young child, that I was quite sure that the company wouldn't mind if I had a quick swim on their beach. However, she told me straightaway that, in fact, she *did* mind me having a swim there – this was a *private* beach! After a brief (but most amiable) chat with her however, she soon revised her objections. I later wrote in my diary: 'During our conversation, this expatriate wife expressed a most arrogant attitude towards Cyprus in general, in which she was (after all) living as a *temporary guest*. She told me that she thoroughly disliked all Cypriots – to which I replied (again most amiably) that I had

282

always found the Cypriots a most friendly and pleasant bunch. Anyway, after making my point on this issue, and after having my refreshing swim, I resumed my journey towards Morphou without more ado'.

Morphou lies at the centre of a wide, well watered valley, and it was in 1953 a most important area for growing oranges and all other citrus fruits. Nowadays, this lucrative area has, of course, been lost to the Greek Cypriots living in the south of the Island. Since 1974, this region has been part the Turkish Republic of Northern Cyprus, and as a consequence, all the names of the towns in the north have now been changed – Morphou for instance is called Güzelyurt; and Kyrenia, is called Girne; and so on.

I drove through Lapithos (as it was then called), and went along the north coast towards Kyrenia. Similar to the previous evening, I parked the car by a deserted beach overnight. After reading another chapter of Neville Shute's *The Far Country,* I settled down to another night's sleep in the car. Afterwards, I wrote in my diary: 'a restful enough night'. Such is youth!

A northern bay with village bread kiln where I stayed the night

On this last day of my trip, I was again up at the crack of dawn for my early morning swim, and I then went along to the village, and had a chat with the friendly local baker whilst he baked his bread for the day. I bought one of his olive-loaves as he took it from his kiln, and I then went to the near-by tavern overlooking the bay, for my breakfast, this time costing 3 shillings (15 pence!)

On the way back to Nicosia that day, I decided to take a circuitous route over roads going east from Kyrenia and then southwards through the mountains, which were mostly quite unknown to me. I wrote:– 'The drive was really beautiful, but it was also often quite dangerous and difficult, due to the width of the road and the speed of some of the oncoming traffic. But the coastline again was magnificent to look at, although much of the sand on the beaches was unattractive and dark in colour, and other parts seemed much too rocky for any good swimming.'

When I hit the main road not far from Famagusta, I drove back to Nicosia and then 20 miles beyond, to have another look at the well-known 10th century church at Peristerona, built by the side of a dried up river-bed. The

10th century church of Peristerona

The road between Nicosia and Famagusta

Famagusta battlements

Kyrenia harbour at dusk in 1953

detour was well worth the effort, because this Greek Orthodox Church is really quite exceptional, and the inside is extremely ornate. I noted that all around the walls there were many ancient paintings and icons depicting the Saints of old.

That evening, when I returned the Morris Minor to the garage, I recorded faithfully in my diary that we had driven over 575 miles during the past week, and used just 14 gallons of petrol – that's about 41 miles to the gallon.

It was very pleasant to be back at Greta's Garden Hotel for those last two days of the holiday. Not

On leave in Cyprus

286

only was the hotel comfortable, and Greta a friendly and welcoming host-
ess, but I had also made friends with a group of young American guests who
were still staying at the hotel when I returned. There were also some other
tasks to be completed before I left:– I had to confirm my return flight to the
Suez Canal Zone with Air Movements; and to collect the jackets and
trousers from the tailors; and to buy some more Van Heusen shirts; and
also to walk round the city and to say my goodbyes to a number of friendly
shopkeepers I now knew. But furthermore, before I left this cornucopia of
goodies in Cyprus, I also wanted to send off some food parcels to my poor,
deprived family at home!

This may seem strange to us today, but rationing didn't end completely
until July 1954, and many of these 'goodies' were still seldom seen in the
shops in Britain. I noted in my diary exactly what I sent and the cost,
including postage:

1lb box of Milk Tray chocolates (9s/4d (47$\frac{1}{2}$ pence)
Large box of Scotch Shortbread (9s/3d (47 pence)
Chocolate coins (4 shillings (20 pence)
Postage: 10s/6d (52$\frac{1}{2}$ pence)

And in the second parcel:–

1lb raisons (1s/1d (5 pence))
2lb sultanas (4s/4d (22 pence))
2lb currants (4s/8d (23 pence))
2 tins of cream (2s/8d (13 pence))
2lb of ham (16 shillings (80 pence))
$\frac{1}{2}$lb of almonds (2s/4d (12 pence))
Postage: 12 shillings (60 pence)

***

It is extremely difficult for an outsider to fully understand the reasons why
an apparently contented, prosperous and friendly population like the one I
saw in Cyprus during 1952 and 1953, can so quickly deteriorate into an
uncivilised, murderous, racist community, riddled with hatred and recrim-

inations. The only possible answer seems to be: that innate and fervent desire for 'Enosis' which will condone indiscriminate EOKA murder and terrorism, spurred on by a big dose of 'religion' – in other words, much the same ingredients as those which existed in Northern Ireland.

In the case of Cyprus, the bombings and the random murders of Britons, Greek-speaking Cypriots and Turkish-speaking Cypriots, carried out by Grivas – a Greek, not a Cypriot – and his EOKA terrorists, eventually led the whole Island into a bloody civil war, which resulted in ethnic cleansings and a totally divided country.

So what led up to all this turmoil and strife? And why was Britain so much involved in Cyprus anyway? And how long had 'Enosis' been such a driving force for the Greek-speaking Cypriots? After all, the Greek Cypriots are descendents of the Mycenaean Greeks who settled on the Island over three thousand years ago, and their language is a strange version of the one now spoken on mainland Greece. In addition, very few Greek Cypriots had ever visited mainland Greece, and the people are really far less 'Greek', than the Australians or the Canadians are English, Welsh, Irish or Scottish.

More than anything else, Enosis and the innate bond between all Greek-speaking peoples has been caused by thousands of years of confrontation and conflict with the neighbouring Turks, and in recent centuries, with the subjugation of their peoples by the Turks in the eastern Mediterranean. From this starting point therefore, here is a very brief summary of events, which attempts to explain some of the main ingredients of this complicated conundrum:–

From 1500 BC, the Island of Cyprus has been annexed in turn through the centuries by Egypt, Assyria, Persia, Rome, Byzantium, the Knights Templar, the Lusignans; and in more recent times, from 1489 until 1571 by the Venetians, and then by the Ottomans (or Turks) until the British took over in 1878.

It was in 1571 that the expanding Ottoman Empire had defeated the Venetians in Cyprus; and from then onwards, for nearly 300 years, the Island was governed neglectfully by the Ottomans with most of the taxation money being returned directly to Istanbul whilst only minimal improvements to the province were ever made. It was during this period also, that most of the Turkish-speaking Cypriots were sent to settle in the country. These were a real mixture of people, but the majority consisted of about 20,000 Janissaries, the soldiers pressed into the Ottoman Armies from all the Empire's subject countries.

During the reign of Catherine the Great (1762-1796), Russia doubled the size of its landmass by conquests, and by the 1840s, it was looking more and more aggressively towards the south, and in particular, towards the possessions of the crumbling Ottoman Empire. This attitude in turn caused alarm in Britain and in France, because aggression in this direction could easily develop into further expansion into the Levant, and also into the whole of the Middle East, and this could eventually lead into Persia, and then onto India. This rationale was the main reason why both Britain and France were encouraged to support the Ottoman Turks against Russia in the disastrous Crimean War which lasted from 1853 until 1856.

Because of Britain's alliance with the Ottomans during that War, and due to the continuing threat of Russia in the region, Turkey and Britain signed an agreement in 1878, whereby Britain undertook to safeguard Turkey against further Russian aggression, but in return would take over the administration of Cyprus, although Turkey would continue to retain sovereignty over the Island.

At this stage (1878), most Greek speaking Cypriots were happy with this arrangement, because they expected Britain to soon transfer Cyprus over to Greece in the same way as it had done with the Ionian Islands in 1864 – mainland Greece itself had won its independence from the Ottomans in a bitter war in 1829.

But Britain soon found that Cyprus – situated as it was so strategically near to the British-owned Suez Canal and also on the most direct route to India – was ideally placed for basing its troops to guard the region. But another important consideration which prevented its immediate transfer to Greece was the fact that some 18% of the population now consisted of Turkish Cypriots, and they were *totally* against *ever* becoming *Greek* citizens! In any case, the Ottoman Government had made it quite clear from the start that it was also totally against any transfer to Greece.

So the years passed by, and instead of Enosis, Britain gave the Greek Cypriots a much better administration on the Island, reforestation, improved farming methods, an end to banditry, a British legal system, good policing, new water supplies, new roads and the stamping out of disease and locusts. All these improvements were most important and beneficial to the inhabitants, but the changes were soon accepted as the norm, and this had nothing to do with Enosis, for which all the Greek-speaking Cypriots craved so deeply.

When Turkey entered World War I on Germany's side in 1914, Britain immediately annexed Cyprus, and in the Treaty of Lausanne which followed the end of that war, Turkey had to renounce all future claims to the Island. Britain however, waited until 1925 before officially making Cyprus a British Crown Colony, and they went ahead with this in spite of continued rumbles for Enosis. Not long afterwards, in 1931, there were some civil disturbances on the Island, when Government House was burned down, but order was restored after a period of martial law, and the situation was soon returned to normal. During World War II, just a few years afterwards, both Greek and Turkish Cypriots fought alongside the British forces in Europe and North Africa.

The Germans and the Italians occupied mainland Greece and Crete during World War II, and after their expulsion in 1944 (with the help of British troops), the USSR under Stalin tried to incorporate the country into the Eastern Block by promoting a civil war there. In spite of this threat, Greece maintained its independence, much with the help of British troops. After all this upheaval, and also due to its inept Government, Greece remained impoverished well into the 1950s, and was therefore sure to be a poor and unhelpful partner during any association with Cyprus, which was comparatively much more prosperous. Nonetheless, the possibility of a drop in living standards made no difference to the Greek Cypriots, whose minds were firmly fixed on unification with the homeland of their ancestors.

By the 1950s, muted demands for Enosis were beginning to grow slightly louder amongst a section of the Greek Cypriots, encouraged by the Greek

Orthodox priests. Even so, by the time of my first visit there in 1952, signs of the campaign were insignificant, except perhaps for a tiny amount of isolated graffiti here and there. During 1954, members of EOKA – translated 'National Organisation of Cypriot Fighters' – started to be recruited in Cyprus by Grivas and Archbishop Makarios, and they decided to start their terrorist campaign in the following year by setting off explosives all round the Island on 1 April 1955. Random killings and haphazard violence followed throughout 1955 and 1956, when the EOKA terrorists murdered British servicemen, innocent civilians, pro-British Greek and Turkish Cypriots – as well as left-wingers and any others who disagreed with their views. These indiscriminate killings inevitably spread hatred and distrust throughout the Island and this completely divided the population.

All these months, the Greek Cypriot population condoned these random murders and acts of terrorism, and showed little or no consideration nor concern for the feelings of their compatriots, the Turkish Cypriot minority. As a result, these became increasingly uneasy about the violence and the possibility and prospect of joining up with Greece. In due course, it was this lack of understanding which eventually proved to be the Greek Cypriots' undoing.

The independent Republic of Cyprus was launched in 1960, but by then Grivas and his EOKA terrorists had destroyed all goodwill within the two Cypriot communities. Within 3 years, there was serious sectarian violence, and the Turkish Cypriots retreated into ghettos for protection, and also formed their own terrorist Resistance Organisation (TMT) to counter the EOKA.

In an attempt to keep the peace, the United Nations established a force on the Island by 1964, but there was now so much hatred between the Greek-speaking Cypriots and the Turkish-speaking Cypriots that violence was never far below the surface.

By the end of the terrorism, the death toll of innocent people caused by Grivas and the EOKA terrorists had climbed to the appalling figure of nearly 600, and of these, 346 young British servicemen had been murdered, whilst the remainder were policemen, or just about anyone else living in Cyprus who disagreed with them!

A few EOKA terrorists were killed in the fighting, but when 9 of the convicted murderers were hanged in 1956, in spite of all the indiscriminate murders they had perpetrated, there were violent protests in Greece and elsewhere in the world, and relations between Britain and Greece plunged to an all-time low! Such is the way of the world.

The problem continued to simmer, and it remained unresolved during the 1960s in spite of many attempts by the UN to find a satisfactory negotiated solution. However, perhaps this was never a possibility after Grivas and his band of murderers had opened their Pandora's box.

The Turkish Government eventually mounted a full-scale invasion of the Island during July 1974, and their forces quickly occupied all the northern part of the country, including Famagusta on the east coast and Morphou in the west (about 37% of the Island). In the process of this drastic action, many Cypriots were killed, and some 200,000 Greek Cypriots were evicted from their homes in the North and sent to the South; whilst conversely, about 100,000 Turkish speaking Cypriots were moved northwards from their lands in the South. Since that time, Cyprus has remained a divided country, and the result of that bloody conflict has been a lasting antagonism between the Greek Cypriots and the Turkish Cypriots on the Island.

Looking back on the contented Island I saw during my short visits there, it is clear that those years of 1953 and 1954 were a watershed in the history of Cyprus, and there must be many Cypriots who now would wish to go back to those halcyon years again, and to let the country evolve without all the bloodshed and bitterness. How will history and the inhabitants of Cyprus eventually judge the part played by Grivas and his EOKA terrorists in the fate of Cyprus?

To end these brief comments about Cyprus at this time, I have included an interesting and pertinent extract from Lawrence Durrell's book, *Bitter Lemons of Cyprus*, which he wrote about his life in Cyprus during this period soon after the dawning of 1954. He spoke the Greek language well, and he was living at that time in the northern hills near Bellapais, just south of Kyrenia.

Here he relates an incident which happened whilst he was having a convivial evening at a local tavern run by his friend Clito, when a local Greek Cypriot called Frangos, became increasingly drunk and loose-tongued in voicing his true feelings about British rule and Enosis. There must have been many mixed feelings amongst the other customers in the tavern. The anecdote also illustrates the dilemma in which many other Cypriots found themselves in their attitudes towards the British, after years of friendliness and harmony together:–

'Every time he has a Name Day in his family he drinks. He's a strange one.' 'Strangeness' in Greek means 'a character'. One indicates the quality by placing one's bunched fingers to the temple and turning them back and forth in a manner of someone trying a door-handle. Clito made the gesture furtively and let it evolve into a wave – towards a chair from which I could watch the fun. 'His name is Frangos,' he said, with the air of a man who explains everything in a single word.

'Who dares to say I am drunk?' roared Frangos for perhaps the ninth time, blowing with the same breath a squeak or two from his handsome brass flute. More guffaws. He then began a splendid tirade, couched in the wildest language, against the damned English and those who endured them with such patience. The policemen began to look more alert at this, and Clito explained hastily: 'When he goes too far...pouf! They cut him off and take him away.' With his two fingers he edited a strip of cinema film. But Frangos seemed to me a formidable person to cut off in this fashion. He had shoulders like an ox. One of the policemen patted him awkwardly and was shaken off like a fly. 'Why,' bellowed Frangos, 'do you tell me to shut up when I am saying what everyone knows?' He gave a toot on his instrument and followed it up with a belch like a slammed door. 'As for the English I am not afraid of them – let them put me in irons.' He joined a pair of huge fists dramatically. A couple of timid English spinsters peered nervously into the tavern as they passed. 'Let them fire on me.' He tore open his shirt and exposed an expanse of breastbone curly with dense black hair with a gold cross nestling in it. He

waited for a full half-second for the English to fire. They did nothing. He leaned against the bar once more, making it creak, and growled on, lashing his tail.

Frangos took another stately draught of the white cognac before him and turned a narrow leonine eye upon me. 'You observe me, Englishman?' he said with contemptuous rudeness. 'I observe you,' I replied cheerfully, sipping my drink. 'Do you understand what I say?' Somewhat to his surprise I said: 'Every word.' He leaned back and sighed deeply into his moustache, flexing his great arms and inflating his chest as prize-fighters do during a preliminary work-out. 'So he understands me,' he said in coarse triumph to the world in general. 'The Englishman, he actually understands.'

I could see from everyone's expression that this was regarded as having gone a bit too far – not only because I was English, but because impoliteness to any stranger is abhorred. The policemen stood up and braced themselves for the coming scuffle. Clito wagged his head sadly and uttered an apologetic po-po-po. This was obviously the point where our friend got himself edited like a strip of film. The policemen showed an understandable reluctance to act, however, and in the intervening silence Frangos had time to launch another derisive shaft at me. He threw up the great jut of his chin squarely and roared: 'And what do you reply to me, Englishman? What do you think sitting there in shame?'

'I think of my brother,' I said coolly.

'Your brother?' he said, caught slightly off his guard by this diversion, which had just occurred to me.

'My brother; he died at Thermopylae, fighting beside the Greeks.'

This was a complete lie, of course, for my brother, to the best of my knowledge, was squatting in some African swamp collecting animals for the European zoos. I put on an air of dejection. The surprise was complete and a stunned silence fell on the wine-impregnated air of the tavern. Clito himself was so surprised that he forgot to turn off the tap in the great cask of red wine and a stain began to spread across the dusty flea-bitten floor. Frangos looked as though someone had emptied a slop-pail over him, and I was rather ashamed of taking this easy advantage of him. 'Your brother,' he mumbled slowly, swallowing, not quite knowing which way to turn, and yet at the same time being unwilling to be so easily discountenanced.

'The Cypriots forget many things,' I said reproachfully. 'But we don't forget. My brother's corpse does not forget, and many another English boy whose blood stains the battlefield....' I gave them a fragment from a newspaper peroration which I had once had to construe during a Greek lesson and which I had memorized for just such occasions. Frangos looked like a cornered bull, sheepishly turning his great head this way and that. A fleeting expression of shy reproach crossed his face. It was as if he had said aloud: 'How damned unfair of you to introduce your brother just when I was getting into my stride. Perfidious Englishman!' I must say I sympathised; but I was unwilling to lose my advantage. It was clear that if I harped on my imaginary brother it would not be long before Frangos could be wrung out like a wet dishrag. 'Your brother,' he mumbled again, uncertain of the proper mood to wear. I saved him now by calling for more drink and he subsided into a smouldering silence at the end of the room, casting a wicked eye at me from time to time. He was obviously turning over something in his mind.

'Englishman,' he said at last, having worked the whole thing out to his satisfaction, 'come and stand beside me and drink to the palikars (the Greek soldiers during the struggle for independence from Turkey) of all nations.' This was indeed a handsome toast and I lost no time in honouring it in brandy.

Bitter Lemons of Cyprus, first published in 1957, Faber and Faber, pages 39 to 41.

Travelling round the Island during 1952 and 1953, I met and spoke freely to all types of Cypriots – on buses and boats; in taverns, restaurants and cafés; in queues and shops; and in a multitude of other public places. Everywhere I went, I *always* found the Cypriots well disposed towards the British, and I never ever came across any hint of animosity or rancour displayed towards me because I was British. Everywhere I went, I met with friendliness and an unreserved welcome. We humans are a strange, puzzling, capricious group of creatures – especially when religion, tribe, nationality or dogma influence our attitudes!

So back to Thursday 27 August 1953:– I had already booked a flight back to Fayid on that day, but when I arrived at the Airport, I was told that I should have to wait until the following day.

This was no problem for me, because I knew that I could easily find a bed for the night, and I was also quite certain that 29 Field could exist without me for another day! I therefore went along to Wayne's Keep, the nearby army camp where 49 Field was stationed, and I was soon made to feel welcome in their spacious Officers' Mess. I always found a great camaraderie in the Army in those days, and I also considered that there was an extra friendliness between Gunners in these circumstances – but perhaps I am romanticizing!

I soon saw some Subalterns I had met during 1952. Two of them, Philip Vaughan and Frank Samworth, had attended our cocktail party at Government House in November, and two Regulars, David Holmes and Robert Darrell, had been to one of the Governor's luncheon parties in October. I mention their names here, because it is quite possible that some of them may be known to others reading these recollections. Two other Subalterns I met in the Officers' Mess that evening, were David Bastin and Bill Jesson, both of whom I gave a good write-up in my diary!

On the following day Frank Samworth, who was soon to be demobilised, drove me to the Airport down the road, and saw me off.

Thus ended another episode in these recollections; and with no particular feelings of sadness, I was quite happy to return once more to the great sand-pit – and to complete my last four months soldiering with 29 Field.

CHAPTER 14

More About Life in MELF

The desert area to the west of Ava Camp was set aside as a Gunnery Range, and this was in constant use by all the Gunner Regiments in 1 Infantry Division and 3 Armoured Brigade. To prevent accidents during firing, there were many strict safety measures in force, and one of the most important of these was to have an independent Safety Officer attached to each Troop of guns firing.

The Subalterns in all the Field and Light Regiments were often given this task to do, and although the role included considerable responsibility, it was certainly not an arduous job, and I think most of us enjoyed being away from the routines of camp life for a few days. We used to drive off with our small teams of Tec Accs (or TARAs) and attach ourselves to our assigned Troop of guns, and then make sure that we interfered with them as little as

Leaving Ava Camp for firing on the ranges

25 pounder of 41 Field firing on the ranges

possible. We looked after ourselves, arranged our own meals, and brewed up whenever we wanted to, and slept at night without the need for guards. We only needed to be on duty when the guns were preparing to fire or when they were firing. We then had to check carefully to prevent any gross errors in the calculations, or in the laying of the guns. The most crucial time was when the guns were firing over or near to their own OP (those in the Observation Post directing the shoot), because that is the time when any shortfall in range could be really dangerous. The range set on all the guns could always be simply checked by confirming that all the barrels were parallel in elevation.

One of our sister Regiments in 1 Infantry Division, 41 Field, had their Practice Camp on 18 and 19 February 1953, and I noted that Dick Brimelow, Harry Cotter, Tom Keeble, John Stansfield, Mike Logan and myself were all acting as Safety Officers for those two days. On 18 February I wrote: – 'I am taking Slater and Brown as my TARAs and Snape as my driver for George Baker (my 4-wheel drive GPO vehicle). We loaded up with all the technical equipment needed and plenty of tins of food: – picnic lunches, spam, tomato soup, beans, potatoes, condensed milk, tea and sugar – and arrived at the meeting place at 9 o'clock, where I attached myself to Dog Troop of 105 Battery'.

'When they moved off, we followed them down the Cairo Road as far as Gebel Iweidid, and then we cut inland, and past the 'railway station', and took up a position just inside the Range. It was lucky for Dog Troop that they did-n't start firing from that location because the Regimental survey of their position was completely wrong; and I also found that one of their guns was set up 10° off for line! We (in 29 Field) were not at all impressed by all these dreadful mistakes, but then we were happy to be merely observers and able to take a completely detached view of their predicament! Later, after the day's firing, I slept out in the open, but since it was mid winter in Egypt, I regretted not having brought my greatcoat with me'.

My GPO Truck, George Baker

The following morning I wrote: 'It was very cold during the night, so I was longing for the sun to rise again. I stirred our blokes at 6.15 (0500 hrs was reveille time for the toilers!), and we had our breakfast of spam and beans, plus a jam sandwich and a mug of sweet tea. The meal last night, which 41 Field gave us, was a horrible stew. We also thought that the Subalterns in 105 Battery were not at all hospitable towards John (Stansfield) and me. Before lunch we advanced yet again to the final Gun Position; and the end of Practice was declared at 2 o'clock. For lunch we cooked up a super 'stew' of tomato soup, spam, beans and potatoes, which went down very well indeed! I think that we have all quite enjoyed being out during these last two days. It is always quite satisfying to be able sit back and watch other people do all the work! On the other hand, the main trouble with being Safety Officer is that there is always the possibility of having to 'take the can back' if ever there is a calamity!'

'I was very pleased to see Tony Opperman again (who I knew from Oswestry days), and I had a long chat with him, and have always enjoyed his company. By chance, he was one of the TARAs in Dog Troop, and yesterday I suddenly heard his voice jabbering away in the Troop Command Post. I was very sorry when he failed to pass his WOSB, because I am quite sure that he would have made a really good officer. Nonetheless, he says that he is quite happy in 41 Field. When we returned to Ava Camp that afternoon, instead of taking the easier, longer route south and back along the road again, I decided to take the more direct route eastwards by driving on a compass-bearing right across the miredahm. We found our way back and avoided all mishaps without any problems.'

I wonder how many nineteen year old youths of today ever have an opportunity like that, of driving more than 30 miles across the trackless desert completely on their own? National Service certainly had its benefits, as well as its disadvantages.

Further on the subject of Safety Officers, a few months later, I experienced some Mortar Batteries in action for the first time. I include this extract from my diary, mainly because these notes also give some further insight

181 Light Battery firing their 4.2 Mortars

into life in Ava Camp: – 'Since I am Safety Officer today with 181 Light Battery, I had to get up early this morning, and be ready to meet them at 6.15, so they could start firing about 7.30. At first, it was rather strange checking these 4.2 mortars, but after a few shoots I found the job quite easy. I was told that all I really had to do was to ensure that the line of fire didn't go within 900 yards of their Observation Post. I therefore only had to worry about the change in line they made on the mortar. They didn't fire for long but packed up a 11 o'clock'. (I expect that their allocation of ammunition was in short supply!)

I went on: 'Since I am ROO today, John (Stansfield) looked round the camp for me in my absence (this 'stand in' arrangement often happened between Subalterns) but I took over as soon as I returned to camp. Brigadier Davies was our guest at the Dinner Night tonight, since he has just taken over as our new Brigade Commander. He looked rather like an over-nourished American businessman, but he seemed to be quite a pleasant individual. I turned out the Guard at midnight. There is no water supply in the Ava Camp again at the moment. We are told that there is a blockage in the pipe, but really, this has been a problem on and off ever since I first arrived in the Canal Zone! It is so annoying not being able to have a shower whenever you want to, especially after sport. The Regimental water trucks are continuously on the go to keep up our supplies. A few weeks ago we also had another electricity power cut for part of the day!!'

Before I finish these remarks about firing the guns, I ought to relate an extraordinary occurrence we sometimes saw on the ranges: – the shells we fired in 25 pounder guns had copper driving-bands round the outside of the casings. These were put there to enable the shells to rotate in the air for greater accuracy, after being propelled through the rifling in the barrel. When the shells later exploded, these copper bands were scattered all over the ground, and of course, the bits of copper metal were comparatively valuable. The local Egyptians soon realised this fact, and strange to relate, we sometimes saw them searching for these pieces of copper on the ranges, even when we were still firing the guns! Heavens knows how many were injured during the course of a year.

***

Major Rex King was the Battery Captain of 8 Battery – Barney's second-in-command – and since he had a far more relaxed attitude towards soldiering than Barney, he was an excellent foil to him in the Battery. He was a bachelor and a heavy smoker, and he had originally trained in the Indian Army. He was one of the great characters in the Mess and a most amusing raconteur. During the War had fought for many years on the Burma Front against the Japanese, and he told us many tales about their suicidal fanaticism. He was a most friendly and congenial character, and he always had time to talk to the Subalterns. He had a yacht moored on the Great Bitter Lake at the Officers' Club in Fayid and often sailed with my friends John Stansfield, Mike Logan and Ray Kelly.

As you know, many Middle Eastern countries in 1953 maintained strong links with the British Armed forces, and often asked for our officers to be sent to their armies as advisors. Rex King was one of those who was seconded to the Iraqi Artillery for a spell during my time with 29 Field, and on his return, he told us plenty of interesting tales about his experiences there.

He told us that he was not at all impressed by the standards he saw in the Iraqi army, and I recorded just two examples of his remarks: He said for instance, that it was quite common to see one of the Iraqi officers suddenly fly into a temper and to violently strike one of the unfortunate Iraqi soldiers standing nearby! But he also told us that whenever the Iraqi Gunners went out on the ranges for some firing practice, he noticed that every time they went to the same very few positions for their guns. This, of course, made it much easier for them to survey their exact gun positions on the map, and also to calculate all the angles and ranges. In addition, it made it much simpler for all those in the Observation Post to quickly identify all the targets and map references on the landscape presented before them!

Quite naturally, Rex attempted to put a stop to this slack practice straightaway. He strongly advised that the next time they went out firing on the ranges they should occupy a completely new and unknown position on the map. The Iraqis in charge immediately objected most strongly to this suggestion, and a near riot ensued. After further explanations from Rex, it was eventually agreed to do as he said. He thought that he had won the day, but when they next went out on the ranges, the Iraqis completely disregarded his instructions, and doggedly went back to one of their old familiar haunts!

This example of bad training in the Iraqi Army epitomized the state of many other Middle Eastern armies in those days (with the exception of the Israeli Army and the Arab Legion) – and the Egyptian Army in 1953 was a classic example of this.

It was well known from our Intelligence information that the Egyptian Army was many times larger than the four, under strength, British Brigades stationed in the Suez Canal Zone, but the training and the calibre of the Egyptian soldiers was known to be extremely poor. Also, although their army had many more modern tanks than MELF, very few of them were ever in good working order at any one time! Luckily, this evaluation was never put to the test during my time in the Zone, but later in 1967, during the Six Day War against Israel, the Egyptian Army was soon shown to be of very low military value.

A few words about 'God's little creatures' we saw whilst in the Zone: –

Apart from the swarms of mosquitoes in certain places, and the trillions of horrible, persistent, resistant, irritating flies – some of which could bite through the socks – it is strange to relate that we saw very few other unpleasant insects or creatures during all our time in Egypt. For instance, I don't remember ever seeing a scorpion, although we were always warned to shake out our slippers in the morning before putting them on!

There was however, one isolated incident that should be included here. One evening when everyone was dressing for dinner, a loud bellow was heard from one of the officers' tents. Jim Cummins had been lying on his bed relaxing, when he suddenly saw an enormous spider stalking across the ceiling of his tent! The commotion which followed soon brought most of us along to see what was happening. After the monster had been put under observation, there were plenty of suggestions about how to subdue and entrap the invader, and before long, it had been caught in an upturned basin, and put to death with some chloroform provided by Dr Bill Cattell! It was nearly 5 inches long, and when someone suggested

The 'Camel Spider'

authoritatively that it was a 'camel spider', we all agreed that this sounded a most appropriate name for it – and so it was 'christened' at its demise!

One of the few mammals that exist in this part of the wilderness is the desert fox, although they must have been quite rare. I did catch sight of one once, but that was only in the far distance. On one occasion, some of us also saw one of these animals during a Battery scheme west of Port Suez. During a slack period in the radio transmissions, we all suddenly heard Rex King excitedly shouting: 'Tally-ho! Tally-ho! Yoicks! Yoicks!' as he gave chase to one of these desert foxes in his Land Rover – to no avail of course! We all had a good laugh at the time about this trivial incident. Sudden tomfoolery of this ilk, adds much to the spice of life in dull moments!

Another jocular remark from Rex which went the rounds at the time and caused some fleeting mirth, happened during a scheme we had deep in the unknown desert south of Port Suez. After a quick move south-westwards into unfamiliar ground, the Commanding Officer visited Rex King's Command Post unannounced.

End of Exercise – now for a bathe in the Gulf of Suez

'So where are we now precisely, Major King?' enquired Colonel Shoreland quite seriously.

Looking quickly at the map, Rex replied heartily: 'At this precise moment, sir, I should say that we're somewhere between Gebel and the deep blue sea!' We much enjoyed relating these in-house witticisms.

***

Although I was quite a mediocre cricketer, I see that I played the game quite frequently during my time in the Zone, both for Baker Troop as well as for 8 Battery. Cricket in MELF was played on concrete wickets covered with matting, and most of the matches seemed to consist of just 20 overs per innings – an arrangement not dissimilar to the One Day Matches played in First Class Cricket fifty years later. In the Suez Canal Zone, these local rules meant that everyone had to bat urgently, and all the innings were bound to be short-lived. There were also plenty of run-outs during the matches we played!

On 11 July 1953 for instance, I wrote about a particular match between Baker Troop and Charlie Troop of 79 Battery: – 'Langford and I were the

305

only two batsmen to score many runs!! He got 33 and I got 25. Fortunately the bowling was atrocious. My maxim in cricket is to block all the straight balls about to hit the wicket, and then swipe at anything which is off the stumps! Baker Troop scored 70, and we got them out for 34.'

I bring up this subject, because a short time afterwards, an incident regarding my involvement in the Baker Troop's cricket team really annoyed me at the time. I wrote: – '79 Battery guns are out shooting on the ranges this morning (which included Mike Logan, my tent-mate). I gave TocL Baker (the Baker Troop Leader's vehicle) its 406 inspection for the month. Nothing else much happened this morning.

'Barney made me furious over lunch in the Mess. He came up to me and said that he wanted me to take over the captaincy of Baker Troop cricket team from now on. This is just typical of Barney, and I really wanted to tell him not to interfere with things that he had nothing directly to do with. After all, it is a Troop affair and not a Battery one, but it is not possible for me to speak frankly to Majors like this. I always like the ORs to manage their own cricket team, and only to ask me to play in the team if they really want me to, and not just because I'm an officer – in exactly the same way as happens with the Troop soccer team. Still I have to do as I am told by Barney. To make matters worse, this afternoon we lost a match against RHQ, and I didn't excel myself either. I dropped a catch, and was involved in two run-outs! It was therefore not a good day for me. I was really furious with Barney for interfering like that though'. This was yet another irritating example of the 'Army Game' in action!

In hindsight, I can see that it was a moot point. Barney must have felt strongly that it was demeaning (or not militarily correct) for me to be playing 'second fiddle' to the ORs in the team! In 1953, even the County and Test Cricket teams had different changing rooms for the 'Gentlemen' (amateurs) and the 'Players' (professionals); and it was always a 'Gentleman' who captained the MCC touring side. It is interesting to note that when (Sir) Len Hutton was appointed England's first modern day professional captain in 1952 (to be succeeded by Peter May, an amateur), many people in cricket's establishment were strongly against the decision. Furthermore, in spite of this significant break with tradition, the hidebound Yorkshire Committee adamantly continued to appoint only amateur captains to lead their own team!

***

Other than Regimental commitments and sporting activities, to keep us all occupied and entertained, our biggest relaxation was the open-air cinema at nearby 10 BOD. When I later read my diaries for 1952 and 1953, I was astonished to see just how many times we all went to the cinema whilst in the Army. I would guess that I must have sat through more than a hundred films during those two years! Without any television available, the three main ways to keep in touch with the outside world were the newspapers and the cinema and the radio (or 'wireless' as it was called in those days).

The cinema at 10 BOD was very popular with the troops, and the programmes must have been changed at least three times a week (I can't recall). Although it was an open-air theatre, I remember that I always returned after a session at the cinema with my shirt smelling very strongly of tobacco-smoke, because most people in those days seemed to smoke incessantly during the films.

Whilst mentioning smoking; I personally never smoked whilst I was in the Army. My father had promised to give my brother, my sister and myself a £100 each if we didn't smoke before we were 21, and I believe that we all won that bet – although all three of us smoked to a certain extent in later years! When my wife and I tried this same ploy with our own children – but for £1,000 in later years – it proved of no value whatsoever. They all completely disregarded the possible reward, and just puffed away as if no bargain had ever been struck!

In addition to the cinema, the radio in the Canal Zone was a great boon to all of us living in our isolated cocoon. The local Forces Broadcasting Station was well organised and very popular with the troops for sending out news and music request programmes; and many of us also set up special aerials for receiving stations from all over the world – especially the Overseas' Service of the BBC. This was my own favourite station, and I found that they frequently had excellent programmes on current affairs, foreign reports, music and radio plays. I see that two of my favourite radio series were *The Scarlet Pimpernel* (played by Marius Goring) and *Horatio Hornblower* and I always listened to these episodes with great enjoyment whenever possible.

Ava Camp, Gineifa

The chance of listening to serious music didn't finish with the radio, because a Regular Subaltern in 29 Field, John Flinn, had his own gramophone player and a selection of 33¹/₃ rpm classical records in his tent. As a result, those interested regularly met for a listening session and discussion after dinner. John Flinn seems to have had a good selection of records, because I noted in my diary that during those months, we listened to such works as Beethoven's *Emperor* Piano Concerto, and his Violin Concerto; Mozart's Horn Concertos and his 39th Symphony; Schubert's *Great* and his *Unfinished* Symphonies and Brahms's 3rd Symphony – but there must have been many others.

From time to time, the Regiment also organised its own stage shows to keep the troops entertained, and it was always surprising to discover how much talent there was lurking within the ranks.

My diary entry of Sunday, 25 October 1953 records one of these concerts. I wrote: – 'this evening we had an inter-Battery Entertainment Competition, and all the Batteries were asked to prepare as many acts as they wished. After all the performances, the audience was then asked to decide, by popular acclamation, which of the acts was thought to be the best. All the acts

8 Battery Lines at Ava Camp. In the distance is the OR's Dining Room where we held our Entertainment Competitions.

contained some merit and amusement, but the outstanding performance of the evening was the one given by 79 Battery, and this had us all laughing in stitches:

'All the players entered the stage one by one, each dressed up in the weirdest and most outrageous outfits, and each one casually took up his position in the band – similar to the style of Spike Jones and his City Slickers. Each person held an object or instrument: – a mouth organ; a comb and paper; a whistle; a little bell; a bottle; a tin-can, or anything else that could produce some sort of noise if it was blown or struck! There was a long pause whilst each member of the 'band' settled down. Then, at a given signal, they all started to play together with mouth organs or combs and paper playing the tune, whilst the percussion 'instruments' backed them up with the beat. They played a number of different tunes for about 30 minutes, and during that time, the whole audience clapped and split their sides laughing (I certainly did!) Also, as they played, they each swigged liberally from a beer bottle as they went along!' They played a good selection of current tunes and also some from Spike Jones's own repertoire, but unfortunately, I omitted to note which ones they included in their programme!

I also wrote: – 'Sergeant Dewar appeared dressed up as a woman for his turn, and was really quite amusing. When he first arrived, he walked past some of the officers sitting at the side, and said, 'please don't stand up, gentlemen!' – And he later, suddenly jumped up and screamed, 'that gentleman pinched me!' And so the entertainment continued with various other turns, many containing a good measure of coarse humour! It was all good fun, but at the end of the show, there was no need to vote on which act had won the competition!'

***

Remembering the illiteracy of some recruits I witnessed at Oswestry in December 1951, I was pleased to see that there was some consideration given to education in 29 Field during my time with them.

On 12 January 1953, for instance, I wrote in my diary: – 'I am assisting (Captain) Peter Brereton (8 Bty), John Flinn (79 Bty), and Ian Sinclair (145 Bty), in running the 3rd Class Examinations today. About 100 people have been selected, and they were given 3 separate papers: – 'English' (written and oral), 'Maths' and 'General Knowledge'. The persons included in this examination were a very mixed bunch, although I thought that they generally coped with the papers rather well. On the other hand, some were surprisingly bad in General Knowledge and Geography. For instance, I noted that some had no idea where the Suez Canal Zone was on the map, nor such places as Gibraltar, Malta, Israel, New York or Sydney.

'One question asked was: 'How did you travel out here to the Suez Canal Zone?' In answer to this, two papers I saw were completely blank, and at least ten were pure guesses, showing routes ending up in such places as Siberia! The 8 Battery ORs seemed to be the best of the bunch, whereas 79 Battery included most of the dunces in the Regiment! After the 'Oral English' had finished in the afternoon, we started marking the English papers, with each of us marking one particular question. It was really quite a lengthy business.'

Next day I wrote: – 'I helped Peter Brereton to correct the Math's papers. We came across 2 blank sheets, and one bloke had written pathetically, 'I

310

haven't met questions like this before, and don't know how to answer them'. But I noted that about 70% passed the paper without any trouble, and everyone except three passed the English exam.' Sadly, I ran out of space in my diary, so I was unable to write any further details about the contents of these examinations. I made no mention in my diary about anyone being unable to read or write, so I am fairly sure that no one was revealed during this examination.

***

A little more about Dinner Nights: – It will be recalled that these were normally held on Wednesdays or Thursdays each week, and they were rather special and enjoyable events – although sometimes things could get out of hand if the drinking was particularly heavy. I suppose these periods of foolishness and outrageous behaviour helped us all to retain our sanity whilst being isolated in these unusual circumstances. 'Blues' uniforms or in summer, white dinner jackets and black bow-ties were worn instead of the normal shirt and tie, and the dinner was conducted in a more formal manner. After proposing the Loyal Toast, 'The Queen our Captain General', smoking was allowed, and Madeira wine as well as Port were passed round to the left. Speeches were also given if called for, and these dinners were the occasions when guests were entertained from other Regiments and newcomers were 'dined in' and those leaving 29 Field were 'dined out'.

After the meal had finished, there might be sing-songs, or sometimes, things could become noisily exuberant: Boisterous inter-Battery games were played, and these were always best enjoyed when everyone was well oiled!. On other occasions there might be other puerile high jinks involving buckets of water or home made thunder flashes and fireworks, made from igniting the discarded ammunition charge bags of the 25 pounders! These explosive antics must have been quite unpredictable and dangerous at times.

Mess Nights were the time when everyone was entitled to misbehave and to let off steam, and on one occasion during a particularly drunken party, Barney Brooke-Fox and Rex King both climbed up on the roof of the Mess Tent, and were seen sliding down, – and in the process, ripping the material badly with their spurs. I wondered how all this damage was explained away in the sober light of day, but I expect that we all paid for these repairs later on our Mess Bills! (Tom Keeble clearly remembered that incident when I spoke to him in later years.)

Soon after Lt Col G.A.Shoreland joined the Regiment as our new Commanding Officer, I wrote on Wednesday, 1 April 1953: – 'It was a Mess Night tonight. The meal was not at all good, because we had some really tough meat. The main reason for this Dinner Night was to 'dine in' the new CO, as well as the new Signal's Officer, and John Chapman, a new National Service Subaltern. The CO made a very good speech, saying that he was looking forward to learning more about 29 Field. After dinner, Chapman and Spears underwent their initiation. It is the first time I've seen this initiation nonsense. I must have missed my own initiation by some stroke of luck, or perhaps someone like Griff has just introduced the ritual. The poor initiate has to hang by his toes on an uplifted table, and then have water poured over him and down his trouser legs' (in my sober state, I thought all this was rather puerile and unnecessary!) 'They were both just soaked by the end! We then played the usual games, and Col Shoreland joined in with the rest. He is quite a small man, and in 'high cockerlorum' he had 3 hefty blokes astride him at one stage – and he just collapsed like a pack of cards! He was very sporty about it, and didn't seem to mind about this at all, but just went on. The evening didn't finish until about 2 o'clock.'

I drank very little in those days, and I never really thought these stupid antics were a particularly clever or sensible way to pass an evening. However, in spite of my true opinions, I participated with great gusto along with all the rest! Heavens knows what Col 'Tiny' Shoreland really thought about this new Regiment he had just joined!

A fortnight later I wrote about an even more riotous night: 'we had a Dinner Night tonight which turned out to be the most hectic one to date – which is saying something! (Major) Bill Moberly (the second-in-command) was dined out at this Dinner and made an excellent speech, whilst Will Warner (another new National Service Subaltern) was initiated in the usual style. After this, water was thrown freely around, started by Griff (Capt Griffiths of 79 Battery), who was afterwards set upon by some of the others, and de-bagged, and then dragged round the Mess. He took it all very well.'

On some more sober occasions after dinners, one of the less energetic contests was 'putting the beer bottle', and since I was tall, fit and slim (in
those days!) I was normally one of the finalists in this competition. The
rules were quite simple: – there was a starting line on the carpet, and in
the prone position with both feet behind the starting line, each competitor
had to 'walk' along resting on an upright bottle in each hand, then place
one of the bottles as far forward as possible, and return again behind the
starting line by using the one remaining bottle as a prop, and without
touching the carpet in between. Height, weight and fitness were important
in this competition, and Geoff Denis, a tall, fit young Captain
in 145 Battery was one of the experts in this game. It must be
said that these competitions normally finished with him and me trying to
place that wretched bottle just a fraction of an inch further than the other!
I expect that the honours were fairly even between us, but if this game
went on for too long, I remember that it had a grievous effect on the
stomach muscles during the following day!

Before I conclude this chapter, I shall mention just one more Dinner
Night that happened on 16 September 1953, when Tom Keeble was being
dined out, and about to go home after his two years of National Service. I
mention this occasion in particular, because for me, this was the end of an
era – a watershed. Tom was the last of that really congenial batch of
National Service Subalterns who had been in the Regiment, and had
welcomed me, when I arrived in August 1952.

It is significant to recall that most of the National Service Subalterns who
joined the Regiment just before and after that time, although mentioned in
my diary by name, left little impression upon me, and have since been lost
to the memory. I do remember Jim Cummins, who took over from me as
Gun Position Officer in Baker Troop, and also John Potts, who became a
friend of mine – but otherwise, I have little or no recollection of the others,
such as Mike Stokoe, David Carter, John Chapman and Will Warner.

I wrote about that Dinner Night at the end of September: – 'We are
dining out Gordon Stadward (a Captain in 79 Battery who was being
transferred to another Regiment) and Tom (Keeble). After the meal, came
the speeches. Gordon made a short one, but Tom made a rather good one.

He told us jokingly, that now he had completed his two year's 'holiday' in the army, he was going back to studying medicine once again, when he hoped to qualify as a doctor.

After the Dinner, there were plenty of explosive bangs, and in the absence of Barney (who had now left the Regiment and normally prepared the explosions) it was Griff who took over the fire-works, and he almost blew up the Mess! Griff was obviously less experienced in handling the charge bags than Barney, because there were a series of large bangs, and then an almighty one which seemed to include several ammunition-bags ignited in one go. It must also have been very close to the building, because the result was 13 broken panes of glass! One of the thunder flashes also somehow reached the roof of the marquee and started a fire – but luckily, Tom Keeble had the gumption and initiative to act quickly, and get up on the roof to put the fire out before it spread. Otherwise, I am quite sure that it could have been quite serious'.

Tom Keeble was therefore dined out with a big bang! Now that he had left the Regiment, I knew that my own turn would arrive in two months' time!

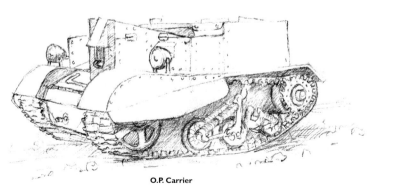

O.P. Carrier

Vicky Saumarez

CHAPTER 15

On the Home Stretch

After I returned from leave in the Levant and Cyprus on 28 August 1953, I realised that there would shortly be many changes to my life in 29 Field. Firstly, I was soon to be transferred from 8 Battery into Regimental Head Quarters Company (RHQ); but secondly, and more importantly, all my National Service friends and colleagues who had been with me in the Regiment since I arrived a year ago, were all coming to the end of their two years, and were about to leave for home. Nothing, of course, ever stays the same for long, but it was clear that my social life in the Mess and at Ava Camp would be quite different from now onwards – and more than ever, this encouraged me to look forward to the end of November, by which time my own demobilisation 'number' (51.23) would be arriving. I felt that I was now on the home stretch!

The Suez Canal near Kabrit on Little Bitter Lake

Whilst I had been away on leave, my closest friend of the seven, John Stansfield, had already been demobilised, and I missed his regular companionship straightaway. We had been the two Gun Position Officers for Able and Baker Troops in 8 Battery for over nine months by now, and we had a great rapport together and always saw plenty of each other in and out of duty during that time. John had toyed with the idea of remaining in the Army as a Regular, but prior to joining up he had accepted a place at Cambridge to read Engineering, so in the event, he decided to attend University as planned. He lived in Norfolk then, and although we wrote a few times to each other, it was virtually impossible to keep in touch with all the many people we knew during those years, and sadly, we never met up again after he had left (but see Chapter 17).

Apart from John Stansfield, the other six National Service friends of mine who would be leaving before the end of September were, Mike Logan (79 Battery), Ian Sinclair (145 Battery), Harry Cotter (145 Battery), Dick Brimelow (79 Battery), Tom Keeble (79 Battery) and Malcolm Ross (79 Battery). We were all about twenty years old and 'birds of a feather', so over the past year we had naturally spent much of our leisure time together, although this was in no way to the exclusion of others in the Mess. Luckily, there was never any cliquishness, nor any hint of a 'them' and 'us' divide between the Regulars and the National Servicemen – although the more senior field officers were naturally treated with all due respect.

Of the six mentioned above Tom Keeble, Ian Sinclair and Malcolm Ross were the three that I had the least affinity with, but the other three were really very close friends of mine. Mike Logan and I shared a tent together for over six months, so he was the one I knew the best, and although he could be rather wayward at times, we always got on very well together and I can't remember us ever having a cross word together. He had been to school at Aldenham, and was a tough looking individual and very cultured and well read. He was also a very likeable and congenial friend and always good fun to be with. He told me that before he joined the Army, he had seldom if ever drunk any alcohol at all, but it was quite clear that he was making up for lost time during his stay in the Suez Canal Zone!

On 29 December 1952, soon after we started sharing the tent together, I wrote in my diary: – 'Mike Logan seems to be a very pleasant companion to share with, and although he drinks more than some others, he never gets belligerent when he's tipsy!'

After the Dinner Night on 14 January, I also noted that he came back to bed in a somewhat inebriated state, and I have to say that there are a number of other mentions in my diary about this condition, but there was never trouble. Perhaps he couldn't hold his drink very well, or maybe he was led on by others who were more used to heavy drinking – and there were plenty of those in the Mess!

Mike came from Bournemouth, which he said was full of old people and a very boring place to live. To illustrate his point, he told me that the imposing Bath Hotel on the front, was the place where the 'Bath-Chair' was given its name! Mike Logan and Ian Sinclair were being demobbed together, and by the time they were allocated their flights home, all the ORs in their draft had already left weeks before – much to Mike's vociferous annoyance and frustration! In the end, they went off to the Airport on 11 September and I noted in my diary: – 'poor Mike (true to form!) missed the first aircraft home because he was the last in the queue – and also because he had excess baggage!' Mike was a really good friend and companion and he left a big hole when he eventually departed.

Harry Cotter and Dick Brimelow also left just a few days afterwards, and these were two other convivial friends whom I missed very much during my last few months in the Suez Canal Zone. In those days, it was necessary to sign on with the Territorial Army after finishing National Service, and since we all lived round London, we tried to join the same TA Regiment – the Surrey Yeomanry – but in the event this was not possible. By the time I had returned home, they were both away at University and sadly, the three of us never met up again (but see Chapter 17).

Soon after Harry had departed, I heard about his initiation in the Regiment as a 'new boy'. Harry was always forthright in his opinions and comments, and on his very first dinner in the Officers' Mess, he was foolish enough to 'cross swords' with one of the senior Regular Subalterns, John Kenny. John was complaining about the soup which he thought was far too peppery – when Harry, from the other end of the table, commented in a very loud voice: 'I think this soup is perfectly alright; there's nothing wrong with it at all. In fact, I think that it is really rather good!' There was a stunned silence, after which the conversation round the table continued as before. Later that night, a party of Subalterns paid a visit to Harry's tent, and firmly turned him out of bed as a penalty for his bumptiousness! Thus began Harry's term with 29 Field, although after this censure had been shown, I feel sure that there were no further recriminations! He was one of the characters in the Mess

John Kenny was one of those young Regulars in the Regiment whom I always regarded most highly. John had been the Subaltern during May, who had led the 'In-lying Picket' to the Water Filtration Plant in my place, when I had made my dreadful gaffe. I was always quite friendly with John, and I later worked with him for a spell in the Regimental Office during my final October, when he was acting as Adjutant. In fact, it was during those weeks in the Office that he had told me about the incident of Harry Cotter's early indiscretion.

Regimental Office at Ava Camp

I always thought that John Kenny would progress to great things in the Army, because I considered that he possessed all the attributes needed to take him onwards and upwards. However, I heard later that whilst on holiday with his girl friend in Wales, he had been driving through the Welsh countryside, when he stopped the car to have a piddle. Without looking, he vaulted over the stonewall at the side of the road – and promptly fell to his death down a quarry! That was just another example of the f-ing fickle finger of fate in operation! Furthermore, it also shows clearly that 'fact' is so often much stranger than 'fiction.' For instance, how could a writer of fiction ever include that sort of death in one of his novels?

***

With eleven weeks of National Service remaining in 29 Field, and with most of my closest friends already departed, I was transferred from 8 Battery on 11 September to become the Intelligence Officer at Regimental Head Quarters (RHQ). This was a rather grandiose title given to the dogsbody at RHQ, whose main duties included acting as Assistant Adjutant or doing any other administrative job needed for the Regiment, as well as acting as the Commanding Officer's assistant on schemes. My friend Dick Brimelow had held this position during his last few months with the Regiment, and he told me that he had found the job really quite interesting at times, and he also added that it was far less demanding than that of Gun Position Officer in one of the Batteries.

My exit from 8 Battery was made far less painful for me than I had originally imagined, because about the same time as my own transfer to RHQ, many of the other officers in the Battery were also on the move, and I considered that most of the replacements were far lesser souls than the ones departing.

By the end of August, Jim Cummins had taken over from me as Gun Position Officer of Baker Troop, and Captain John Orde had replaced Mac as Baker Troop Commander. Mike Martin had moved to RHQ as the Regimental Surveyor and been replaced by John Rogers (a newly arrived Regular); whilst Mike Stokoe (another National Serviceman) had taken the place of John Stansfield as GPO in Able Troop. Also, Major Barney Brook-

Fox and Major Rex King had both left 29 Field and moved on to other Regiments. Following all these changes, the only two 'originals' remaining in 8 Battery, were Captain Peter Brereton and Lt John Gilmour, both of whom I was friendly with and both I considered to be first class officers.

This sort of move around in the Gunner Regiments was not at all unusual in those days, because the Royal Artillery is by far the largest and most diverse arm of the British Army, and these postings were beneficial and indeed essential for Regular Gunner officers so that they could widen their experience and scope. It also gave them a chance to assimilate the diverse branches of the Royal Artillery: – the Mortars, the Locating Batteries, the Light and Heavy Ack Ack, as well as the Heavy and Medium Field Artillery. There were many different aspects of Gunnery for them to be conversant with.

I knew Jim Cummins quite well by this stage, because he had been acting as my Baker Troop Leader (the GPO's assistant) since May, and I have to say that within a few days of working with him, I knew that he was not my type of man at all! Jim had started as a National Serviceman, but after Mons, he had decided to sign on for a Short Term Service Commission, which meant that he was paid the same as a Regular for three years. (This was a method of inducing National Servicemen to stay on as Regulars). He had been a contemporary of John Stansfield at Wellington, and John and I had soon agreed that he was far too cocky about his mastery of Gunnery for his own good. However, we both knew that he would soon discover that theory and practice in Gunnery were two quite different matters!

On a fairly windy day a few weeks later, I was acting as Safety Officer for Baker Troop during some firing on the Ranges, and I noticed that Jim had incorrectly laid out his gun position with his Command Post well down-wind of the guns. This was soon to cause him much difficulty when shouting his orders clearly to the guns. As a result, right in the middle of the first shoot, he had to run out the tannoy lines hurriedly to the guns so that his orders could be received properly. That evening, I faithfully recorded all these happenings in my diary – no doubt with just a *soupçon* of satisfaction!

Jim Cummins was unlucky enough to have Captain John Orde as his new Troop Commander in Baker Troop, because John was just the sort of officer in this 'Army Game' whom I disliked the most: – firstly, he thought that he 'knew it all'; and secondly, he acted superciliously towards the ORs; and thirdly, he frequently 'pulled rank'.

On 31 August I wrote: – 'A few weeks ago, I wasn't very happy about handing over to Jim (Cummins) in Baker Troop and moving temporarily to BHQ (8 Battery Head Quarters), but now that John Orde has replaced Mac as Troop Commander, the Troop is not the same at all. John Orde is already very unpopular with the blokes as well as with Jim, because he makes such a nuisance of himself on schemes by interfering unnecessarily in the Troop Command Post. On one occasion, I saw him telling off a signaller for using the wrong procedure on his wireless set, although in fact, it was proved later that the signaller had been quite correct all along. Worse still, after John's mistake had been proved to him, he just walked away without even apologising to the signaller for his error. Jim Cummins has already had cross words with him about this sort of conduct.'

On 9 September, I recorded another newcomer to 29 Field who was, in effect, a replacement for one of my demobbed, departed friends in the Regiment. I wrote: 'A new Subaltern called John Rogers has just arrived from the UK this afternoon. He is a Sandhurst man, and I hear that he will be joining 8 Battery, and will also be replacing my friend Mike Logan in my tent.'

I soon realised that this newcomer was a far less congenial companion than my friend Mike Logan. I wrote critically at the time: – 'Now that I have lived in the tent with John Rogers for a spell, I have to say that I don't like the man at all: – for one thing, he is far too pushy, and already treats 'our' tent as if he owns the place. The only good thing about the situation is that I know my time is now fast running out, so I only have to put up with him for another 8 weeks or so! Evidently, he passed out from Mons before going onto Sandhurst so he has already seen plenty of Service – but to my mind, he is much too pleased with himself. He always speaks as if he knows everything there is to know about Gunnery (another one!). He will in future be working in the 8 Battery Command Post, so he will be under John

Gilmour (a most clued up and competent Gunner), so he will soon find out that he has plenty more to learn on the subject!'

Another extract from my diary, written just over a month later is pertinent to be included here: I see from my notes on 9 November 1953, that there was an 8 Battery Dinner to celebrate its 'Battle Honour', *Alma* (a Battle in the Crimean War) and although I was now with RHQ, I was invited to attend this function because of my past connections. I wrote about this event: – 'The food was really quite good, and there was plenty of beer available for everyone. During the meal, I spoke to Rouse, who I know quite well because he had often played with me in the Baker Troop Soccer XI, and had also joined up at exactly the same time as me in December 1951 (Batch 51.23). He is now 'demob-happy', and with some others I know well in Baker Troop, we had quite a long chat together about the current situation in 8 Battery (this was of course most indiscreet of me!) Dunn and Ross in particular, had quite a lot to say for themselves on the subject. The ORs always make full use of these unofficial sessions to have a good 'tick' (the army slang for 'grumble') about their officers, and it is quite clear that all of them loathe John Orde and John Rogers, because both are so arrogant. I was not in the least surprised to hear all this!'

Although Major Barney Brook-Fox was never my favourite man in the Regiment, I grudgingly admired him for maintaining such high standards, and I always felt that he was the sort of dedicated soldier who had made the British Army such a formidable fighting force – no one ever messed about with Barney! He was 'dined out' at the end of September, and went on to greater things in a rather more 'senior' Regiment – 6 Field, a Regiment with self-propelled 25 Pounders in 3 Armoured Brigade, which had similar status to that of an RHA Regiment. His abilities and influence were being rightly acknowledged for the outstanding role he was playing in the 'Army Game'.

Reading my diary entry for Saturday, 26 September (just after I had moved from 8 Battery), I was amused to hear that Barney had made his final Battery Inspection a most memorable event by giving everyone involved a real ticking off for their negligence and idleness! I wrote: 'At lunchtime, all the 8 Battery blokes came into the Mess really fed up after Barney's

Saturday Inspection this morning. He had evidently pulled everything to bits and given them all a real bollocking for slackness, as he had done so often to us in the past! Afterwards, Mike (Martin) and I had a really good laugh together about all this'.

***

Now that I had moved over to RHQ, Captain Lionel Savin was my immediate boss, so I spent much of my time with him during the normal working day. I don't recall now exactly how the Regimental Head Quarters Company was run, but I suppose it just gathered together all those individual sub-units not directly involved in the three Batteries: – namely, all the REME mechanics in the vehicle workshops and the Royal Signallers, which were organised quite separately; the Regimental Surveyors, now under Mike Martin; the Adjutant and all those involved in the Regimental Office; all those in Catering as well as the Medical Unit and the Quarter Master's Stores and Armoury. I believe that the total number of soldiers was slightly lower than that in each of the three Batteries, because RHQ normally came fourth when involved in competitions with the other three Batteries.

Although Lionel was an amiable colleague to work with, he was one of those recent additions in the Regiment whom I considered much smaller fry than the younger regulars who had been in 29 Field when I had first joined the unit in September 1952 – namely, Ted Burgess, Geoff Denis, John Flinn, John Gilmour, Nigel Hacking, Ronnie Hambleton, Ray Kelly, John Kenny, Mike Martin, Ted Prescott and Doug Spittle – all of whom, I considered capable of proceeding to much greater things during their Army careers.

I soon became tired of Lionel telling me how he 'used to do it in the Ack-Ack', and I noted more than once that he acted 'like a nattering old woman'! However, he was a pleasant enough person, and also intelligent, but I always considered that he would have been much better suited to life as a schoolmaster or in some other academic position, rather than as a career officer in the Army.

On 18 September, I wrote: – 'On parade with RHQ this morning. I am not at all impressed by the way Lionel acts as the Troop Commander for these morning parades. When he goes down the ranks making the personal inspections, he checks almost every single person, which I think is just ridiculous! Also, he doesn't differentiate between the NCOs and the other ORs when he does this. This can't possibly be the correct way to do it.'

Although life in RHQ was less interesting than 8 Battery, there was really no reason for anyone to feel bored in 29 Field. To keep us all busy, there were always plenty of camp and Regimental duties to be covered, as well as a continuous stream of sporting activities available for everyone interested. At various times, there was athletics, cross-country running, swimming, rifle shooting and boxing – and then there were games to either participate in or to watch, such as tennis and squash, or team games like hockey, basket ball, water polo, cricket, soccer and even rugby on that horrible rough and rocky ground! During my time in the Zone I participated in all of these pursuits – but I kept away from rugby, after seeing Tom Keeble's badly grazed knees on one occasion!

I see that I played more basket ball and hockey than any other sport during those last few months, and I mention this in particular because it was due to hockey that I ended up in Hospital – *just four days before* the inter-Battery Athletics Competition I mention in detail later.

On Saturday, 3 October I wrote: – 'This afternoon I played in a hockey match against 10 BOD, which turned out to be a very dirty, badly umpired game. About half way through the first half, I received an almighty swipe with a stick on the forefinger of my left hand, so I found it difficult to play my best after that! I think my finger might be broken because it looks an odd shape, and it soon started to swell up after the game.'

Foolishly, it wasn't until Monday that I eventually showed my injured finger to our new doctor, Jock McGuinness. He just gave it a cursory glance, and immediately drove me off in his Land Rover to the British Military Hospital (BMH) at Fayid to have it ex-rayed. Sure enough, one of the top bones in my finger had been fractured, so I found myself in a Hospital bed for the night. After my little operation that evening, my finger and fore-arm were really quite painful, so I was only able to sleep fitfully during that night. I also found that, whenever I eventually managed to drop off to sleep, the night nurse seemed to come round and wake me up again, by roughly examining my fractured finger!

During those few hours stay in the BMH, I quickly realised that the whole place was primarily run for the satisfaction of the régime and to comply with the strict rules laid down, rather than for the benefit of the patients being treated therein! For instance, after my disturbed night's sleep, all the inmates in my ward were woken up at 6.30, irrespective of their ailments it seemed, and they all had to be washed and shaved by 8 o'clock without fail! Also, before I was allowed to dress and have my breakfast, there was much fuss and bother in the ward in preparation for the morning inspection which was carried out by some high-up Military Doctors and senior Matrons. Apparently, the main objective of this ward inspection was to see that all the beds and belongings looked neat and tidy, rather than to ensure that all was well with the ailing patients. It was quite clear to me that no one had come into BMH for a restful time!

To make that night even more memorable for me, whilst I was sleeping fitfully during the early hours, there was the noisiest thunderstorm and the heaviest cloudburst of rain I experienced during the whole of my time in the Suez Canal Zone. I wrote about our journey back to Ava Camp next morning: –

'The tarmac roads in the Zone are very uneven, smooth and badly cambered, so the surfaces are quite unable to cope with a heavy downpour we had last night. This morning, there were big puddles everywhere, and the shiny surfaces of the roads were extremely slippery. We saw a number of accidents on our way back to camp, caused by vehicles driving too fast and just skidding off the road. I noticed that a large truck from 71 HAA (my school friend John Bayman's Regiment) was involved in a bad accident. Our Land Rover was in a filthy state from the spray by the time we arrived back in camp, so it needed a really good wash-down. I find that I am ROO today, so I performed the usual duties. I was sorry that this prevented me from going out for a short training run in preparation for the athletics in 2 day's time. My finger is still not past the throbbing stage, so I can see that it will be quite a nuisance when I run. I had to turn out the guard at 0115.'

The Treaty Road near Ismailia

With the BTE inter-Regimental Athletics Championships coming up in November, the emphasis was now on athletics in 29 Field from the end of September onwards. As a result, Mike Martin, Lionel Savin and I decided that we should make a real effort in RHQ to do our best in the forthcoming Regimental Competition. We first searched for all the hidden athletes we had lurking within our diverse pack, and we soon found that there were a good number of potentials. We then organised some training sessions at the Kabrit athletic track. Whilst Mike and Lionel mainly supervised those competing in the Field Events, I trained the track runners, and made sure that we practiced plenty of baton changing. By the time of the Competition, we were really quite hopeful about our prospects.

On 8 October 1953, with my finger still throbbing from my hospital visit just two days before, I wrote: – 'The inter-Battery Competition started with the 3 miles event, which was not a relay race. I thought that we might win this event because we had two really good runners, but in the event, the race turned out to be a disaster for us. L/Bdr Whittaker developed a stitch half way through the race and finished well down the field, and our second runner O'Donovan, misunderstood the number of laps he had completed, and came in sprinting in front of all the other runners – only to be told that he still had another 440 yards to run! He collapsed exhausted and said he could do no more, so RHQ scored no points at all!

'The 880 yards x 4 wasn't very successful for us either, owing to our weak second runner, who was a substitute. He was not up to it, and lost the lead given to him by Latham, as well as about 50 yards to the next two runners! When Ian Spear (the Royal Corps of Signals Subaltern) took over, he was unable to gain any appreciable distance, so when I ran the last leg, the two leaders were so far ahead, it was just impossible to make up the lost ground. We therefore came in 3rd.

'RHQ did well from then onwards, although worse in the sprint relays than I had hoped. We won a number of the Field Events, and also the hurdles, and then we came to the last two track events of the day: – the one mile race, and the 4 x 440 yards relay. RHQ just romped away with both of these races. In the mile race our runners came in first and second; and in 440 yard relay, we also had a strong team. Moss of REME is a very good athlete, so I decided that he should run the last leg, and that I would start the race. I managed to give RHQ a good lead on the first leg, and we maintained this throughout the race to come in easily first. The final score was: – 79 Battery 55 points; 145 Battery 52 points; RHQ 49 points; and 8 Battery 42 points! I am glad that we managed to beat one of the Batteries, but I felt sorry that it had to be 8 Battery!'

With the RHQ teams normally finishing a poor fourth in these inter-Battery competitions, we felt quite pleased with ourselves about coming third – although we couldn't help thinking what the result could have been, if only the 3 mile race had been re-run. But such is life!

***

A few weeks after I became Intelligence Officer at RHQ, it was time for 29 Field to have its all important yearly inspection by the CRA – the inspection I had fortunately missed whilst in Cyprus last year. This year, I wasn't involved at all in the excessive painting and polishing which always goes before these inspections but a few days before, I spent some time collecting facts and figures about Regiment so that the CO was ready to answer any awkward questions. The Adjutant told me that I should be acting as Col Shoreland's ADC during the inspection, and would be escorting him and the CRA round the camp. He also told me that, 'it was my job to ensure that they didn't get behindhand with the schedule!' On this last point, I commented in my diary: 'some hope I've got of influencing the CRA in the heat of the chase!'

Since it was now the end of October, the Regiment was dressed in battle-dress for the early morning parade and inspection, and after that, the whole morning was spent touring Ava Camp from the gun parks, the slit trenches and the perimeter wire, to the Armoury, the canteens and the kitchens. I noted that, 'the CRA seemed well pleased with what he saw, and when he had departed after lunch with us in the Officers' Mess, most of us decided to settle down for a good dose of Egyptian PT!'

***

One of the most interesting parts of this job in RHQ was acting as the Colonel's assistant on 'Skeleton' schemes – those with HQ staffs but no troops. These Divisional and Regimental schemes were organised to give the senior officers and their HQ staffs experience in working together during a moving battle, and they involved all the Divisional and Brigade staffs as well as those of all the Infantry Battalions and their supporting Gunner Regiments.

We had a four day Exercise like this in the middle of October (called *Caesar's Witch*), and this took us halfway along the road towards Cairo, and then many miles deep into the desert southwards through some impressive mountainous terrain north of Gebel Khaliya – parts of which were nicknamed 'Cheddar Gorge' – and then south-east through the Wadi Hugul, until we eventually reached the Gulf of Suez near Bir Udeib (Well of Udeib). It was during these days in the wilderness that I came across masses of fossilised wood scattered on the surface of the desert – and fortunately, I thought of picking up a suitable sample for displaying years later on my bookshelf at home!

In preparation for *Caesar's Witch*, the day before, I marked up all the maps for the Colonel, and I noted in my diary: – 'the CO's Land Rover and mine with trailer are all ready this evening. We are taking 3 boxes of compo (prepared Army rations), and also burners in case we are self-supporting. We have 4 extra jerry cans of petrol and 5 of water. We shall not be leaving tomorrow before 0700 hrs, so I don't need to get up much earlier than usual. The Battery Commanders, the Adjutant, the Second-in-Command and the Signals Officer will all be leaving before us. Bed early.'

Next day, Tuesday 13 October I wrote: – 'We pulled out of camp at 0715 hrs, and drove south towards Gebel Ataqa (a prominent mountain of some 3,000 feet near Port Suez), then travelled westward past Gebel Iweidid (1,700 feet) and about 40 miles along the Cairo road as far as the 'Pink Palace' (the ruined Palace of Abbasi), and took up a position in sight of the ruins which stand up on the hills. The Brigade HQ is in the wadi south of the Green Howards, the Cheshires and the Inniskillings' (the Infantry Battalions supported by 29 Field Regiment with its 24 x 25 pounder guns). 'It was the first time that I have ever seen a Brigade HQ in operation, so I found this really interesting. By the end of this exercise, I expect that I shall have learned a few insights into the workings of a Brigade'.

'The wireless sets are giving a lot of trouble (a frequent occurrence for us on schemes) and Ian Spear (the Regular Royal Signal's Subaltern now attached to 29 Field) frequently had to be called to our position. The CO was really annoyed (quite rightly) because both of his sets, the one on Brigade net and the other on the Regimental net, were both unreliable. My own set was also not behaving itself properly! Eventually, after we had moved into close *laager* for the night, the innards of the sets were changed round and from then onwards they all worked well for the rest of the night. We had supper at 7.30, and I allotted times to the drivers and operators for looking after the sets during the night. The CO has been out for most of the day on reconnaissance. It was quite cold tonight, so I was pleased to have brought my sweater. I didn't undress for the night, but as usual just loosened my boots and took off my belt.'

I have included some more of my contemporary diary jottings to give some more insight into what happens on these Exercises. On Wednesday morning for instance I wrote: – 'I put the drivers on the wireless sets from 12 to 3 since this is the quietest period of the night. I didn't do a stag last night because everyone is fresh at the moment, but I shall take a turn tonight. From now onwards the blokes will be getting progressively more tired. At 2 am we were attacked by some paratroops who made a mock night attack on the HQ. They managed to get through our sentries and the slit trenches. I slept quite well during the night. At dawn we moved out of close *laager* and went back to yesterday's position and camouflaged again.' The camouflage netting was always taken down after dark, in case a night move was necessary. Smoking under camouflage netting was also a constant hazard in those days.

Later that day I wrote: – 'The (wireless) air was full of messages – the enemy had attacked along the line of the 'railway' to the north of us, and the BCs were putting fire down on them. The way our CO was giving instructions to the Adjutant etc, showed that he was very competent at his job. He also gets on extremely well with his fellow COs in the Battalions.'

There were two more days of this movement, action, inaction and confusion – and there were also many changes in the situation organised by the umpires to ensure that we were all kept on our toes! I see that I mentioned more than once about the problems we had with our malfunctioning wireless sets, and this was due mainly to the state of this old equipment. I wrote: 'some of these wireless sets are as clapped out and 'U/S' (Army slang for unserviceable) as some of our old Army vehicles!' In retrospect, it seems ridiculous that this old equipment was allowed to continue giving such constant problems, especially when communications between units is such a crucial matter. What is it like today one wonders?

I was also interested to read from my diary notes that on Thursday night, towards the end of the Exercise: – 'I notice that the Brigade Major has lost too much sleep at this stage, and is liable to fly off the handle at times if things go against him!' With some officers, this was a common occurrence after a day or two of these fast moving schemes.

Caesar's Witch finished on the morning of Friday at 5.30 am, so after a good breakfast, the CO and I attended a conference, at which we discussed the events of the past few days and constructively examined all the lessons to be learned. The general feeling was that the Exercise had been a success, although the wireless sets came in for much criticism. I thought to myself at the time, that the one person who probably learned the most from this whole Exercise, was a certain 2nd Lt Goodliffe – and he was shortly to be demobilised!

Before leaving this subject, I have to comment on how much I was impressed by the way our Lt Col 'Tiny' Shoreland conducted himself during my few days working closely with him. I thought that he had all those attributes which my father had always told me were essential in a 'good leader': – he kept cool, and was a good example to those under him – he was enthusiastic about the job he was doing, which was infectious to those under him – and he was always ready to give praise and encouragement when this was deserved – but also fair when he found fault. Without doubt, my father would have approved of our Colonel.

**

In my position as Intelligence Officer in RHQ, there were times in camp when I felt distinctly under employed. However, a very big plus to the job

An Egyptian dwelling near Fayid on the Treaty Road

was the need for me to travel on behalf of the Regiment to other parts of the Suez Canal Zone. For instance, the administration of 29 Field involved calling at the Divisional HQ Offices in Fayid and Ismailia for Regimental Orders, and for collecting wages or other supplies for the Regiment – and these trips round and about were much to my liking.

I see from my diary that I often collected cash for the ORs' pay and on one occasion I had to drive down to Bir Udeib, some 25 miles south of Port Suez, to pay our Royal Signals detachment located there for some reason at the time. I also went to the main storage depots in the Canal Zone – such as El Tell el Kebir, Fanara and 10 BOD, for collecting various food and other necessities for the Regiment.

It was during one of these visits to Fanara Depot that I was told a most unlikely story (although I have to say that I readily believed it, knowing the ways of the 'Army Game' as I did by that time): – It was a fact, that when stores were checked in the Army in those days, there were normally some items that were habitually hidden out of sight. The reason for this was to ensure that the numbers of articles being checked matched up *precisely* with the numbers recorded on the *official* inventory sheets. The only way to

A common fellow traveller on the Treaty Road

receive 'full marks' in these Army stock checks – and to avoid any awkward questions being asked – was to present *exact* numbers!

Talking to those in charge at Fanara Depot, I was told that once they had a Jeep on the site, of which there was no record on any of their inventories. Furthermore, no one in the stores had any idea whatsoever where it had originally come from. Whenever there was a periodic inspection, the Jeep was therefore hidden discreetly out of sight and this subterfuge went on for several months. As time passed however, it became more and more of an embarrassment and so eventually, to avoid any awkward questions being asked, the vehicle was driven out far into the miredahm and just blown up! In this way, the potential problem was finally solved!

***

At one of my last Dinner Nights in 29 Field, Lionel Savin demonstrated one of his previously hidden talents, which made a lasting impression upon me. We had finished our Dinner and had retired into the Mess Room, when Lionel suggested that he should show us a little demonstration of hypnotism that he had picked up along the way. I remember that some of us were rather apprehensive about this suggestion, because we felt that it was delving too much into the unknown and playing with something that nobody really understood – including Lionel!

However, before any meaningful discussion could take place, Mike Stokoe had eagerly volunteered to be the guinea-pig, and before we realised what was happening, the show had begun: The lights were turned down in the room, and Mike was very quickly put into a trance by Lionel, and most of the bystanders were shocked by this sudden transformation.

Lionel then told him firmly that the temperature in the room had become 'extremely cold' – at which Mike immediately started shivering all over, and acted as if he was freezing to death! Lionel let him continue in this state for some time, but then completely reversed his instructions: 'The room is now stiflingly hot, and you can hardly breathe'. Straightaway, Mike gave the appearance of being in great distress, and was frantically struggling to undo the top button of his Blues Uniform!

Lionel Savin, Mike Stokoe and John Potts playing the fool

All this drama was of course taking place just a few feet away from us all, and many felt quite relieved when Lionel eventually ended his little demonstration, and deftly brought Mike out of his trance again. There is no doubt about it, the episode was absolutely genuine. There was definitely no subterfuge or collusion whatsoever between the two of them. After the show was all over, many of us felt quite relieved that Mike Stokoe was back to normal once again, rather than being left suspended in a trance in the middle of the Gineifa wilderness!

***

Looking back after so long, I can't fully understand why I mention so little about most of the replacement National Servicemen who joined the Regiment after all my initial friends had departed. The fact remains that John Potts was the only one that I really befriended and remember well – all the rest have been lost in the mist of time.

John Potts came from the North-East and after leaving Newcastle Grammar School, he had qualified as a Chartered Accountant before joining the Army. He must have been quite a talented accountant, because he was constantly being asked by the other officers in the Regiment to help them in sorting out their minor accounting problems. He told me that he was quite confident that he could earn at least £70 per week within a few years of leaving the Army – which seemed an immense amount of money to me at the time.

John and I frequently socialised together, and one of the many mentions I made of him during 'the home stretch' was on Sunday 15 November, when I wrote: – 'I went to the Evening Service with John Potts and Jim Cummins. Supper in the Mess was not at all good this evening, so afterwards, John Potts and I went off to his tent together and heated up two tins of 'compo' stew and a tin of vegetables. It was really good and rich, and went down very well indeed! He is a good deal older than the other NS Subalterns, and he is an extremely convivial companion. We stayed up talking together for some time.'

On another occasion I recorded a discussion John and I had about officers who have been commissioned from the ranks – referred to as 'rankers'. There were only two rankers in 29 Field at that time: Bill Lacey, the Regiment's Quarter Master Captain (this job appointment was quite common in the Army), and Major Eve, John Potts's Battery Commander. In those days, when snobbery was far more rampant than it is today, this move from being a Warrant Officer to a Commissioned Officer was sometimes a difficult change to make successfully – as shown, for example, by the unfortunate Major Austin of 84 Mauritian Guards Company (mentioned in Chapter 10).

If they were unable to adapt themselves readily to their altered status, they might quite easily find themselves out of place with their peers as well as with the Warrant Officers and the other non-commissioned soldiers under them. Major Eve must have been promoted during the war years, because by then, he seemed to have assimilated satisfactorily with his fellow Field Officers. Even so, it was noticeable to me, that out of all the senior officers in the Mess, Major Ede was the one who was just a little more touchy about his position and rank; and it was *he* who stood on ceremony just a shade more than any of the other seniors.

This whole issue is obviously a contentious one and there are many contrary views on the subject, but it was certainly a widely expressed generalisation in the Army in those days, that most of the Warrant Officers and ORs preferred their officers to be Sandhurst-trained, or at least to come from the traditional 'officer class', rather than those promoted from the ranks. This may or may not be a fair and objective assessment, but then I certainly heard this view expressed across the spectrum.

**

I notice that during that last November there were plenty of events in 29 Field to keep us occupied, even though the days still seemed to move on slowly for me. For instance, we entertained 250 sailors and officers from the Cruiser *HMS Glasgow* as well as those from Lord Mountbatten's accompanying frigate *HMS Surprise* when both these ships were passing through the Suez Canal from the Far East. This event was a great success. During the day, we showed them round Ava Camp, demonstrated the guns in action and played some amicable sports matches with them, including a most entertaining tug-of-war competition. Also, to ensure that the day went with a swing, we had collected many essential supplies from the main NAAFI Stores at Fanara, including 21 crates of beer – about 1,000 bottles!

Another reason for mentioning this particular event is to pass on two little snippets I duly recorded in my diary. Firstly, we were told by the sailors that it was common knowledge on board the *Surprise* that Lord Mountbatten's wife was a 'domineering b—ch' and that 'she threw tantrums and bossed him around all the time'! Oh dear, I thought, what a dreadful reputation to have freely discussed around the ship! The other point which I noted was that *HMS Glasgow* was far too old by 1953, to be of much use on active service. I was told that after the ship had fired a few broadsides, bits of the radar started falling off, which made it virtually useless for modern warfare!

Otherwise, during my last few weeks with the Regiment: – on 8 November, we had the usual combined Remembrance Day Parade with soldiers from local Regiments – and soon afterwards, 79 Battery organ-

**Lt Col Shoreland, Capt Peter Brereton, Maj Pat Warren and
Dr Jock McGuinness studying the form at the Donkey Derby**

ised a 'Donkey Derby', using mules provided by Animal Transport of
RASC – then I see that I also had another day out as Safety Officer on the
Ranges, and had to organise the manning of the Road Block outside Ava
Camp, which was normally called for whenever any Army vehicle was
stolen in the Zone.

**Road blocks were mounted on the Treaty Road if ever army vehicles
were stolen**

Then on Saturday, 14 November, it was also 8 Battery's turn to give a Gunnery demonstration for the benefit of all the officers in the Regiment. I wrote in my diary about this display: – 'Peter Brereton took the first shoot from the OP (Observation Post) on the Miniature Range, and provided us all with the usual laughs – Peter always loved to have an audience. The Battery Command Post worked very well, and clearly showed us that John Gilmour is the best Battery Command Post Officer in the Regiment. John has a moustache, which suits him well, and is such a friendly and convivial companion to be with. He's one of those persons who always has a ready smile on his face. Jim Cummins and Baker Troop had their guns in action, and it was quite nostalgic for me to hear Stacey (the Tec Acc during my time as GPO) calling out the ranges and angles in his thick Norfolk brogue. Jim fired once before he had received the order, but otherwise he did quite well as Gun Position Officer.' That last comment seemed a little grudging to me, reading it in retrospect!

The days continued to drag, and it was on 16 November, that some of the ORs in my Group (51.23 – i.e. December 1951), including Rouse, received their orders to report to the Airport on the next day. However, there was still no word about my own return flight!

Just afterwards, on 18 and 19 November, for the second time during my stay in the Suez Canal Zone I was involved in the Divisional RA and BTE RA Athletics Championships in Fayid stadium. I recorded that 29 Field came second in both these competitions which we thought was quite satisfactory. I also recorded in my diary on the second day that: 'there was barely an hour's interval for me to recover between the 440 yard relay and the 880 yard relay, so at the end of the second race, I was completely whacked out!'

It was in the middle of these championships that I was 'dined out' of the Regiment at the same time as my friend Captain Ronnie Hambleton of 145 Battery, who was to be posted to an Ack Ack Regiment. Like most Regular Field Gunners, he told me that he was not at all enthusiastic about being transferred away from Field Gunnery, because he considered Ack Ack to be very tame in comparison. Ronnie was another first class Regular officer in 29 Field who would be very difficult to replace with another of similar stature. I knew Ronnie well by this stage because he had been with the

Regiment when I joined it in August 1952 – and he was also one of the officers who congregated regularly to hear and discuss classical music in John Flinn's tent.

Two days later, I wrote in my diary: – 'Just before lunch Lionel (Savin) told me the welcome news that I am to report on Tuesday 24 November at Fayid Airport for my passage back to the UK!' However, in spite of this excellent news, I tried not to get too excited because I had learned long ago that *nothing* is certain until it is *certain* – and so it transpired, because within two days I heard that the date had been changed. I wrote on Sunday 22 November –

'I spent this morning packing my trunk which I am sending by MFO. At lunchtime Lionel told me that my departure time has been put back after all! I shan't be leaving now until the end of the week, reporting at Fayid Airport on Saturday 28 November. I'm not particularly surprised, but this really is a most frustrating business. I now realise just how annoyed Mike Logan was when he was delayed for so long'.

'Lionel is now acting Adjutant and since John Rogers is ill and was down for ROO, Lionel has asked me to stand in for him. I agreed to do this to help him out, even though it is certainly not my turn. I thought that he would at least let me choose my own time for turning out the Guard – but no! He insisted that I drew my time out of the hat as usual. I reasoned with him, but to no avail! I finally decided that he was just crass stupid!' Even though I was doing him a real favour, and even though I was to be demobbed in a few days, I still had to abide by the immutable rules of the 'Army Game'!

When leaving a Regiment in the Canal Zone, it was always a problem disposing of unwanted uniforms and other possessions, but I see from my diary that I gratefully received £10 from the impecunious John Rogers for my radio, shorts, stockings, KD suit, and dressing gown. All my other surplus kit I left with John Potts for him to pass onto the next Subalterns arriving in the Regiment.

Later that week, I took the new recruits in RHQ for rifle shooting practice on the small-arms ranges, and on my last day (Friday 27 November), I was involved in organising the course for the RHQ cross country run, in which everyone under 35 years old was obliged to participate.

I wrote about this event: – 'Up at 6.20 this morning. I went down to the lines at 6.45 and took a Land Rover and also the flags for marking out the course. I left soon after 7, and had just reached the rubbish dump when I heard the starting whistle go. I then had to rush like mad to keep ahead of the forward runners. I went up the track past the dump and then turned right along the hills. I used 4-wheel-drive most of the time to make sure that I didn't get bogged down in any loose sand. I just made it! As I hammered in the last flag, the first runners came running up to me!'

I continued in my diary: 'There were the usual batch of 'skivers' on the run, so they will all be sent off again on Monday! Lionel finished 38th, and Sgt Shrimplin – who tried hard to be excused the run – finished in front of Lionel!'

'I said my farewells to everyone tonight at dinner and drank their health – and so to bed at 10. The last night in Gineifa!!!!!!'

Since all of the guns are out firing on the Ranges that morning, I saw very few people in the Mess before I finally left Ava Camp for the last time. I noted in my diary: – 'The weather is really dreadful this morning. There is a fierce north wind blowing, and it is overcast, and we even had a light drizzle of rain later on. I eventually left at 12.15, and appropriately enough, as I was driving out of Ava Camp, the guns from Baker Troop were just returning from the Ranges.'

'Once again Air Movements in Fayid Airport was totally disorganized about *my* movements, because when I asked at the desk in the Transit Camp, they searched in vain for my name on the flight list. Nonetheless, they promised me a seat on a Hermes Flight leaving on the following day. I noticed in the Mess Book that David Rose – who was with me in Fox Troop at Mons until he was relegated last July – had left from Fayid Airport yesterday. It also gave me a *soupçon* of satisfaction when I confirmed that one or two other 51.23s were also flying out tomorrow at 0400 hrs'.

Last year at the end of August 1952, when I had arrived at Fayid Airport, all the facilities were badly unfinished and disorganised, but in the intervening year many improvements had been made on the site. The tents and Ante-Room had now been upgraded and the food I had in the canteen was really excellent. I had a satisfying lunch and dinner for 5 Akkars each, and on Saturday afternoon I spent the time strolling in Fayid village and having a look round the shops.

I was told that I would be leaving on Sunday afternoon. I wrote: – 'Breakfast was an excellent mixed grill. I reported in at 10.30 and had my luggage weighed. It was just a few pounds overweight but they didn't seem to mind. After lunch at 2.30 we went to the Airport. Our flight eventually left Fayid about 4 pm local time'.

Sitting finally in the aircraft, I wrote in my diary: – 'They can keep all their flies and sand and sun! I am a little comforted to find that there are just a few 51.23 ORs on this Hermes with me, so I can see that I am not the *very* last of my group to leave this sand-pit! After a pleasant flight to Malta, we touched down in a rainstorm at about 10 pm Egyptian time. We had a good meal at the restaurant here; and I see that, like Fayid, it had been greatly improved since I last passed this way in 1952. After a wait of about two

Last look at the Suez Canal from the Hermes

hours, we were eventually told that there was fog at Blackbushe Airport, so our flight would be delayed.

'I recognised a Gunner from 145 Battery in our group so I went over and spoke to him. His name is Martin. He told me that he is going home on compassionate leave. He also said that he was on Lakeside Guard duty last night so he was rather sleepy! At 12 midnight we were driven about 5 miles to the Transit Camp through winding lanes and between stonewalls. We were told that we would be called at about 3.30 am.'

Then on Monday 30 November I wrote: – 'After a few hours sleep we were woken up again, and then waited for our transport to take us all back to the Hermes aircraft. Unfortunately we could see virtually nothing of Malta because it was still before sun-rise. We eventually took off at 5 GMT and reached Blackbushe after 11 am. Oh boy! It was really wonderful to step off the 'plane and to feel that brisk, cool breeze, and to see the green grass and civilisation again! I 'phoned home at 12 and said that I'd be returning at about 3 pm. We left by coach soon after that, and arrived at Goodge Street

Arrival at Blackbushe Airport – Home again!

at 2.10. I had just got off the coach and was making for the reception room when I saw Dad waiting for me. Thoughtful as ever, he had made sure that he was there to greet me and to drive me home'.

That night at home we all had a fish and chips supper together, and after that, I had a luxurious soak in a hot bath – my first since Government House in Cyprus, over twelve months before – another lasting memory!

Before the crack of dawn on the following morning, as usual, my father and Derek (my elder brother) were up and off to work at OCS. A few hours later, I drove to Woolwich to collect my Release Papers. I was also pleased to note that a grateful Army had paid me right up to 26 December, which I thought was very generous of them!

So ended my two years involvement in the 'Army Game'. During those two most impressionable years, I had been given a full measure of adventure, responsibility and experience that I could have gained in few other ways. These extraordinary and important years of my growing up were to influence my perspective and outlook on life for the rest of my days. I can appreciate now, that I had enlisted as a 'young lad' and had finished as a 'young man'. Many others must have found the same.

Strangely enough, the diaries which I had written so conscientiously during the whole of 1952 and 1953 were allowed to remain unread and discarded for many decades on my bookshelf. It was only when I delved into them in more recent years that my interest grew, and I found that many long forgotten memories had come racing back.

Luckily, I had normally recorded my experiences – both mundane and remarkable – in sufficient detail to remind myself about long forgotten events. Although there are also some other episodes about which I fervently wish I had written more. Time and space often determined how much I could write down, but on occasions, I also know that I saw little point in mentioning more details about some matters which were so very familiar to me at the time. Having said this, my main problem through-out the writing of *Recollections* has been in deciding how much to include and how much to discard.

In the foregoing chapters, I have attempted to give you an accurate, rounded and objective account of my experiences. I hope in so doing, that I have not been too long-winded nor included too much tiresome esoteric detail. I must also reiterate at this late stage, that if you believe I have made up or embellished any of the episodes related in these pages, then I reply that you are in error. I am reminded of Marco Polo's telling reply when some denounced him for exaggerating his experiences; he remarked disarmingly: 'I haven't even told you the half of it!'

Regarding the photographs that I took during those two years – now here I have many regrets. I just cannot understand why I took so few photographs of *people* – my close friends and colleagues. That was an omission that I can neither explain nor fully understand.

So the foregoing chapters are all that I have decided to include about my Army experiences from 6 December 1951 until December 1953. I was now back in Britain, twenty years old and fancy-free. As long ago as January 1953, my 'first love' Jennifer Chisholm had written me a 'Dear John' letter, which caused me much unhappiness at the time – although by my return, I had reconciled myself to this sad loss.

I was now ready to start living my young life – unlike the poor unfortunate David Nicoll, killed in Korea – and the whole world was out there waiting for me......

Within a few months I had rejoined Office Cleaning Services Limited at their newly acquired Smart's Laundry in Earlsfield, South London, and it was in this dilapidated and ramshackle old plant that I finally put the 'Army Game' behind me, and started my working life – as a trainee dogsbody!

It was not dissimilar to playing *Snakes and Ladders:* – I willingly went down one of the snakes back to square one. Meanwhile, I imagined with a few regrets that most of my erstwhile National Service friends in 29 Field were by now firmly established in their Universities.

Such is life! But read on...

CHAPTER 16

Postscript from 2003

Towards the end of 2002, whilst I was still in the midst of writing Chapter 15 of *Recollections*, my curiosity increased about the possibility of finding out what had happened to some of those congenial friends of mine, who were so well known to me during my time in National Service. Fifty years had passed since we had all left the Army, and yet I remembered meeting just four of them since we had all gone our separate ways in 1952 and 1953. Where were they all now? I realised that some of them might well have fallen off their perches, but in any case, since we were all over 70 years old by now, it was essential that I should start my search straightaway.

In this Postscript Chapter, I have decided to print in heavy type, all those persons I have mentioned in earlier chapters.

As you will know, I had frequently met **Ian Lucas** (Oswestry and Mons) after 1953, because we had both joined the Surrey Yeomanry Territorials together, and often saw each other at Parades and at the yearly Firing Camps at Larkhill, Sennybridge or Otterburn. I was also one of the godfathers to their son David. Also, when Ian and I were working in the City of London during the 1950s, we had often met up for lunch together, and sometimes asked **Bob Bartlett** to join us.(another colleague of Oswestry and Mons). In due course however, Bob and I went our separate ways.

Bryan Ingham (in Fox Battery at Mons) was another person I met in Macclesfield whenever I went to Manchester during the 1960s and 1970s, although he became ill in about 1985, and I always concluded that he must have died about that time.

Richard Davies should also be mentioned in this respect, although unlike the other three, our friendship went back to our schooldays and had nothing at all to do with our time in National Service. Richard now lives near Leicester, but whenever he visits London, we regularly meet for a stimulating lunch together. In fact, Richard, more than anyone else, encouraged me to persist in completing these *Recollections*.

So apart from these four, at the end of 2002, I decided to start my search in earnest for six of my other main friends from National Service days. After pursuing a number of fruitless lines of enquiry, it suddenly dawned upon me to contact their Old Boys' Associations, so I started telephoning the relevant schools enthusiastically: –

- Wellington College for **John Stansfield**;
- Haileybury for **Dick Brimelow**;
- Marlborough College for **Harry Cotter**;
- Aldenham School for **Mike Logan** – my four main friends in 29 Field in MELF;
- and then Harrow School for **Jerry Treherne-Thomas**, my friend at Oswestry and Mons;
- and Downside Abbey for **Jack Collett** – my particular friend at Oswestry who went into the Intelligence Corps.
- For obvious reasons, I discounted any attempt to locate my close friend at Mons, **Brian Jones**!

I soon discovered that, due to the Data Protection Act, school associations are now very circumspect about revealing any information over the telephone. Nonetheless, all agreed to forward any letters I sent to them straightaway. Only those at Harrow School and Haileybury trusted me enough to sensibly take pity and to forget the rules. From these two I learned straightaway that poor **Jerry Treherne-Thomas** had died in Pittsburg, USA in 1994 – whilst **Dick Brimelow** was alive and well and now living near Macclesfield.

Dick's telephone number was easily found from Directory Enquiries, and when I telephoned him, he nearly fell off his chair! We quickly bridged the fifty year gap, and we had a half-hour long conversation together about times past and present. He told me that the only one of our former colleagues in 29 Field he was still in touch with was **John Stansfield**. Dick also reminded me that we had in fact met up a few times after returning to

England – about which I had completely forgotten – and went on to say that I had been an usher at his Wedding in 1958! He was very keen to read *Recollections*, so I posted off a few draft Chapters to him, and promised to let him know if I managed to contact any of our other mutual friends.

This was a most encouraging start to my enquiries, and having sent off the other four exploratory letters, I soon received a welcome response from both **John Stansfield** and **Mike Logan**; however, as the subsequent weeks passed into March and April 2003, I still failed to receive any response from either **Harry Cotter** or **Jack Collett.**

But flushed with these early three successes, the other person I decided to telephone, was **Geoffrey (Greg) Peck**, my Old Carthusian colleague in both Charlie Company and Fox Field Battery at Mons. I looked him up on the school list, and managed to speak to him straightaway. Like Dick Brimelow, Greg was extremely surprised when I telephoned him out of the blue, but the past came flooding back, and we had a long chat together, and promised to meet up. He was now living in Tenterden in Kent, and as I expected, he was still in touch with his three great friends in Fox Battery – always called the 'gang of four' – namely, **John Morley** (one of the 'Gladiators'), **Mike Gibbon** and **John Moore**.

When we were all at Mons Officer Cadet School, these four always kept together whenever possible. All four had been friends since the beginning of their Basic Training at Oswestry, and all four had 'Failed Watch' together on their first attempt at WOSB, but then, all four had passed together on the second attempt. They had all started at Mons at the same time as me, and all four had sailed through the hazards of OCTU without a hitch and were Commissioned from Fox Troop with me – which shows the importance of including 'Failed Watch' within the WOSB test.

When I sent **Greg Peck** Chapters 3, 4, 5 and 6, he was delighted, and sent copies onto the other three without delay. Sure enough, within a few weeks, I received letters from both **John Morley** and **Mike Gibbon**. **John Moore** was away in South Africa.

Therefore, as a result of my initial enquiries during December and early

2003, I was now in touch with seven of my former National Service colleagues, and as time went on, I also contacted **Tom Keeble**. Many letters were exchanged between us, and I also met some of them for lunch in the meantime.

Each one of them passed on various remembrances and anecdotes about their own experiences during National Service, and in this postscript of *Recollections,* I have included a selection of their comments and anecdotes below, which supplement aspects of Army life already touched upon in other chapters.

***

To start with, I have included the remarks made by my friend **Richard Davies**, who preceded me in National Service by a few weeks – much to my advantage. When I told him in 2002 that I was in the midst of writing up my National Service diaries for the benefit of my children and grandchildren, he was most eager to read some of the draft Chapters, and he gave me some helpful advice and encouragement. Richard is a very cultured and well-read individual, and he avidly devoured all the Chapters I gave to him. So much of the contents reminded him of his own experiences – especially about Mons – that before long he sent me the following comments: –

'I think I remember several of the names you mention – **Harry Cotter**, of course, and also both **John Stansfield** and **Dick Brimelow** seem to ring a bell. But the names that really jump off the page are **RSM Brittain, CSM Storey** and **CSM Bennett**.

'My first and unpleasant encounter with **RSM Brittain** happened early on at Mons, and involved my boots. My Army issue boots pulled on my heels which became bruised and blistered. I therefore went to an Army surplus store and bought a pair which were much more comfortable and, so far as I could see, looked identical to the ones the Army had given me. At the next Parade on the Square, Brittain strutted down the line, stopped in front of me, and in his usually stentorian voice, screamed at me: 'Are those regulation boots, Mr Davies?' My faltering explanation produced an even louder, 'Sergeant! Put him in the Guard House!' I seemed to be lifted bodily and rushed into a cell in the Guard House. I was denied the single phone call which is granted to all criminals upon arrest, but a kindly Orderly slipped me a cigarette through the bars while I contemplated a return to my Unit (an RTU), the ruin of my military career and even, possibly a Courts Marshal!

'Then my guardian angel appeared in the form of **CSM Storey**, our Mons mentor, who immediately 'sprung me' and took me to see the Medical Officer:

'**CSM Storey**: 'I'll do the talking'.

Richard Davies: 'Yes, Sir'.

Then, when in front of the MO, **CSM Storey** said: 'This man has trouble with his regulation boots, Sir. He needs a certificate to say that he must use medically approved ones.'

Doctor: 'That sounds a bit fishy ? but OK'. The Certificate was handed over.

Next morning, at Adjutant's Parade to deal with the previous day's defaulters, **CSM Storey** told Richard: 'I'll do the talking, understood?'
Richard Davies: 'Yes, Sir'.

After being called in, the Adjutant, **Captain Webb-Bowen**, of the Welsh Guards: 'Charged with wearing non-regulation boots on parade; why?'

CSM Storey: 'A slight misunderstanding, Sir. His boots are non-regula-tion, but these have to be worn on Medical Officer's orders.' The MO's Certificate is placed in front of the Adjutant.

Captain Webb-Bowen, after a long stare at both of us, eventually says: 'It sounds a bit fishy to me – but OK – case dismissed'.

Richard Davies said that he always wondered whether or not his painless release from this critical situation had been due entirely to the fact that **Captain Webb-Bowen** and **CSM Storey** were both from the Welsh Guards! Looking at this 'amusing' anecdote now – though certainly not 'amusing' for Richard at the time – I, myself, am quite certain that this whole charade was just another example of the 'Army Game' in action during the 1950s!

Richard continued with his recollections of fifty years ago: – 'Several weeks after this episode, I was selected as one of the 'Stick Men' who you may recall wore large diagonal white strips across their chests and a pace stick under their left arm and slow-marched up the steps, escorting the visiting General at the end of each Passing Out Parade. On the great day **RSM Brittain**, trying to look inconspicuous, glided along just behind me and I heard the almost inaudible words slipping from under his bristly little moustache, 'Well done Mr Davies! Just keep that steady pace. You're doing fine!' Either he bore no grudges, or he had forgotten all about the boots episode, because on that occasion he was kindness itself, and clearly showed me that he had a heart of gold under that terrifying exterior!

'**CSM Bennett's** 'soft centre' was certainly not visible when I was doing an extra drill (jankers?) with him in a damp and wind-swept Gun Shed one night. He ran us up and down for the best part of half an hour with a brief pause for what he called a 'quiz'. From behind me he shouted loudly into my right ear: 'What's the colour of the hat band of the Coldstream Guards?' 'White Sir', I replied. 'I should think so too,' said Bennett. That question was burnt into my brain and has stayed in my memory without the slightest difficulty for 52 years!

'Finally, a few words about **Harry Cotter**, who was in my Battery at Mons: Harry often seemed to be badly organised when it came to being on parade on time and in good order. I remember one of the weekly rehearsals for a Passing Out Parade in particular. The scabbard of Harry's bayonet was badly chipped and he had forgotten to re-paint it in time. Nonetheless he put it in its frog and attached it to the back of his belt, and then asked me to paint it in situ with what he optimistically called, 'quick drying paint'. Once on the Square, **RSM Brittain** with his uncanny flare soon homed in on Harry's bayonet and proceeded to pick it up. Next minute, Harry was flying across the Square to the Guard House, while Brittain did his best to remove the black paint from the palm of his hand with his white handkerchief!'

***

Dick Brimelow, my friend in 79 Battery of 29 Field, the first of my erstwhile colleagues I contacted at the end of 2002, was also the first to write me a letter. He immediately remembered **Richard Davies** when he read about him in *Recollections,* because both he and **Harry Cotter** had trained at Mons in the same Battery. Dick went on to relate a few of his own memories.

He told me that after National Service, he had read Law at Oxford, and was later called to the Bar in 1957. He met his wife at Oxford, and after starting his career with ICI, he moved onto the Swiss Chemical Company, CIBA-GEIGY, where he became a Company Secretary. He and Elizabeth have five children.

About his time at Mons, he told me that during one of the training schemes in the Field Batteries, it came to his turn to take over as Gun Position Officer. He was given a map reference by his Troop Instructor, and then told to go on ahead and lay out the next Gun Position for the guns. On a fast moving day scheme like this, when jobs are changed between cadets, it was often difficult to pick up the map for the first time, and then to quickly decide your exact position and work out exactly where you had to go. Unfortunately for Dick, he completely misread his position on the map, and went driving off in the wrong direction. When he did eventually find his way back to the correct map reference, his guns were already there, waiting for him to arrive! He therefore had to lay out each gun position as quickly as possible, so that they could occupy their positions! He could easily have been relegated for such a bad faux-pas, but he luckily survived with just a severe ticking off! (As I mentioned in Chapter 6, *I* had a similar experience to this at Mons.)

Dick said that so many of the happenings he read about in *Recollections* had reminded him of his own experiences – 'long since buried in the sands of time!' He entirely agreed with my comments about the congeniality of our National Service colleagues, and he also agreed wholeheartedly about the high calibre of the Regular officers we had in our Regiment. They made a lasting impression upon him, especially since he was then such 'a very callow nineteen-year-old youth' (Dick's words). It is easy to forget now, just how *very young* we all were.

On his journey to join the Regiment after Mons, Dick had travelled slowly on the troopship *Empire Trooper* (like most of the earlier arrivals in 29 Field), so when he eventually reached the Regiment to start his soldiering again, his Gunnery knowledge had not been tested for nearly two months. However, Dick was very soon thrown into the deep end. He told me: –

'On my arrival at Ava Camp, the Regiment was out firing on the Ranges, so I was driven out in a Land Rover to the Observation Post, where a group of officers, including the Commanding Officer, **Lt Col Chris Hutt**, were directing the shoots. I was looking forward to learning a few pointers from all the other experienced Gunner Officers around me, but when the next shoot started, the CO turned to me and said that he would like *me* to take the next shoot! Oh dear! I just about managed to cope with this unfair ordeal, but I thought that it was a ridiculous decision for him to have made. Perhaps it was this sort of illogical decision which had made him generally disliked by many of the Regular officers in the Regiment – as I later learned.'

When **Dick Brimelow** wrote to me, he also mentioned that one of his lasting memories of 29 Field was the outstanding success of our Regimental Soccer team in the BTE Championships at the end of 1952. Maybe because the competition was well underway by the time I returned from Cyprus at the end of November, I wrote few meaningful details about this tournament in my diary, so I now remember surprisingly little about it. But I do recall that our team was very successful, and also that much of this success was due to the flamboyant **Malcolm Ross,** who I knew little before he left the Regiment. Dick on the other hand was Malcolm's colleague in 79 Battery, so they knew each other well. He wrote: –

'The one National Serviceman who impressed me immediately that I arrived was **Malcolm Ross**, a cheerful extrovert, and a most unmilitary type with wavy, ginger hair and freckles, and also a rolling gait which was quite unsuited to the parade ground! His great achievement was to inspire the Regimental Soccer Team to become the Suez Canal Zone Champions. He did this by sheer force of personality and enthusiasm, even though he had no particular bent for football. The team loved him and their successes were a terrific boost for the whole Regiment.'

From what I do remember, I agree entirely with these comments of Dick, so a little more needs to be said about **Malcolm Ross** at this point: – he really was a most humorous character and he often kept us amused in the Mess by his strange antics and histrionics. He was the sort of person who could easily have made a career for himself on the stage. He was always ready to organise an entertainment show for the troops, and I expect that it was Malcolm who had written that clever skit about a Troop Command Post as seen by William Shakespeare (referred to in Chapter 9). He was very adept at writing parodies, and **John Stansfield** luckily sent me a parody on *Paradise Lost* which Malcolm had written soon after his arrival in the Canal Zone. Part of which ran as follows: –

'Is this the region, this the soil, the clime?'
Said then the forlorn Gunner.
'This, the seat that we must change for Ballah,
This mournful gloom for that celestial light?'

'Be it so, since he who now is CRA (Commander RA)
Can dispose and bid what shall be right.
But farthest from him is best, whom reason hath equalled,
And force hath made supreme above his equals'.

'Farewell happy fields where joy forever dwells;
Hail horrors, Hail infernal world, and thou
Profoundest Hell receive thy new possessed: –
One who brings a mind not to be changed by place or time'.

'The mind is its own place, and in itself
Can make a Heaven of Hell, a Hell of Heaven.
What matter where, if I still be the same, and what I should be,
All but less than he whom pips hath made greater?'

'Here at least we shall be free.
Here we may reign secure, and in my choice,
One pip is worth ambition though in Hell:
Better to reign in Hell than serve in Civvy Street!'

I am sure that these words from **Malcolm Ross** illustrate the man.

As I say, I never knew Malcolm very well. I expect that he went on to become a barrister, or maybe a politician! But as Dick says, the way Malcolm managed to fire up our Regimental Soccer Team was an object lesson on team motivation. I suppose he must have had some of those ineffable qualities possessed by the likes of Alf Ramsey, Matt Busby and Brian Clough.

***

I was really delighted when I received some newsy letters from my particular friend in MELF, **John Stansfield**. He replied immediately after receiving my first exploratory letter, and I sent him most of the Chapters of *Recollections*.

He told me that after taking his degree in Engineering at Cambridge University, he had worked in various Companies until he moved to IBM, where he remained until his retirement in 1993. With IBM he had been transferred to Paris in 1971, where he married his French wife Brigitte. They lived then in Montesson, to the west of Paris, with their two daughters.

He sent me an excellent photograph of **RSM Brittain**, which I have been able to include in Chapter 5, *Infantry Training at Mons*, and he also related a typical anecdote about Brittain, which had stuck firmly in his mind after all these years! He wrote: –

'I recall one fateful drill day on the Parade Ground with about 5 Squads under the eagle eye of **RSM Brittain**. On this particular morning, when I was in a great hurry to get to the drill parade on time, I forgot to attach my frog and bayonet to my belt. You can imagine that I was on tenterhooks during that drill parade, waiting for the dreaded order: 'Fix bayonets!' Sure enough, the order did come, so I went through the motions as if I had a bayonet! Then we started marching up and down again. Since I was in the middle of the Squad, there was still a chance that I wouldn't be observed – but not a bit of it! There was suddenly a high-pitched shout from Brittain: – 'Get that man! – That one without a bayonet!' **CSM**

Storey quickly identified me, and hauled me out in front of our Squad. Brittain came over quickly and towered above me – and called me a string of names that I now forget – except that none of them was in the least bit complimentary! The result was that I was given extra drills and had my weekend leave cancelled. All this may sound rather amusing now, but I can assure you, that at the time, it was anything but funny!'

John also sent me a copy of the brief diary which he kept during his time with 29 Field. This was most interesting for me to read, but unfortunately the remarks were written in such a brief way that they failed to include many details or (more important) any of his opinions. He just recorded the bare facts. Nonetheless, he did fill in some gaps which I had left out from my own version of events in *Recollections*, and confirmed how often we went to the open-air cinema in 10 BOD

For instance, (because I never sailed) I had forgotten just how much sailing was done on the Bitter Lakes during my time in the Zone. I see that **John Stansfield** frequently went out sailing in the afternoons with **Mike Martin**, **Mike Logan**, and **Ray Kelly**, as well as with **Barney** and **Rex King**. Also, I learned that many other Regulars also had sailing boats moored in the Great Bitter Lake near the Officers' Club at Fayid.

I was also amused when he wrote succinctly after finishing a session running one of those dreadful night Road Patrols: — 'In the afternoon I spent the time doing some 'Egyptian PT'. This was the term we used when we rested on our beds for a sleep!

But I have also included below, just a few more random snippets from his diary about life in the Suez Canal Zone in 1953, which expand upon my own comments – including the unfortunate death of one of our soldiers which I omitted to mention, and also the problem **David Carter** had after just 5 days in the Suez Canal Zone!. Here are some of the notes that John made at the time: –

'**11 January**: **1953:** – Went through the accounts of 'Pieces of Eight' (the 8 Battery OR's Mess) with Battery Commander (**Barney**). Strong cold wind blowing.'

'**31 January 1953:** – In the evening, we dined out **Lt Col Hutt OBE,** who is leaving the Regiment after a year's appointment as CO. He was taken around the camp in a Quad and Trailer.'

'**2 February 1953:** – Bombardier Spiers died in hospital of meningitis.'

'**9 February 1953:** – Checked Bombardier Spier's kit all afternoon with BC. ROO today. Many 'westernised oriental gentlemen' outside 10 BOD last night – 4 were killed. Inspected Guard at 04.00 hrs.'

'**11 February 1953**: – Watched the final of the 1st division football championship at Fayid with 29 Field v 3 Grenadier Guards which ended in a draw 2 – 2. Rowdy Dinner Night this evening.

'**1 March 1953:** – 29 Field v 25 Field Regiment Royal Engineers in Semi-Final BTE Soccer Cup. Won in thrilling game 6-4. Went to Church in the evening.'

'**5 March 1953:** – Played rugby in the afternoon, and took half the skin off my face when Sgt Field tackled me. Went to bed early with a slight headache.'

'**10 March 1953:** – Orderly Officer today. Turned out the Guard at 03.20. Saw a desert fox to the north end of the camp. Electricity went off in the camp this evening. In charge of Road Patrol tomorrow night.'

'**18 July 1953**: – Had BC's Inspection – not too bad – followed by laying tests. In the afternoon, sailed *Barbara* with the Adjutant; came 3rd. We went to the flicks to see *One Piece Bathing Suit* with Esther Williams. 105° F in the shade today.

'**23 July 1953:** – **David Carter** (a NS Subaltern) arrived yesterday. Took laying tests in the morning. Went swimming with **Brian Goodliffe** and **Mike Logan**; we had the swimming pool to ourselves. Saw very good film, John Mills in *The Long Memory*.'

'**27 July 1953** – Preparation for course shooting. Did Battery survey with

Mike Martin. Played **Dick Brimelow** tennis in the afternoon. Rather a strong wind. **David Carter** suffered from heat stroke. Taken to BMH.

'**30 July 1953** – Did Safety Officer for Easy Troop. **Ray Kelly's** fix was 1,300 yards out. I spotted this on my 1/25,000 map. The second round landed 50 yards from OP as I had expected. The CRA came to GP and agreed with my map spot.

John also reminded me about the role played by our local friendly Egyptian called 'Busty', who lived and operated in an Army-issue tent just outside the entrance to Ava Camp. He had a little shop there, from which he sold delicacies from Cairo, such as excellent Turkish Delight. In addition to this, he also provided an important dhobi service (i.e. laundry service) for all those in the Regiment who wanted to use it. I clearly remember how he ironed the shirts after washing, by sucking up some water in his mouth, and then spitting it out onto the shirts whilst ironing them to perfection!

He used to also grow tomatoes and other vegetables in a small vegetable plot outside his tent, and it was interesting to see just how fertile the desert sand was for these crops – so long as the plants were watered and tended properly. Also, the added bonus for those living in that part of the world, was that sometimes, as many as three crops could be harvested during the course of one year!

Unfortunately, due to the antipathy of the Egyptian Government towards the British Troops in the Suez Canal Zone, the authorities put restrictions on these Egyptian entrepreneurs from time to time, and towards the end of my stay, I wrote in my diary on 11 November 1953: –

'I hope that Busty will be able to get some Turkish Delight for me to take home. The Egyptians have recently tightened up their controls, and have made it much more difficult to bring in these goods from Cairo. We have just heard about one trader has been fined £E100 and been given 3 months imprisonment! They are stupid people these Egyptians; they could so easily make plenty of money from the British troops in the Zone if they were more sensible.'

Also, **John Stansfield** told me more details about some of the individuals mentioned elsewhere in these chapters. For example, he knew our mutual friend **Mike Martin** very well. He had been on holiday in Greece and Cyprus with him, and had kept in touch with him after National Service had finished. He told me that in 1956, Mike had been appointed ADC to Sir John Harding, the Governor and Commander-in-Chief in Cyprus in the middle of the troubles. Sadly, it was soon after this appointment that he had suddenly contracted a severe dose of polio – which was very prevalent in the 1950s – and so, was immediately sent back to the Churchill Hospital in Oxford. John had seen him there whilst he was undergoing treatment in an 'iron lung' machine. Sadly, this treatment was to no avail. Just a few months after this visit, poor Mike died.

Mike Martin was my first mentor after joining the Regiment from Mons, and he was a most helpful, congenial and generous-hearted colleague to work with. One of his favourite comments was 'splendid!' – and he would exclaim this word with great enthusiasm whenever he felt that his approval was called for. Like many sons of vicars, he was educated at St John's School in Leatherhead, and after Sandhurst, had joined 29 Field just before it was sent to the Suez Canal Zone. He was a very keen and competent young Subaltern, and I am quite certain that he would have progressed well in the Army had he lived longer. His tragic, early death underlines once again, just how grossly unfair this mortal life on earth can be! Is there anyone up there listening?

John Stansfield also knew Captain **Geoff Denis** very well – my great competitor in the 'bottle game' mentioned in Chapter 14. They had travelled out together in the Troopship *Empire Windrush* when they had first joined 29 Field in April 1952. Geoff was an Old Wykehamist, and another of those first-rate officers we had in our Regiment at the time. John told me that Geoff had started off as a Guards' Officer before he had transferred to the Royal Artillery, and was always proud of that training. He particularly liked drill parades, and made sure that he was one of the smartest officers in the Regiment. He was also a great lover of classical music, and I know that he was a regular attender in **John Flinn's** tent for our record sessions.

John Stansfield also told me that after his second year at Cambridge, he and Geoff had been on holiday together through France and Spain, when they had driven Geoff's old Mercedes. He said that they had kept in touch with each other until about 1977. Geoff was stationed in BAOR for a period, and whilst he was there, he met **Mac** (my Troop Commander in Baker Troop). Apparently, poor **Mac** had been involved in a bad motor accident whilst he was there, and this had resulted in much plastic surgery as well as a long spell in hospital. This was yet another example of the f—-king, fickle finger of fate playing its part with my erstwhile colleagues in 29 Field.

Many of the Regular Officers after the War found it difficult to settle down and to find suitable jobs in civilian life, and **Geoff Denis** was another example of this. He was a most personable man, but even so, **John Stansfield**, knowing him well, said that 'he couldn't imagine Denis moving easily from his role in the Army to a solid 9 to 5 job, especially in a large organisation like IBM'.

John Stansfield also knew **Jim Cummins** well from his school days at Wellington, and after reading my comments in Chapter 15, John said that he had thoroughly concurred with my remarks about him. He went on to say that he was really quite surprised that Jim had passed through Mons as he did, and also that he had signed on for the extra year as a Short-Term Regular. John reminded me that Jim was a pious person – which I had quite forgotten – and that he frequently pontificated to us on religious matters. One of his favourite sayings was 'God moves in strange ways'. It should not be surprising to learn therefore, that after leaving the Army, he had been ordained as a clergyman in the Church of England. When John met him in later years, he found that he was in charge of a parish near Norwich, which was not so far from where John lived at the time. Sadly, one of his three children had Down's syndrome.

***

Mike Logan, my erstwhile tent-mate in 29 Field, also wrote to me before Christmas 2002. Mike was then living in Lincolnshire, and he sent me a very newsy letter. He told me that I had in fact attended his Wedding to Sheila in 1956 – which I had also completely forgotten – and furthermore, that my Wedding present to them was three volumes of Winston Churchill's

History of the English Speaking Peoples! In my defence, I must confirm that Mike had specifically requested this set of books as a present from me!

Mike had attended Reading University where he read Agriculture, and after his marriage to Sheila, they travelled to Borneo to take up an appointment as a District Administrator where they remained for fifteen years. Unfortunately, after Independence, the country became part of Malaysia, and this resulted in his Service Agreement being terminated. As a result, he found himself back in the UK without a job. He eventually found a suitable appointment as the Group Secretary of the National Farmers' Union in North Lincolnshire, and there he happily spent the rest of his working life.

Mike told me that the only other person he had kept in touch with after leaving the Regiment was his friend in 79 Battery, **Tom Keeble** (Chapters 7 & 14). Tom had joined the Regiment about two months before me, and he was one of the National Service Subalterns I didn't know very well. He was a year or two older than most other National Servicemen, and I think that he was friendlier with the older Regular Subalterns in the Regiment like **John Kenny** and **Ray Kelly**. Before joining up, Tom had spent some years training to be a doctor but had failed to pass his final examinations. I remember Tom as being one of those people who looked upon his two years of National Service as a waste of time, and was always impatient to return to the UK. This was because he was anxious to have another attempt at qualifying as a doctor.

Dick Brimelow, who shared a tent with **Tom Keeble**, told me about one of the lighter moments Tom had in the Suez Canal Zone: – Dick remembers Tom stretched out on his bed, rolling helplessly in laughter, after **Mike Logan** had lost his spectacles down the officers' latrines after a heavy drinking session on one of our Mess Nights! Dick felt guilty about passing on that indiscreet tale to me after fifty years, but we are all the same, aren't we? Nothing remains more firmly in our memory banks than an amusing gaffe like that!

Mike Logan told me that after demobilisation, Tom had returned to his training as a doctor, and had qualified successfully on the second attempt, after which he had joined his father's Practice near Newbury. He had later married again, and on retirement had moved over to live in France near Paris. After our recent correspondence, Mike was able to tell **Tom Keeble** that he was living quite near to **John Stansfield**, so they got in touch with each other, and planned to meet up.

Mike was particularly interested to read Chapter 6 in *Recollections* about Fox Battery at Mons, because he had passed through Mons by the same route just a few months before me. In his letter to me, Mike wrote: –

'I can remember **Major Hamilton**, but we didn't have **Major Tice** like you, although it was **CSM Bennett** who was the one firmly imprinted on my whole being! We didn't call him 'Sergeant Major', but 'Sir'. When we arrived in front of the Battery Office, he said that he would call us 'Sir', and we would call him 'Sir'; but the only difference would be that *we* would really mean it! But in any case, there *was* a difference: – we called him 'Sah' to rhyme with 'car', whilst he called us 'Sur' to rhyme with 'cur'. But despite his fierceness, he was really a softee – with a bark much worse than his bite! – (**Richard Davies** would certainly not agree with *that* comment!)

'We had some illustrious people in our Battery: – there was Jeremy Mackay-Lewis the Master Gunner's son (his father is mentioned in Chapter 9), and we had Lord Medway as well. Bennett made sure that he kept them on his side. Lord Medway was highly amused when he was given a pep talk at the outset by Bennett who said: 'now then; let's get this straight from the start, Mister Lord f-ing Medway.....'

'In the Passing-out party, Bennett finally let his hair down, and I remember that he told us that he had made love to women of every race and creed, and the ones that stood out as perfect, were the Yugoslavs! I have met about 3 women of that race, and I must admit that I have always looked at them with especial interest as a result of that remark of Bennett's!'

Mike went on to tell me about two other remembrances he had about two of our colleagues in the Regiment. He wrote: –

'You mention **Mac** in 29 Field, who was an Ack Ack Gunner doing his prescribed stint with a Field Regiment, and I always thought that there was a certain antipathy between him and the other Regulars in 29 Field. I remember also that on an Exercise in the desert once, he was wearing a red silk scarf, when **Colonel Hutt** said to him: **'Mr Mackenzie**, you have the looks of a cowboy with that scarf round your neck.' As quick as a flash, Mac replied: 'I would be looking like a Red Indian without it Sir!' Isn't it strange how we remember such trivial incidents after so many years?

'The other remembrance I have is of **Gordon Stadward** (mentioned in Chapter 14), who was a Captain with me in 79 Battery. He used to long to be with his wife and family all the time, and was really fed up with Army life – but he couldn't think of another way of earning his living'. (This predicament was quite common after the War). 'I remember that he had a fervent hatred of flies, and would chase them furiously with his fly swatter whenever he was worried by them.'

Before I move on, **Mike Logan's** comments about **CSM Bennett** reminded me of another snippet passed onto me by another friend of mine who went through the mill of Fox Battery at Mons. During an inspection, Bennett was heard to shout forcefully: 'That's just damned idle Sir! – I bet you went to Eton or 'arrer!'

***

As a result of all the exchanges of letters and copy letters between **Dick Brimelow**, **John Stansfield, Mike Logan** and myself, I also heard from **Tom Keeble** in Paris.

Tom had very mixed views about those months we all spent together in the Suez Canal Zone. He wrote: 'It was for me a complete waste of time, and yet in retrospect it was a missed opportunity. I was clearly not designed for army life, and found military logic very frustrating. It didn't matter how logical *my* solution seemed to be, it was always necessary to follow the military route. Discipline is one thing, but stupid 'logic' is quite another. After reading your *Recollections*, I am only sorry that my boredom showed as much as it appears to have done!'

It seems from his remarks that Tom didn't fully appreciate that he was merely playing his allotted part – like us all – in the 'Army Game'!

Tom Keeble wrote me the following anecdotes: 'For a good while I was responsible for the 29 Field Officers' Mess catering at Ava Camp, and although we had a very good reputation for our high standards, I have to say that this was mainly due to circumstances entirely outside my control. Firstly, our Mess Sergeant had previously been trained at the Grosvenor House Hotel in London, and clearly knew exactly how things had to be done without any help from me. And secondly, very soon after I took over the job, a 'westernised oriental gentleman' called Ali, turned up most helpfully at the Mess Back Door, and started offering us fresh vegetables, chickens, eggs, fruit and many other appealing goodies, which until then had been extremely difficult to come by.

'Anyway, this most useful supply continued to arrive regularly for many months, until one day when a Mess Dinner was due, without any warning, Ali failed to turn up! We learned later that he had been jailed because he had been supplying some of our needs liberally from the Commander-in-Chief's garden!'

Another incident Tom recalled about his time with 29 Field, was a memorable duck shooting expedition which he made 'towards the end of his stint' with two of our Regular Subalterns, **John Kenny** and **John Flinn**: – 'This involved a pre-dawn start, a long drive, and also getting very wet by wading through some marshes for over an hour. Although we sighted no ducks at all during this time, we were greatly encouraged to keep on searching, because we frequently heard a quacking sound nearby. Eventually, we realised that all this quacking was only being made by the noisy local frogs! We returned back to Ava Camp, tired, wet and empty handed!'

There will be more about **Tom Keeble, Dick Brimelow, John Stansfield** and **Mike Logan** in the next Chapter.....

***

Next, a few words about **Geoffery (Greg) Peck**, who was my contemporary at Charterhouse, and who also trained with me in the Companies as well as in Fox Battery at Mons Officer Cadet School.

Our paths had seldom crossed at school, and as I have said, even when at Mons together, Greg and I had our own particular friends, so we saw no more of each other than the rest of our colleagues in Fox Battery. Of the 'gang of four', I suppose that I knew **John Morley** better than the other three, because he and I were both one of Tice's 'Gladiators' – John was a very competent three mile runner.

After leaving Mons, Greg's three friends, **John Morley, Mike Gibbon** and **John Moore**, were all posted to various Regiments with BAOR in Germany, whilst Greg himself was returned to 17 Training Regiment at Oswestry. I thought that this was an unfortunate posting for him to have been given, but then he had made the cardinal mistake of actually *mentioning* a posting to Oswestry as his third choice, which had virtually 'guaranteed' him a posting there! In the event however, he found that this posting – as with everything else in life – had its plusses as well as its minuses. He told me that he had passed a pleasant year there playing plenty of cricket and other sport, as well as taking frequent periods of home leave. My elder brother **Derek** had also been posted there after Mons, and he had really quite enjoyed the life in a Training Regiment in Park Hall Camp, with its low-key soldiering, and plenty of cricket, golf and fishing.

After leaving National Service, Greg had become a schoolmaster and taught at a number of schools, including Loretto and later had become an Educational Consultant before he retired.

After National Service, Greg told me that 'the gang of four' were variously occupied: – **John Morley** went into car fleet management, **Mike Gibbon** ran a privately owned Printing Ink Company, and **John Moore** had immigrated into South Africa.

It was **Greg Peck** who reminded me about the command shouted out to us in Charlie Company by **CSM Wilkinson** whilst we were marching to a Church Parade: 'Now remember Gentlemen, you're goin' to Church this mornin' – so for *Christ's sake SING!?*

He also remembered **Sgt Snaith** remarking once: 'That's just idle, **Mister Knowles** – *you* will end up in the Guard'ouse – and *I* – just couldn't care less.'

***

John Morley was the second person from the 'gang of four' to contact me, and since he was an outstanding long distance runner and one of Tice's 'gladiators' in Fox Battery, I saw much more of him than the others during my time in Fox Battery at Mons. Luckily, John had also written an interesting account of his time in the Army, and many of the points he recorded about his weeks before and during Mons supplemented my own comments. For instance, I had completely forgotten that our pay as Gunners was just 28 shillings per week (i.e. £1.40 pence in today's deflated currency), so I understood straightaway why we usually walked or took buses whenever possible, instead of using expensive taxis! He also reminded me about the revolting tea we were given at Oswestry, which was heavily laced with bromide to curb our aggression and sexual urges!

After Oswestry, whilst the 'gang of four' were waiting to retake their WOSB after 'Failing Watch', they were all posted together to 5 RHA Field Regiment (Royal Horse Artillery) at Larkhill. John wrote that, during their time off, they sometimes went into Salisbury together, and he reminded me that hitch-hiking was a very common way for servicemen to travel in the country areas in those days. I do remember that most motorists would stop in the 1950s whenever they saw someone in Army uniform hitch-hiking, and John said that on one occasion, they were lucky enough to be picked up by a kind middle-aged lady who straightaway took them to a suitable pub, and treated them all to a slap-up meal! It really pleased my heart to read that endearing little anecdote, which I'm quite sure was not at all unusual in those days.

I also found that John's reaction and comments after arriving at Mons OCTU were most interesting – and so very true. He wrote:

'An Officer Cadet at Mons OCS was a strange person. He still held the rank of 'Gunner' yet was called 'Sir' by all the Non-Commissioned Drill

Sergeants and Instructors. Nothing, however, could convey greater contempt than the intonation of that title when used to draw attention to some piece of stupidity or neglect on the part of the cadet! A white plastic disc was worn behind the Cap Badge to denote one's status in this strange place which was Mons Officer Cadet School.

'The Officers and NCOs in charge of us were a pretty good bunch on the whole. At times their bite was every bit as bad as their bark, but as the Course progressed, a mutual respect and recognition developed. However, if there was any sign of a Cadet being 'idle' – a favourite Army term of abuse which covered a wide spectrum – this brought instant retribution. **BSM Bennett** was quite a fierce character and rather enjoyed making the cadets jump about. He later melted completely however, at our Battery Passing-Out Party at the end of our Course, and was helpless with laughter at the antics and conjuring tricks of **Mike Gibbon** – a natural comedian and a member of the Magic Circle. No doubt, the fact that Bennett had been liberally supplied with beer throughout the evening assisted the unwinding process!'

After **John Morley** had received his Commission at the same time as me at Mons, he was posted for the rest of his National Service to 2 RHA (Royal Horse Artillery) which was considered one of the 'senior' Regiments in the Royal Artillery. The Regiment was then stationed at Hildesheim in BAOR 26, in the British Sector of West Germany. It should be recalled that in 1952, the Cold War with Russia was at its height, and Britain was providing many Divisions to the NATO Army Force in Europe. These soldiers were constantly 'on the alert' to counter any aggression shown by the massive Russian Army on the Eastern side of the Iron Curtain. This tension and alertness of the Regiments of BAOR in the 1950s, is difficult for us to fully appreciate today. Nonetheless, the USSR was a very real threat to the 'free democracies' in 1952 – and it was really difficult for many of us involved in those days, to excuse the antics and antipathetic views expressed by left-wingers like Michael Foot and Wedgewood Benn (and many others during that tense period) who ostensibly 'encouraged' their followers to stab the 'free' Democracies in the back in favour of the murderous Stalin's uncompromising Communistic ideology.

As we know, there was always much emphasis on sport of all kinds in the British Army, and **John Morley** gives some insight here into aspects of his life in BAOR in 1952/53:

'The accommodation and facilities which 2 RHA occupied were superb. They were situated on a former Luftwaffe Airfield, two miles from the town of Hildesheim. It was a vast area, and it was ideal for training and recreation, and included stabling for horses, squash and tennis courts, an athletics track, and an indoor riding school in one of the hangars. The other buildings were used for housing and maintaining the tanks and guns. All the new officers were expected to horse ride, and received early morning schooling if they needed it. The experienced riders took the horses far and wide over the Airfield and beyond, and some even went hunting with a pack of hounds whenever there was a meet! I learned to ride quite well, and enjoyed it, though I found that it conflicted later with my athletics training, to which I gave priority.'

I have to say that all John's descriptions about 2 RHA sound much more lavish than anything we ever had in Ava Camp in the Suez Canal Zone. But to rub it in, **John Morley** went on to say that he sometimes organised Regimental skiing trips into the Harz Mountains!

***

Mike Gibbon wrote to me soon after I had heard from **John Morley,** and like many others, it was **CSM Bennett** who had stuck firmly in his mind after fifty years. Mike wrote: – 'I have only managed to squeeze just a few drops of Army-related juice from my brain: –

You mention **Brian Angell**. Now he is a person that I *do* remember. I recall that he always had difficulty with the drilling at Mons. He must have dreaded that Parade Ground, because he was one of those people who swung his left arm when he put his left foot forward – he always got very confused at first, poor chap. That brought about a famous remark from **CSM Bennett**: – '**Angell?** You're no f-ing angel!' And it was also Bennett, whilst standing outside the church door as we filed in during one Church Parade, who said: – 'take yer 'at off in the 'ouse of the Lord, you c-t' "

Mike Gibbon continued: 'I was posted to 40 Field Regiment in Dortmund after we passed out of Mons, and I spent the rest of my service time there. It was all quite cushy really. My most dangerous task was dealing with the violent, highly-strung German chefs! Our accommodation was an ex-Luftwaffe Mess, which was a magnificent centrally heated castle-like building with a large, attractive cellar, ideal for parties. We used to improve our food in the Mess by selling off our cwt of issued prunes in the local market, and then buying some more luxurious food with the proceeds. This was of course highly illegal, but it made out Regiment very popular with the guests we invited to dine with us in our Mess!

'We had a reputation for good nosh in our Mess, and I recall one rather special Mess Night, when we were inviting a number of important guests from some of the neighbouring Regiments. When I went to check up on the kitchen about an hour before the dinner, I found the chef lying on the tiled floor and having an epileptic fit! It was a dangerous job being Mess Officer! That evening was rescued in the nick of time, by borrowing a chef from the Sergeants' Mess, which cost us the proceeds of our next cwt of prunes!

'Many an evening in the Mess, the German civilian barman used to regale us with horrific stories of everywhere he had dropped bombs in England. He could give precise, lurid details of his various sorties, smacking his lips, and pulling himself pints as the tension heightened. Apart from that, he was really quite a decent chap!'

***

On 15 April 2003, a letter arrived from Australia; it was from **Harry Cotter**! He told me that after much travelling – and retiring three times –he and his wife Olive finally settled down in the small coastal town of Woonona, about 50 miles south of Sydney.

He told me that he read Physics at Cambridge University, and after a spell of teaching at Cambridge, he soon found himself deeply involved in religious matters, particularly in the Church Missionary Society. He later moved out to work in Kenya for many years, and it was here that he met and married his wife Olive, and started raising their family of three girls and a boy.

After my sending Harry some more chapters of *Recollections* and replying to his letter, I received a second letter from him in September 2003. He wrote how much he enjoyed reading my account of our travels together in the Levant (Chapter 12), and also made the following comments on his disjointed remembrances of our journeys together: –

'On the flight from Fayid to Aqaba, I remember being surprised by the backward-facing seats in the aircraft, and also by the piles of animal carcasses put alongside the seats (this was the regular flight which took meat supplies to the British troops garrisoned in Aqaba). Luckily, due to the rear-view seats, we didn't see the wreckage of a recently crashed aircraft on the runway until after we had landed safely!

'You wrote about our shopping in Ma'an before we left for Petra, and I remember how the three of us stood outside the store – I can't imagine why – whilst a number of helpful but very grubby and snotty-nosed little boys stood by watching and giving their comments. Samples of each of the shop-keeper's suggestions were passed along the ring of dirty hands, so by the time the flat loaves of bread reached us the thought of eating them was clearly unthinkable – and so they went back the same way to the stall!

'Also, on our first day at our little hotel in Nicosia, Cyprus, I remember that we debated briefly about what we should wear for dinner on the first evening: – should it be ties as well as shirts? And jackets as well? Eventually, we decided to wear all three, just to be on the safe side. When we walked into the dining room, we found two American Servicemen sitting there bare from the waist up. I don't know who was more embarrassed, them or us!'

Isn't it interesting how our memories work after fifty years? Normally, we retain just the broad brush of our experiences in our minds, which become dimmer and dimmer as the years pass. But in addition to this, like **Harry Cotter**, we also clearly recall just a few isolated, trivial incidents – like individual stones of a lost mosaic.

Harry ends his letter on a much more serious note, and indeed, very much echoes the remarks made in Chapter 12. Regarding our visit to Jerusalem, he wrote:–

'I also have a lasting memory of the Arabs we met in Jerusalem and around. Everyone had a story to tell about a Jewish atrocity, or a dead relative, or lost land, or of other Arabs (or was it Jews?) who dug up graveyards and put a pick through the skull to make one less for the resurrection. And I have a lasting memory of the Arabs in the refugee camps, and the sense of hatred and evil I felt hanging around the place, like the build-up to a khamseen. I am not a psychic sort of person, but I remember being really depressed by all this. It fits in with the continuing hatred we still see in that unhappy country'.

As **Harry Cotter** commented: – 'In the new millennium, the situation in Palestine is just as tense as it ever was – and the inveterate hatred which we all witnessed as young lads in Jerusalem in 1953, still exists in the same measure as it ever did over fifty years ago'.

Having received the welcome response from **Harry Cotter**, I had no idea how I was going to bring these rambling *Recollections* to a conclusion.

Before long, **Dick Brimelow** and **Tom Keeble** came to my rescue. Hence the final Chapter, which follows........

CHAPTER 17

Short Postscript from 2004

The circulation during 2003 of the early drafts of *Recollections of Gunner Goodliffe*, immediately stimulated a renewed interest in the happenings of 1952 and 1953 and during the whole of that year there were many communications between the five of us who had served together in 29 Field Regiment. Not only were there letters and telephone calls, but a number of lunches were also arranged between us.

During a visit to London in May 2003, **Dick Brimelow** and I had a most enjoyable lunch together at Manzi's Fish Restaurant in London (sadly closed down in 2006), and although we had not met each other since I had been an usher at his Wedding in 1958, we immediately renewed our past friendship. By the time we eventually left the restaurant at 4 o'clock, we had seen all the other luncheon customers away! On another occasion, Dick had met **Mike Logan** at Hathersage in Derbyshire; and over in France, **John Stansfield** and **Tom Keeble** had also met in Paris.

Early in 2004, **Dick Brimelow** told me that he had been in touch with **Tom Keeble** in France, and that they proposed to organise a Reunion Lunch, together with wives, in Paris during the following June. This was an excellent idea, and before long all five of us had expressed enthusiasm to join the party. In due course, the date was fixed for 17 June 2004, and **Tom Keeble** selected Le Grand Colbert as a suitable venue, and agreed to make all the arrangements.

As it happened, I also saw a friend of mine who had served elsewhere in the Suez Canal Zone during the 1950s, and he told me that we are now entitled to wear the 'General Service Medal' in recognition for defending the Suez Canal so well against all comers! With our reunion coming up therefore, I made arrangements to buy some of these medals, so that I could present these to the others on the day.

I had also told **Harry Cotter** about our forthcoming lunch together, and a few days before we left for Paris, I received a welcome telephone call from him in Woonona, Australia, asking me to pass on his best wishes to the others. I had really hoped to have a letter from him to read out on the day, but nonetheless, a telephone message would serve as well.

In mid-June therefore, **Dick and Elizabeth Brimelow**, and **Cynthia** and I stayed two nights together at the Hotel Bedford in the centre of Paris, and **Mike and Sheila Logan** stayed at some lodgings they knew near Montmartre, whilst **Tom and Georgina Keeble** and **John Stansfield** met us at le Grand Colbert for lunch at 12 noon on the day. Unfortunately, **Brigitte Stansfield** was unable to join the party after all – or maybe it was because she just couldn't face five old British codgers reminiscing together!?

In the event, the food, the wine and the ambience were just right. The presentation of the General Service Medals was much appreciated – and the whole get-together proved to be a most memorable, worthwhile, enjoyable and convivial event.

Just have a look at the photographs!

So ends this whole saga.

Cynthia Goodliffe, Sheila Logan, Elizabeth and Dick Brimlow, Mike Logan

Georgina Keeble, Cynthia Goodliffe, Dr Tom Keeble, Dick Brimelow and
John Stansfield

John Stansfield

Dr Tom Keeble

Mike Logan

Dick Brimelow

Dick Brimelow and John Stansfield

Dick Brimelow, Brian Goodliffe
and Mike Logan

Elizabeth Brimelow, Sheila Logan, Georgina Keeble and Cynthia Goodliffe

Recollections of Gunner Goodliffe

List of Officers in
29 Field Regiment RA
(during 1952 & 1953)

Brereton (Peter)	Captain in 8 Battery
Bridge (George)	Major; Adjutant of 29 Field
Brimelow (Dick)	**2nd Lt; (NS) in 79 Battery**
Brook-Fox (Barney)	Major, BC of 8 Battery
Burgess (Ted)	Captain in 8 Battery (soon left)
Carter (David)	2nd Lt; (NS) in 79 Battery
Cattell (Bill)	Captain; first Regimental Doctor
Chapman (Bill)	Lt; in 145 Battery
Cotter (Harry)	**2nd Lt; (NS) in 145 Battery**
Cummins (Jim)	2nd Lt; Regular in 8 Battery
Denis (Geoff)	Captain in 145 Battery
Eve	Major; BC of 145 Battery
Flinn (John)	Lt/Captain in 79 Battery
Gilmour (John)	Lt/Captain in 8 Battery
Griffiths (Griff)	Captain in 79 Battery
Hacking (Nigel)	Captain in 145 Battery
Hambleton (Ronnie)	Lt/Captain in 145 Battery
Hutt (Chris) OBE	Lt Col., first CO of 29 Field (left early 1953)
Keeble (Tom)	**2nd Lt; (NS) in 79 Battery**
Kelly (David)	Major in 79 Battery (soon left)
Kelly (Ray)	Lt/Captain in 145 Battery
Kenney (John)	Lt/Captain in 79 Battery and RHQ
King (Rex)	Major; BK in 8 Battery
Lacey (Bill)	Captain of QMS
Lloyd (ERR)	Major, second BC of 8 Battery
Logan (Mike)	**2nd Lt; (NS) in 79 Battery**
Mackenzie (Mac)	Lt/Captain; in 8 Battery
MacGuinness (Jock)	Captain; second Regimental Doctor
Martin (Mike)	Lt/Captain; in 8 Bty & RHQ

Miller (Peter)	2nd Lt, (NS), RHQ (soon left)
Moberley (Bill) OBE	Major and 2 I/C of 29 Field
Orde (John)	Captain in 8 Battery
Potts (John)	2nd Lt, (NS) in 145 Battery
Prescott (Ted)	Captain in RHQ
Pritchard (Bill)	First Captain of Royal Signals in 29 Field
Roberts (Peter)	Major; first Adjutant of 29 Field
Rogers (John)	2nd Lt; Regular in 8 Battery
Ross (Malcolm)	2nd Lt, (NS) in 79 Battery
Savin (Lionel)	Captain in RHQ
Secker-Walker (David)	2nd Lt; (NS) in 145 Battery (soon left)
Shoreland (GA,Tiny)	Lt Col; Second CO of Regt (from 1953)
Sinclair (Ian)	2nd Lt; (NS) in 145 Battery
Spear (Ian)	Second Captain of Royal Signals in 29 Field
Spittle (Doug)	Captain in 79 Battery (soon left)
Stadward (Gordon)	Captain in 79 Battery
Stansfield (John)	**2nd Lt; (NS) in 8 Battery**
Stokoe (Mike)	2nd Lt, (NS) in 8 Battery
Taylor (Sam)	2nd Lt, (NS) in RHQ (late 1953)
Warner (Will)	2nd Lt, (NS) in 145 Battery (late 1953)
Warren (George)	Major, BC of 79 Battery

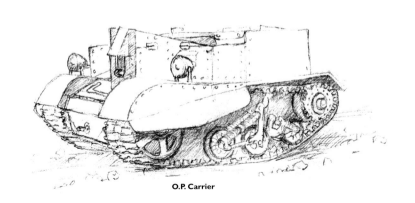

O.P. Carrier

Vicky Saumarez

Acknowledgements

First of all, I should like to thank and acknowledge the support given to me by my wife Cynthia, who has put up with my spending so much time closeted in my study, completing these *Recollections*. Inexperienced as I am in literary matters, I had not anticipated just how many hours and months it would take me to complete this work.

I should also like to acknowledge the help and encouragement given to me by my friends Richard Davies, Dick Brimelow, Mike Logan, John Stansfield and Tom Keeble, all of whom were so enthusiastic after reading the early drafts of these chapters.

All these persons, together with my erstwhile colleagues and friends at Mons OCTU, Greg Peck, John Morley and Mike Gibbon, who also sent me their own remembrances of those far off days, which enabled me to include the varied and interesting 'postscript' in Chapter 16. In this connection, I should not forget to mention and thank Malcolm Ross (in his absence) for his amusing parody on *Paradise Lost* which John Stansfield passed onto me.

Lastly, I am indebted to Vicky Saumarez for producing the attractive sketches of 25 Pounder Guns and other Army vehicles; and I thank Lawrence Durrell for giving permission to include the interesting anecdote from his book *Bitter Lemons of Cyprus*, which complements the earlier comments made in Chapter 13 so well.

The extract from *Bitter Lemons of Cyprus* by Lawrence Durrell in Chapter 13, is reproduced with permission of Curtis Brown Group Ltd, London on behalf of the Estate of Lawrence Durrell.
Copyright © Lawrence Durrell 1957

A Telling Addendum from Modern-Day Jerusalem

(See Chapter 12, Pages 258 and 262)

The following article appeared in the
Daily Telegraph on Monday, 10 November 2008:

Rival monks start brawl in church

By Carolynne Wheeler in Jerusalem

RIOT police had to break up a brawl between monks in Jerusalem yesterday. The fight, in the Church of the Holy Sepulchre, was between Armenian and Greek Orthodox monks. Two of them, one with a bloody gash on his forehead, were taken away in handcuffs.

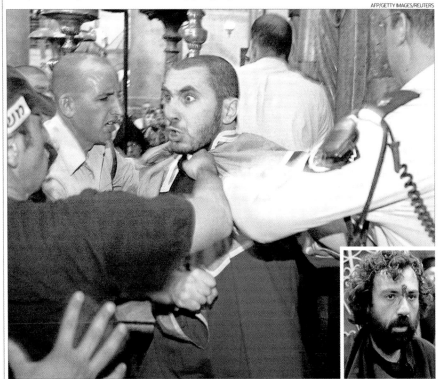

Holy war Argument over worshipping rights turns into a brawl

AFP/GETTY IMAGES/REUTERS

Israeli police rushed into one of Christianity's holiest churches yesterday and arrested two clergymen after an argument between rival monks erupted into a brawl. The Church of the Holy Sepulchre, believed to be the site of Jesus's crucifixion, burial and resurrection, is home to six different Christian sects. The fight erupted after Greek Orthodox monks were apparently refused permission to post a monk inside the Edicule, a structure built on what is believed to be Christ's tomb. Police arrested an Armenian monk and a Greek Orthodox monk bleeding from a gash on his forehead. Watch video of the brawl at www.telegraph.co.uk/tv

Index